PREFACE TO THE FIRST EDITION

Russell's ironical humour is evident in the very title of the book *Unpopular Essays*. The Essays, it goes without saying, are quite the opposite of unpopular. They express the multifaceted genius of Bertrand Russell. Ranging over a wide area—the influence of philosophy on politics, what is intellectual rubbish, functions of a teacher, the future of mankind, ideas that have helped and harmed mankind—the essays are written in a piquant style one does not normally associate with a philosopher and mathematician. The ideas and principles, which were all through his life dear to Russell, are reflected in the essays.

The present critical study of *Unpopular Essays* has aimed at elucidating all the twelve essays, with detailed annotations and explanation of difficult passages. The various facets of Russell's thought and art in *Unpopular Essays* have been critically and exhaustively discussed. For the convenience of students the textual discussion has been arranged in the form of Answers to Questions selected from various Indian University Examinations. It is to be noted that all page references in this book are to *Unpopular Essays* edited by Blackie and Son.

We take this opportunity to thank various literary critics on Bertrand Russell and his *Unpopular Essays* whose views have been incorporated in this book. We also thank Messrs. Unique Publishers for their cooperation in bringing out this book.

S.Sen
K. Kothari
P.S. Chopra
J.K. Chopra

New Delhi
1984

PREFACE TO THE LATEST EDITION

It is a pleasure that our annotated edition of Bertrand Russell's *Unpopular Essays* has been appreciated by a wide circle of students and teachers. We are thus encouraged to bring out a fresh edition.

Suggestions for further improvement will be welcome.

S.Sen

New Delhi

J.K. Chopra

BERTRAND RUSSELL

UNPOPULAR ESSAYS

A Critical Study with Summary of All Essays, Annotations, Critical Appreciation, Explanations with Critical Comment, Discussion of Textual Topics and Select University Questions with Answers

Latest Revised Edition

Authors

DR. S. SEN
M.A., Ph.D.

J.K. CHOPRA
M.A., M.Phil.

Thoroughly revised by

DR. G. S. MANSUKHANI
M.A., Ph.D.
Ex- Head of the Department of English
S.G.T.B. Khalsa College
University of Delhi
&
Retd. Deputy Secretary
University Grants Commission

UNIQUE PUBLISHERS
Education Redefined

Price : ₹ 125.00
ISBN : 978-81-8357-150-0
Code : 2.4

***Published by*:**
Amarjeet S. Chopra
Unique Publishers (I) Pvt. Ltd.
Email : info@uniquepublishersindia.org
Website : www.uniquepublishersindia.org

***Regd. Office*:**
M-51, Lajpat Nagar-II, New Delhi - 110024
Fax: +91 11 46573070

***Delhi Office*:**
4574/15, Padam Chand Marg (Opp. Happy School)
Ansari Road, Daryaganj
New Delhi - 110002
Tel : +91 11 41564400/11/22
Fax : +91 11 43508440

***Corporate Office*:**
B-155, Sector-63
Noida - 201301 (U.P.)
Tel : +91 120 4575555
Fax : +91 120 4575563

***Printed at*:**
Sanjeev Offset Printers

CONTENTS

III. RUSSELL'S PROSE STYLE

IV. RUSSELL'S IDEAS ON POLITICS, HUMANITY, EDUCATION AND MORALITY AS EXEMPLIFIED IN INDIVIDUAL ESSAYS

Examine critically Russell's essay 'Philosophy and Politics'. 176

Q. 6. Narrate, after Russell, the role that philosophy can play in increasing human happiness or well-being.

Or

"Philosophy can give certain things that will greatly increase the student's value as a human being and as a citizen". Elucidate.

Or

Examine critically the ideas contained in Russell's 'Philosophy For Laymen.' 182

Q. 7. "I come to the question: What should be our policy, in view of the various dangers to which mankind is exposed ?" Consider the circumstances that have led Russell to raise the above question. What are the dangers referred to here ? What policy does Russell suggest to avert those dangers ?

Or

Why does Russell, in his essay 'The Future of Mankind', advocate the formation of an international government? How far do you agree with him ?

Or

Examine critically the ideas contained in Russell's 'The Future of Mankind'. 184

Q. 8. Discuss how ulterior motives have made philosophy fallacious. How, according to Russell, should philosophy be cultivated ?

Or

Examine critically the ideas contained in Russell's essay, 'Philosophy's Ulterior Motives'. 189

Q. 9. Why and how is 'superior virtue' attributed to the oppressed classes ? Comment on Russell's views.

Or

"Children were idealized by Wordsworth and unidealized by Freud. Marx was the Wordsworth of the proletariat; its Freud is still to come." Describe in detail how Russell comes to this conclusion.

Or

Attempt a critical analysis of Russell's essay 'The Superior Virtue of the Oppressed'. 192

Q. 10. Describe the prominent features of a modern-minded man as put forward by Russell.

Or

"Our age is the most parochial since Homer." How does Russell elucidate this remark ?

Or

"A certain degree of isolation both in space and time is essential to generate the independence required for the most important work." Discuss in detail how Russell comes to this conclusion.

Or

Examine critically the ideas contained in Russell's essay, 'On Being Modern-minded' 195

Q. 11. "Man is a rational animal." What comments does Russell offer against this contention in his essay 'An Outline of Intellectual Rubbish' ?

Or

Give a critical analysis of the ideas that Russell has put forth in his essay 'An Outline of Intellectual Rubbish'. 198

Q. 12. What remedies for avoidance of false and foolish opinions does Russell prescribe in his essay, 'An Outline of Intellectual Rubbish ?

Or

"To avoid the various foolish operations to which mankind are prone, no superhuman genius is required. A few simple rules will keep you, not from all error, but from silly error." What does Russell mean here ? Analyse and comment on the simple rules suggested by him. 203

1

Introduction to Bertrand Russell (1872-1970)

I. LIFE OF BERTRAND RUSSELL

Early Life. Bertrand Russell, the greatest philosopher of the present age, was born on 18 May, 1872, at Ravenscroft in Monmouthshire. His father, Viscount Amberley, was the third son of Lord John Russell, one time Prime Minister of England who later became the first Earl Russell. His mother, Lady Kate Stanley, was a daughter of Lord Stanley of Alderley. Both his parents died during his early childhood and Russell, along with his elder brother Frank, were left to the care of their grandmother "Lady John".

Education. His early education was provided at home by private tutors. It is recorded that Russell, the author of that monumental classic, *Principia Mathematica*, wept over his first efforts to learn the multiplication table and began with a hearty dislike of Algebra. At eleven he was given his first geometry lesson and was disappointed to discover the subject proceeded from axioms which had to be accepted without proof. The insipient philosopher dared to question Euclid and demanded to be convinced that two things which are equal to the same thing are equal to one another. He read hungrily in his grandfather's copious library and laid the foundation for that vast store of knowledge which was later to earn him the reputation of "the wisest man in Britain". At sixteen he strained his eyes and was forbidden to read or write, so he filled this gap by learning poetry by heart. John Stewart Mill had the greatest influence on his developing mind. Russell had an immediate affinity for empirical philosophy, the common sense belief that all knowledge comes from experience.

When the time came for Cambridge, he was sent to a grammar school to learn Latin and Greek. At eighteen he joined Trinity College, Camrbidge, to study mathematics. He was to add to that extraordinary period of Cambridge history which produced such men as McTaggart, Moore, Whitehead, Eddington, Rutherford, Marshal and Keynes. He was placed seventh in the Mathematical Tripos of 1893, and stayed another year at Trinity to appear for the Moral Science Tripos in which he obtained a First Class distinction.

Marriage with Alys. In 1889, Russell fell in love with Alys Pearsall Smith, a sister of the writer Logan Pearsall Smith. Lady John, who disapproved of the romance, got Bertrand the post of an honorary attache in the British Embassy and sent him away. But he returned home very soon and married Alys in 1894.

Fellowship at Cambridge. Russell obtained a Fellowship at Trinity College in 1895 and held this post till 1901. During these years he published several of his books. These include *The Foundations of Geometry* (1897), *The Philosophy of Leibniz* (1900) and *The Principles of Mathematics* (1903). His great work in the field of Mathematics was the three-volume *Principia Mathematica* (1910-13) compiled in collaboration with Dr. A.N. Whitehead.

Interest in Politics. While he was working on his mathematical books he also found time for politics. In 1907, he stood for Parliament as a candidate of the National Union of Women's Suffrage Societies, but was defeated. He made a more serious bid to enter the House of Commons in 1910 seeking adoption as a Liberal candidate. He was not considered for candidacy on account of his indifference to the Church. Later he became a convinced Socialist and Pacifist. During the First World War he indulged in pacifist activities which brought him into serious confrontation with the government. He was imprisoned for a brief period in 1917. Later he was fined for writing a pamphlet in which he criticised his sentence as a conscientious objector. His anti-war activities led Trinity College to dismiss him in 1916 as a lecturer, a post he had obtained in 1910. In 1918 he was again sent to prison for six months for an article about the use of troops against strikers in America. During this imprisonment he wrote the *Introduction to Mathematical Philosophy.*

His other marriages. Russell believed in the practice of free love and himself had four marriages. He was separated from his first wife Alys in 1911, but was granted divorce in 1921. In the same year he married Dora Black. The marriage ended in 1935 and in 1936 Russell got married to Patricia Spence. The marriage broke up in 1942, and then in 1952 Russell married Edith Finch, an American woman who, more than any other wife of his, made him happy. His fourth wife was a teacher and writer of repute.

Visit to Russia. Russell visited Russia in 1920. There he came to the conclusion that the Bolsheviks were remarkably similar to the Puritans. He wrote : "Their form of government is almost exactly the same as the form of government established in England by Cromwell in the seventeenth century." In Russia he had a talk with Lenin but when Russell said it might be possible to achieve socialism in England without bloodshed, the Russian director "waved the suggestion aside as fantastic." The result of his experience in Russia was a critical analysis, *The Practice and Theory of Bolshevism* which he summed up later saying, "when I went there in 1920 I found nothing I could like or admire".

Visit to China. Later in 1920 Russell went to China and received an enthusiastic welcome. Peking University students launched a special "Russell Magazine" and San-Yat-Sen described him as the only Englishman ever to understand China. He exhausted himself by lecturing in draughty halls and fell desperately ill. Reports of his death were circulated and Russell later had the wry pleasure of reading his own obituary notices. He was nursed back to health by his devoted companion Dora, who later became his second wife. On his return to England he published *The Problem of China*—a remarkable forecast of the future trends in the Far East.

Association with B.B.C. After his return from China Russell remained associated with B.B.C., London, for quite a number of years. During this period came out his progressive work *Marriage and Morals* (1929) which at once drew opposition from the conformists. His next work, *The Conquest of Happiness* also advocated some sexual freedom, and received similar opposition.

Visit to America : In 1938, Russell went to the United States to lecture, first at Chicago University then at the University of California. In 1940 he was appointed Professor of Philosophy at City College, New York. A bishop of the Anglican Church protested against the appointment on the ground that Russell was recognised propagandist against religion and morality. A biased Roman Catholic judge heard the case and gave his verdict against the appointment. Afterwards he went to Pennsylvania to lecture in philosophy at Burnes Foundation. In 1944 he returned to England and was appointed a Fellow at his old college, Trinity. In 1946 came out one of his most illuminating books, *A History of Western Philosophy*.

Awards. In 1949 Russell was awarded the Order of Merit, the most exclusive honour in the awards of the Crown. That same year he undertook a lecture tour of Australia. Shortly after he returned to England, in 1950, he was awarded the Nobel Prize for Literature.

Last Years. At the age of eighty he turned to a new field —fiction. His first stories appeared in the collection *Satan in the Suburbs*. Then began the most publicised part of his life—the campaign for disarmament. His endeavour to create a general awareness of the perils of nuclear and bacteriological warfare, continued till the end of his life. In 1935, he wrote to the Heads of six prominent powers to make an attempt to end the nuclear menace. In 1957 he appealed to Britain to ban the Hydrogen bomb unilaterally. In 1958 he was elected President of the Campaign for Nuclear Disarmanent. In February, 1961, he was sentenced to two months imprisonment on the charge of inciting civil disobedience. The sentence was, however, not carried out for medical reasons. In 1967 came out his book *War Crimes in Vietnam* in which he exposed American atrocities on the Vietnamese people. His eventful life came to an end on February 2, 1970, at his home in North Wales when he was in his ninety-eighth year.

A tribute to Russell : a champion of humanity. This is how Herbert Gottschalk, in his biography of Russell, sums up the greatness of this indomitable man : "The world will not often have the good fortune to witness, in the long life of an individual outliving so many of his contemporaries, such an example of indomitable struggle. He gives, despite all the pros and cons of criticism, new courage and confidence to those in danger of losing heart and inclined to abandon the struggle to preserve human civilization. Perhaps, one day the world will be less interested in Bertrand Russell's philosophical works, and in the details of his personal life, than in the splendid examples of courage and human dignity he has given us. Without sentimentality or pathos, we can say that men like Bertrand Russell are the real champions of humanity. When the world no longer produces his kind, the freedom of man really will be in danger of extinction. Talk of heroism he would not care for, so let us say then that his personality is a striking example of harmonious unity of conscience, word and deed."

II. PRINCIPAL WORKS OF BERTRAND RUSSELL

Philosophical Works

The Principles of Mathematics—1903

Principia Mathematica (in collaboration with A.N. Whitehead)—1910-13

The Problems of Philosophy—1912

Mysticism and Logic—1917

The Analysis of Mind—1921

The Analysis of Matter—1927

History of Western Philosophy—1945

Logic and Knowledge—1956

Political and Social Works

Principles of Social Reconstruction—1916

Roads to Freedom—1918

On Education—1926

Sceptical Essays—1928

Marriage and Morals—1929
The Conquest of Happiness—1930
Power—1938
Authority and the Individual—1949
Unpopular Essays—1950
New Hopes for a Changing World—1951

Biographical Works

The Amberley Papers (in collaboration with his third wife)—1937
Portraits from Memory—1956
Autobiography (in 3 volumes)—1967-69

III. RUSSELL AS A PHILOSOPHER

Russell and Western Philosophy. Bertrand Russell was at once a brilliant philosopher and one of the greatest intellects of the modern times. He was first of all a philosopher and then a mathematician. He has secured a niche in the history of modern philosophy not because he formulated a new system in this sphere but because he demonstrated, in all his works, an unbiased sincere passion for enquiry. In Western philosophy two tendencies have been found to be predominating—Idealism and Empiricism. The cult of idealism is based on the assumption of an Absolute Idea, and interpretation of the universe under this assumption. This idealism was explored and cultivated by philosophers like Plato, Spinoza, Kant and Hegel. Empiricism, on the other hand, is characterised by an altogether different approach. It aims at acquiring knowledge of the universe and life not through any preconceived notions, but through observation, experience, sensation and perception of things. In other words, Empiricism is based on a rational outlook, and, therefore, can also be called Rationalism.

Russell and Empiricism. Russell proclaimed his sympathy with Locke's Empiricism which he equated to a scientific outlook. He inculcated a rational or sceptical temper which allows him to accept things only after finding convincing justifications in their favour. The tendency to believe doctrines gives rise to dogmatic creeds which destroy the ideas of fraternity and tolerance and have brought upon the human race countless misfortunes. Russell advocated Empiricism as "the only philosophy that affords a justification for democracy in its temper of mind" and clearly supports liberty and toleration and opposes absolute monarchy. Also, the empirical mind will not wish to carry political action beyond demonstrable necessity, and will fight shy of inflicting pain in the present for distant and speculative ends, whether these be put forward in the name of religious, social, or racial dogmatism. Russell's choice of the Empiricist philosophy got further impetus from the existing state of things in this world. He felt that with the invention of nuclear weapons the world had reached a stage where it could hope to serve only through a revival of liberal tentativeness and tolerance that can be provided by Empiricism. Locke's philosophy, found in Russell in the form of Liberalism, pervades Russell's entire life and philosophy, and finds expression in his views on religion, morality, education, politics, science, and every sphere of life that he has explored.

Contribution to logic. Russell has contributed a new method of philosophy, obtained, through modification, from an earlier method used by mathematical logicians. Russell has described his method as 'logical-analytic' method or the method of 'logical atomism'. About 'logic of atomism' Russell himself says : "The way to get at the nature of any subject-matter you are looking at is analysis + and you can analyse until you get to things that can't be analysed any further and these would be logical atoms. I call them logical atoms because they are not little bits of matter. They are the ideas, so to speak, out of which a thing is built." Russell prefers this analytical method to those of Idealism or Realism because it is less speculative and more scientific than the other, and can help the analyst to get at what he calls 'atomic facts'.

Contribution to mathematics. Russell's most important work in this field is *Principia Mathematica*, written in collaboration with A.N. Whitehead. The work contains a precise formulation of logic and a detailed proof that the theorems of pure mathematics follow from the principles of logic alone. It shows that all the concepts of mathematics may be defined in terms of the vocabulary of logic. Subsequent developments have indicated that the systems of *Principia* requires only three undefined terms ; Russell describes these as constituting a 'minimum vocabulary' for mathematics, since theoretically all of mathematics and logic can be formulated in these terms alone. A number of important doctrines of *Principia* were published by him in articles written before *Principia*. Among these doctrines are the following :

(i) The Theory of Descriptions. The expressions, "the author of *Warverly*" and "the golden mountain" are instances of what Russell calls "definite descriptions". Such expressions, when they denote anything, denote it by characterizing it uniquely. Russell shows how to define these, making it possible to express uniqueness in terms of the vocabulary of logic. In general, to say "The author of *Waverly* was Scottish" is to say : "Someone has the property of having written *Waverly* : everyone who has that property is identical with him; and he is Scottish", and to say "the golden mountain does not exist", is

to say : "nothing that exists is both golden and mountainous". This theory removes the apparent need for assuming that statements such as "The golden mountain does not exist" assert of something that it does not exist, and then involve a realm of essence containing non-existent entities. Moreover, the theory has introduced an important type of definition, sometimes called "definition in use" "contextual definition". Instead of providing terms which could be substituted for descriptive phrases in the statements in which such phrases occur, Russell's definition provides a method of substituting for the statements themselves other statements of a different structure, not containing descriptive phrases. Russell believed that the possibility of such definitions indicates that the grammatical form of the defined statement furnishes no clue as to its real meaning.

(ii) The elimination of cardinal numbers and classes. Russell shows that all the properties of number can be preserved, if the cardinal numbers are defined in terms of classes. The cardinal number of a given class is defined as the class of all those classes which are similar to that class; classes are 'similar' if their members can be put in one-one correspondence. 'One-one correspondence' is defined in terms of the logical vocabulary. Hence there is no need to assume that, in addition to classes, there are such entities as numbers. Russell shows further that there is no need to assume that there are classes : by contextual definition, statements which appear to be about classes may be replaced by other more complex statements which mention properties but no classes.

Contribution to philosophy. Russell believes that by utilising the logical analytic method of *Principia*, philosophy may achieve a respectable status as a science. Much of his technical writing has been directed by the desire to provide a minimum vocabulary for our non-mathematical knowledge and substitute logical constructions for inferred entities.

In *Our Knowledge of the External World* (1914) Russell shows how the points and instants of mathematical physics may be regarded as constructions upon the crude data of sense, and he suggests that physical objects may be treated similarly. One of the traditional problems of philosophy is concerned with the relation of a physical object, say a tree, to its appearance. Russell hopes to solve this by providing a method for translating statements about physical objects into statements referring solely to their appearances. Thus the tree can be regarded as a logical construction that need not be treated as an inferred metaphysical entity lying beyond the data of sense.

In *The Analysis of Mind* (1921), Russell submits the concept of psychology to logical analysis. He holds that consciousness, belief, perception, memory, and desire are all reducible to the ultimate constituents employed in the analysis of matter. This view is sometimes called "neutral monism", since matter and mind are constructed from the same neutral stuff. Such entities as "the soul" and "the ego" inferred by the older psychology, does not seem to Russell to be sufficiently important even to need construction. Personal identity, he holds, can be secured by various types of continuity, such as continuity of experience.

In *The Analysis of Matter* (1923), Russell holds it probable that physics is fundamental in the sense that the laws of the other sciences including psychology may be reduced to the laws of physics. But the notes that his own views of the universe have certain affinities with idealism, since precepts are among the constituents from which matter is constructed, and since, in precepts, we have an "intimate qualitative knowledge" not derivable from physics.

Conclusion. Logic is thus the basis of Russell's philosophy. He is a consistent monist and a philosophical materialist, with some leaning toward behaviourism and pragmatism. Edmund Wilson calls him a type of the eighteenth century philosopher, ironic, elegant, dry, humanitarian, and anti-mystic. His philosophical views he carries over into the realm of sociology, and it is difficult to define him sociologically except as an advanced individualist. He himself says "...there is no one key : politics, economics, psychology, education, all act and react.....It is necessary to embrace all life and all science.... All that I can do is to make some men conscious of the problem and of the kind of directions in which solutions are to be sought."

IV. RUSSELL'S POLITICAL VIEWS

Political theories. Russell has gone through the theories advanced by political thinkers through ages. He finds Plato's *Republic*, which puts the concept of a totalitarian state, as useless : "That Plato's *Republic* should have been admired on its political side by decent people, is perhaps the most astonishing example of literary snobbery in all history". Plato has advocated war through his concept of education according to which the chief purpose of education is to produce courage in battle. He also suggests total rejection of poetry, music and drama. According to Russell any man who has any regard for the ideals of equality, liberty and fraternity cannot accept Plato's views. Russell also warns us not to be persuaded by the theories offered by Kant and Hegel. These philosophers preached obedience to authority, absolute monarchy, war, and a ban on free speech. Their theories encouraged the Nazis, to a considerable extent, to start the Second War.

Views on Communism. Marx, according to Russell, was influenced by Kant and Hegel. Hegel's idea of perfection *i.e.*, 'Absolute Idea' was Germany. Marx accepted his theory of thesis, antithesis and synthesis, and believed that the Absolute Idea could be achieved only through a revolution...Marx believed in a single party rule and the necessity of violence against the capitalists. Russell finds the Marxian doctrines unacceptable because they advocate an oligarchic form of government and cruelty against opponents. According to him, such theories are based on hatred, intolerance and fanaticism. His experience in Russia, a country where communism is practised, confirmed the irrationality of these doctrines to him. In Russia, there is nothing called liberty, freedom of thought and freedom of the Press. There, anyone who disagrees with the official dogmas of the authority is likely to be liquidated or deported. A Liberal like Russell cannot accept any such doctrine that may be detrimental to individual liberty.

Views on Empiricism and democracy. Russell's innate regard for democratic ideals makes him turn to the theory of Empiricism, propagated by John Locke. Empricism leads to the Liberal theory in politics, advocates toleration and mutual understanding, eliminates fanaticism in political programmes, and opposes absolute monarchy. The Liberal creed is one of live-and-let-live and implies freedom and moderation. Democracy, according to Russell, was invented as a means for reconciling government with liberty. A democratic government cannot misuse power as it depends on popular approval. At the same time it gives necessary freedom to the citizens and imposes the necessary restrictions on them to keep law and order intact. For these reasons, Russell believes, democracy is the best possible form of government.

Concept of World Government. Russell is convinced that the nuclear arms-race is leading to such wars that will bring about the inevitable extinction of the human race. He thinks that the only possible way to avert this danger is to form a single world government which will possess the monopoly of all armed forces and armaments. Only such a government can keep in check the unlawful and aggressive intentions of any country and ensure peace in the world. Attention then will be diverted from meaningless production of weapons to the promotion of human happiness. Russell feels that the present circumstances are ideal for the formation of a world government. There are now only two really independent states, Russia and America. What is now needed is to reduce them to one by agreement, or, if necessary, by force.

V. RUSSELL'S VIEWS ON EDUCATION

Importance of Education. The importance of education in the life of an individual cannot be overrated. Only through proper education will people become ideal citizens of an ideal society when it will be established. Russell offers a liberal definition of education. Education, according to him, is "the formation, by means of instruction, of certain mental habits and a certain outlook on life and the world".

Functions of the teacher. The orthodox system of education is designed to teach children, when they grow up, to be loyal to the 'status quo' and turn them into instruments for carrying out the purpose of the State. It leaves little scope for free development from within. But it is the duty of the teacher to recognise that children have their own instincts and impulses. He is to use them "not as means but as ends" in themselves; in other words, he is to instruct them in a way so that he may bring into full play their separate personalities giving each one the opportunities for a full unimpeded growth. It is his primary duty to encourage in children positive virtues such as courage, vitality, sensitiveness and intelligence, so that they may grow into good men and women in the future. The popular way of looking at goodness is not to regard it as an active force but as a negative virtue that refrains from doing what is contrary to the accepted moral or social standard. There is a whole system of laws and codes, written and unwritten, social and religious, which works through fear and superstition and crushes the healthy instincts in children. The teacher will be failing in his responsibility unless he is able to foster in children a sense of self-respect and an attitude of looking at all questions with a searching, impersonal outlook. They should be encouraged to take the initiative and do what is good for themselves and for others. The teacher must always remember that the most important aims of education are to prevent dogmatism and to spread tolerance. If educational systems, through the efforts of the teachers, can fulfil these aims, most of the misfortunes that now afflict the human race will disappear from the world.

Freedom for the teachers. Under the present system the teacher has been reduced to the position of a spokesman of the official dogmatic creed. A teacher can discharge his duties only when he feels himself an individual guided by his own creative impulses. He can have such a feeling only when he is free from all outside interference. Therefore, if education has to aim at the well-being of its receivers the teachers must be granted complete freedom from intellectual bondage.

University education. There was a time when universities were open only to men of rank and birth. Now they exist for two purposes: (i) for imparting vocational training, and (ii) for encouraging pursuit of knowledge and research for their own sake without any consideration of utility. According to Russell, the time has come when intellectual aristocracy should replace privileged aristocracy. So, as regards the first purpose, students, before they are allowed admission, will have to prove their claims by showing a special aptitude for the work they undertake, while no preference is to be made to wealth for its own sake. The second purpose, in Russell's view, is far more important in its contribution to life's happiness. Liberal education, to be deserving of its name, must have a disinterested love of learning and pursue knowledge for its own sake with no ulterior object other than securing intellectual excellence. Russell does not deny the importance of professional or technical education which has made the world what it is today. But he wants to keep alive the Renaissance tradition in which learning was a part of the *joie de vivre*, whereby the privileged aristocrats sought learning for no interest other than the intellectual and aesthetic satisfaction it afforded. They had the leisure for it and modern science has brought leisure within general reach of men by triumphing over time and eliminating dull work. If this leisure is properly utilised there will be time for unimpassioned contemplation and for creating a culture which would gradually remove some of the worst features of the modern world.

Study of science. In Russell's opinion, the study of science should be considered an integral part of education. It has, according to him, a greater cultural value than a purely classical and literary education. An exclusive devotion to the study of classical subjects is likely to make a man fastidious in taste, and dissatisfied with the present. The study of science will satisfy the creative impulse, and more importantly will develop a scientific outlook and a disinterested love of truth without any bias or consideration of utility. The free intellect, inspired only by love of truth, will look upon the world as it is, without any bias, without any motive, with God-like impartiality solely for the sake of knowledge which is dispassionate and impersonal. Such a philosophic calmness, practised and preserved in the sphere of contemplation, will not fail to influence the individual when he enters the sphere of action.

Study of philosophy. 'Philosophy' means 'love of wisdom', and in this sense should be cultivated by men. Philosophy as a guide to wisdom should be separated from the philosophy of specialists, and made a part of general education. According to Russell, philosophy can help us to attain the right attitude towards science by making clear at once the scope and limitations of scientific knowledge. It can protect mankind against two possible evils—dogmatism and scepticism—and keep suggesting ways of living and looking at life. Study of philosophy can inculcate the philosophic spirit that helps to eliminate fear or self-esteem and lends us the virtues of intellectual sobriety and impartiality. It is not necessary that the study of philosophy has to be allotted as much time as that given to technical studies. But, even in the time that can be spared, philosophy can help increase the student's value as a human being and as a citizen by encouraging in him the habit of exact and careful thinking and providing him with an impersonal conception of his relation to society and the universe.

VI. RUSSELL'S VIEWS ON RELIGION

Attitude towards religion. Russell looks upon religion as a matter of faith. Faith, according to Russell, is "a firm belief in something for which there is no evidence." Religious faiths, which have sprung partly out of our tendency to believe in the existing doctrines and partly out of fear and superstitions, have no intellectual basis. So it is natural that such faith cannot find a place of importance in Russell's rational and scientific mind. On the other hand he is of the opinion that religious dogmas have done more harm than good to mankind. These dogmas have often led to fanaticism and are responsible for countless cruelties inflicted on men. However, Russell's opposition to religion never borders on fanaticism, because fanaticism does not befit a rational mind like his. So, the position he adopts in this case, as he does in all cases, is one of 'rational scepticism'. He writes : "My own view of religion is that of Lucretius. I regard it as a disease born of fear and as a source of untold misery to the human race". On this opinion Brian Carr comments : "Russell's opinion is an uncompromising one, but not one to be rejected without a sincere attempt to meet his arguments. These arguments may be found compelling—indeed, we see in our time much debate between Christians and unbelievers in the claims of Christianity and in its supposed moral and social benefits. The Churches have not always been so ready to listen to criticism levelled against their dogma, preferring, when political power was available, to use such methods as are even now present in totalitarian states for countering unorthodoxy."

Views on agnosticism. Russell, by his own description, is an agnostic—one who holds that nothing is known, or likely to be known, of the existence of a God or anything beyond material phenomena. This agnosticism, inspired by his innate mathematical mind, forced him, even in his early years, to develop doubts about religious doctrines concerned with the existence of God, immortality and free will.

Russell dismisses all arguments put forth by the theologians, to prove God's existence, as fallacious. He is not convinced by the theologians' view that God is the First Cause of everything and therefore, He exists. The argument that God exists as the giver of the laws of nature also does not appeal to Russell's mind. He finds this concept of a 'celestial policeman' to be unnecessary and ridiculous. He finds contradictions in the concepts of God's omnipotence and God's goodness. If

God is omnipotent, no one can act against His will. So when a person commits a heinous crime he does so with God's approval. Such involvement with criminal activities can never agree with the concept of God's goodness.

Views on Christianity. Russell is usually dubbed as anti-Christ and anti-Christian. He does not accept Christ as divine or as an embodiment of goodness. He looks upon Christ as a mortal being given to the feelings of vindictiveness and cruelty. The Christian Church, in his opinion, has displayed greater intolerance than other religious organizations. This intolerance was manifest in the burning of thousands of so-called heretics and witches in the Middle Ages. In those days the most influential text in the Bible was : 'Thou shalt not suffer a witch to live'. The Church declared pestilence, famine, earthquake and flood as merely the instruments of divine justice. Anyone who disagreed with such orthodox views of the Church was liable to be punished as a heretic. According to Russell, Christianity has always stood in the way of progress. The Christian clergy have always fought against the development of science because it has been continually exposing the stupidity of the religious notions of nature and the universe. The Christian belief that all sufferings are inflicted by God for our sins, and the consequent opposition to euthanasia and use of anaesthetics on the ground that they would stand in God's way, do not confirm God's kindness or his sense of justice. If sufferings are punishments for sins, innocent children should never have suffered in this world.

Ideas on future of religion. Religion, according to Russell, is born of fear and man's feeling of helplessness against the forces of nature and evil. Science has helped to reduce religion's grip on mankind by establishing man's supremacy over nature. But the social evils are still there and, so long as they continue to exist, men will keep turning to religion for a supposed protection against these evils. Russell as an optimist hopes that we will one day recognise our irrationalities and shake them off. When we do that, religion, an evil in itself, will disappear from this world.

2

Introduction To "Unpopular Essays"

Writing and publication. The essays contained in the collection *Unpopular Essays* were written by Bertrand Russell between 1935 and 1950. The volume was published in 1950, the year in which he received the Nobel Prize for literature. Three of the essays—*An Outline of Intellectual Rubbish, Ideas That Have Harmed Mankind* and *Ideas That Have Helped Mankind*—had been published earlier in the United States. The last piece of the collection, *Obituary*, had also been published in *The Listener* in 1937.

The Title. In the preface to *Unpopular Essays* Russell himself explains why he has chosen this unusual title : "In the preface to my *Human Knowledge* I said that I was writing not only for professional philosophers, and that 'philosophy proper deals with matters of interest to the general educated public'. Reviewers took me to task, saying they found parts of the book difficult, and implying that my words wêre such as to mislead purchasers. I do not wish to expose myself again to this charge; I will therefore confess that there are several sentences in the present volume which some unusually stupid children of ten might find a little puzzling. On this ground I do not claim that the essays are popular; and if not popular, then 'unpopular'." However, it does not follow that what "is not popular" is "unpopular", and when a great logician writes 'illogically' like this we can assume that he is either jesting or meaning something else. In fact Russell adopted this ironical title to have a little satiric humour at the expense of those reviewers who had expressed those baseless suspicions with regard to his *Human Knowledge*.

Purpose. Russell declares in the Preface that the purpose of *Unpopular Essays* is "to combat, in one way or another the growth of dogmatism, whether of the Right or of the Left, which has hitherto characterised our tragic century. This serious purpose inspires them even if, at times, they seem flippant, for those who are solemn and pontifical are not to be successfully fought by being even more solemn and even more pontifical". In addition, the essays express concern for the race for accumulating nuclear weapons, and advocate establishment of a world government and pursuit of the ideals of liberty, equality and fraternity. Russell also intends his essays to impress upon the readers the necessities of democracy and rejection of superstitions and false beliefs that have made men irrational.

Popular appeal. The *Unpopular Essays,* needless to say, have proved far from unpopular. In 1950, when the volume was published, Russell had been awarded the Nobel Prize and become a literary celebrity. As such the people received the collection with all eagerness and, expectedly, were not disappointed. Because of the concern for the problems of the world and the clear headed approach to their solution the essays readily appealed to the readers; the sincerity of the writer, the ready wit, the humour, and the lucid and clear prose style made them instantly popular.

Synopses of the Essays. Given below are the gists of the different essays.

(1) 'Philosophy and Politics'. *Criticism of Hegel's philosophy.* One of the main purposes of this essay is to expose the dangerous political implications of Hegel's philosophy. Russell dismisses Hegel's concept of the 'Absolute Idea' as one of 'pure thought thinking about pure thought'. He shows that Hegel's philosophy advocates monarchy and war and oppose the establishment of any international organization for settling disputes. The success of Hegel's philosophy to gain a huge following has baffled Russell. Like the Nazis in Germany, Marx too came under his influence.

Merits of empiricism . Russell recommends the pursuit of Locke's philosophy of empiricism. This philosophy, based on democratic principles, preaches mutual toleration, avoidance of dogmatism, and moderation in political programmes.

(2) 'Philosophy of Laymen'. *Necessity of Philosophy.* Men have acquired the scientific skill necessary for dominating over Nature, but have not developed the knowledge of how best to utilise that skill. As a result, instead of using science for the benefit of mankind they have invented nuclear weapons that have become a menace to themselves. Philosophy which means, 'Love of wisdom' should be cultivated because it can provide men with the knowledge of proper utilisation of their acquired skill.

Objects and utility of philosophy. Philosophy has two objects : a theoretical understanding of the world and discovery of the best possible way of life. Philosophy is thus closely related to both science and religion. On the theoretical side, philosophy puts forth hypotheses, many of which have formed the basis for scientific inventions. A hypothesis remains philosophy as long as it cannot be tested; as soon as it is verified scientifically it becomes science. Moreover there are some questions of universal interest like those involving life after death and the relation between mind and matter, which have remained beyond the range of science. One function of philosophy is to keep alive the interest in such issues.

On the practical side philosophy can produce in us the philosophic spirit which can eliminate fear or self-esteem and lend us an intellectual sobriety, the quality of impartiality, and an objective outlook. Philosophy can also increase the value of a person as a human being and as a citizen. It can encourage exact and careful thinking and provide us with a conception of the ends of life and an awareness of our relation to the society and the universe. It can also serve as a remedy for the evils that inflict the human race in today's world.

(3) 'The Future of Mankind'. *The project of a world government* . According to Russell, the present state of anarchy and the increasing hostility between America and Russia are leading humanity to destruction. In his opinion the only way to save the human race from total disaster is to establish a single world government led by America. America is preferred to Russia because in that country there is greater respect for freedom of thought, freedom of inquiry, freedom of discussion, and humane feelings, that are essential in a civilised life. In Russia individuals are denied such freedom, and anyone disagreeing with the policies of the government is either liquidated or deported. A world government dominated by Russia will eliminate all kinds of freedom from the world and, therefore, is not welcome.

Dangers to mankind : Russell points out three dangers that have been confronting mankind. They are (i) the end of the human race; (ii) return to barbarism; (iii) the establishment of a universal slave state involving misery for the vast majority and stagnation of progress in knowledge and thought. In his opinion these dangers can be averted only by forming a single world government by agreement, or, if necessary, by force.

(4) **'Philosophy's Ulterior Motives'.** *Ulterior Motives* . Russell refers to a particular problem that a philosopher usually faces. The philosopher has a tendency to believe in the existing notions; at the same time he finds it difficult to believe them without finding an intellectual basis for them. So very often, in his attempt to find such intellectual justifications for these notions, he resorts to a long process of reasoning. There is every possibility that during this long process he might make a single mistake that would lead him far out in the realms of illogicality. In such cases the philosopher is bound to produce distorted and confusing philosophy. Descartes, the father of modern philosophy, illustrates this peculiar mental temper. The disagreement of

his teachers on various things made him conclude that nothing was a certainty. This prompted his search for certainty at the beginning of which he decided that he would not accept anything that would appear to be doubtful. However, he could not doubt his own existence since if he did not exist he would not be able to doubt. Upto this point he was logical in his approach, but then the ulterior motive of believing in the existing notions overwhelmed him and he lost his reason. In order to prove the existence of God he argued that since he could form an idea of God as a more perfect being than himself, and since God must be the cause of this idea, there is no doubt about God's existence.

Russell goes on to offer a list of philosophers who began well but were later led astray by certain ulterior motives. The list includes philosophers like Leibniz, Bishop Berkeley, Kant, Hegel and Marx. He illustrates how these philosophers, under the influence of their ulterior motives, deviated from the logical approach and produced obscure and ambiguous philosophy.

(5) 'The Superior Virtue of the Oppressed'. *Superior Virtue.* In Russell's opinion some people, especially the moralists, think ill of their fellow-men and admire people belonging to other sections. A form of this admiration is the belief in the superior virtue of the oppressed, such as the poor, the subject nations, women and children.

Case of the oppressed classes. According to Russell superior virtue is attributed to the oppressed by the oppressors with the intention of keeping their respective positions intact. The rich regard the poor as morally superior to them only to keep the poor under their domination. The subject nations are bestowed with charm and noble qualities by the ruler nations. But as soon as they become independent the notion of those qualities in them disappears. Spiritual qualities were attributed to women to keep them inferior to men politically and economically. When they gained equality with men the concept of female spirituality came to an end. Children were idealized in the same manner when parental authority was threatened. Now, the growth of an educational policy emphasising the welfare of children has put limitations on the adult's tyrannical treatment of children. As a result the divinity attached earlier to children has been taken away and they have reverted to being 'wicked' again. The latest victim of such deliberate imposition of superior virtue has been the proletariat. The labouring classes are being idealized now. When they will attain equality with the rest, the attribution of superior virtue to them will cease.

(6) 'On Being Modern-Minded'. *Parochiality of the modern age.* The modern man has a tendency to reject the past and to follow the fashion of the day. He thinks that he has reached the apex of intelligence, and, as such, dismisses the things of the past as things of no significance. He attaches great value to money and admiration and is not prepared to express his personal thoughts and ideas for fear that they might earn the hostility of his contemporaries. The modern man intends to say just what others will say, and is only, perhaps, slightly ahead of others in point of time. In Russell's opinion, temptations of easy money and fame, the continuing swift replacement of theories by newer ones, and the decline in the faith of God and such other noble ideals account for this loss of individuality in the modern age.

Necessity of detachment and objectivity. Detachment and objectivity, in both thought and feeling, have to be preserved. Some amount of isolation, in both space and time, and finding an objective higher than popular applause are essential for the creation of original and individual works.

(7) 'An Outline of Intellectual Rubbish'. *Man's irrationality* . Russell can find ample evidence of the trait of irrationality in mankind. Aristotle's theory that man is rational because he can master arithmetic has been proved false and is no longer accepted today.

Irrationality of clergymen. Russell shows how the clergy, through the ages, have displayed extreme irrationality. The clergymen have always propagated silly interpretations of things and have opposed scientific research that would expose their stupidity. The concept of Sin, as propagated by them, is highly contradictory and unconvincing. Their views regarding the sacredness of human corpses, sex and marriage have never been based on reason.

False beliefs. Russell draws a list of false beliefs prevalent among men. We suffer from a feeling of superiority that leads us to believe that we are better than others and that our countries are superior to other countries. We have a tendency to believe in the marvellous and in rumours without caring for evidence. We also believe, without any reason, that some men are superior to others on account of their 'blood' and 'race'. We also imagine that human nature cannot be changed. Russell proves with illustrations that human nature does change and, on this basis, contends that governments, guided by reason, can impose sanity and reason on their people and can ensure peace in this world. We also have a tendency to generalize upon people and nations, as a result of which we have had such changing attitudes towards women and wrong ideas of national characteristics.

Russell's suggestions . Russell suggests adherence to a few simple rules for removal of false beliefs. They are personal observation, analysis of opinions, avoidance of dogmatism, caution against self-esteem, elimination of fear, and disbelief in superstitions.

(8) 'The Functions of a Teacher'. *The plight of the teachers.* The teacher today has lost the intellectual freedom that he enjoyed in the past. Education has now become a prerogative of the State and as such the teacher today has been reduced to the position of propagandist for the State. He is now forced to infuse fear, subservience and blind obedience into his pupils so that they never question the State's authority. This kind of teaching encourages fanaticism which obstructs the development of an international culture.

Duties of a teacher . It is necessary that the teacher should be protected from intellectual bondage, and made aware of his duties. Imparting definite uncontroversial information is one of his functions. He can encourage patriotism but not at the cost of rationality. He has to act as the main defence against the spread of dogmatism which is one of the main causes of human miseries. He should keep away from political strifes and must infuse into his pupils the habit of impartial inquiry. He must regard himself as a guardian of civilization and endeavour to impart a civilized attitude to his pupils. To do this he has to spread among his pupils an awareness of their insignificance in relation to the world, and an international outlook. He will always try to discover and remove the ills that afflict mankind. A good teacher must possess genuine affection for his students and a desire to encourage their kind impulses by showing them the possibility of delightful activities. He has to avoid every kind of falsehood in his teaching and should implant in his pupils a scientifically investigative desire to always get at the truth. His most important function is to teach them tolerance for opinions which differ from their own.

Freedom for the teacher. The teacher can carry out his responsibilities properly only if he feels himself an individual, guided by his own creative impulses. He can have such feeling only if freedom from outside interference is granted to him. In the present circumstances he must have the liberty to look for loopholes in the present systems; else the systems will destroy all that is best in man.

(9) 'Ideas That Have Helped Mankind'. *Two kinds of ideas.* The ideas discussed in the essay have been divided into two kinds— those that contribute to knowledge and technique, and those that are concerned with morals or politics.

Ideas contributing to knowledge and teachnique. Most important steps were taken in prehistoric times. Language, fire, the art of cookery, agriculture and the act of writing were inventions of those times that have helped mankind immensely. Coming to historic times much advance has been made in the spheres of mathematics and astronomy. The earliest important steps in these fields were made by the ancient

Greeks. In the seventeenth century great progress was achieved by Galileo, Descartes, Newton and Leibniz in the sphere of understanding nature. The Law of Intertia laid the foundations of the purely materialistic physics. In the nineteenth century the progress in geology and Darwin's theory of evolution upset many irrational religious ideas.

Ideas concerned with morals and politics. Scientific progress without a corresponding moral and political progress may increase the possibility of the destruction of mankind. The brotherhood of man is an ideal that was preached by the ancient Greeks and later endorsed by Christ and Buddha. The ideas of equality, liberty and fraternity have religious origin. Equality was practised by the ancient Orphic societies in Greece; later it passed into Stoicism, and subsequently, into Christianity. The idea of liberty first took shape in the form of religious toleration and was advocated by John Locke. Free press, free speech and freedom from arbitrary arrest came to be acknowledged in the nineteenth century. Law and government are two political ideas to which mankind owes a lot. Democracy was invented as a means of reconciling government with liberty.

Necessity of a world government. To avert the present crisis of mankind an international government has to be set up. The present circumstances are conducive to the formation of such a government. What is now necessary is the step from the two independent States, Russia and America, to form one—not by war, but by agreement. If this is achieved, mankind will be transferrred to an era of happiness and well being.

(10) 'Ideas That Have Harmed Mankind'. *Source of human misfortunes:* The misfortunes of human beings are mostly caused by the evil passions of men. Many of them were the product of sadistic impulses. Some organised systems of false beliefs have also contributed to human miseries.

Harmful systems of belief. Of the ideas that have harmed mankind the religious or superstitious ones are the most prominent. Human sacrifice and the custom of destroying conquered races had religious sanction. Christian ascetics condemned physical pleasures but they derived mental pleasure from the contemplation of torture of pagans and heretics in the next world. The ascetic self-denial can now be seen among the earnest communists. Again, the belief that misfortunes are caused by the malevolence of others gave rise to the belief in witchcraft and black magic which caused enormous cruelties until the seventeenth century. One of the most powerful sources of false belief is envy. Envy causes jealousy, and in the international field leads to international hatred and wars. Another source of false belief that is politically harmful is pride of nationality, race, sex, class or creed.

Pride has created rivalries among nations, countries and peoples, and has led to numerous misfortunes.

Importance of world government, democracy and moral qualities : Russell thinks that an international government has got to be formed to avert wars. He also advocates democracy as it is a government set up by general assent. He also emphasises the need for inculcating moral qualities like charity and tolerance which can infuse sanity and clear vision in the people.

(11) 'Eminent Men I Have Known'. *Poets* . Russell in this essay offers his impressions of some eminent persons he has known personally. The poet Robert Browning, according to him was refined, kindly and pleasant but lacked the divine fire of poetic inspiration. Russell hated Tennyson who always 'acted' the poet. He liked Ernest Toller but disliked Rupert Brooke for his Byronic insincerity.

Philosophers and scientists . Among philosophers William James was most impressive for his naturalness and indifference to his greatness. Russell has great respect for Henry Sidgwick, his teacher in ethics, for his intellectual honesty. Russell liked the scientist Einstein for his great intellect and childlike simplicity.

Politicians. Of the seven Prime Ministers Russell had met, Gladstone was the most unforgettable. Only Lenin could come near him in personal impressiveness. Gladstone possessed a terrifying personality. Once left for a *tete-a-tete* with him Russell remained speechless with awe. Profound moral conviction was the basis of his political influence. Lenin, on the other hand, was cruel and unscrupulous. Both of them, however, considered themselves human agents of a superhuman power, and had unshakable conviction of their own rectitude. Gladstone would impress a stranger at first sight, but in such a situation Lenin would seem a fanatic and a cheap cynic. Lenin lacked leadership qualities and would never have been successful in peaceful times.

Others: Russell has been impressed by some persons of no eminence. He remembers an illiterate gardener as a perfect type of simple goodness. He can never forget E. D. Morel who gave up his shipping clerk's job to fight against King Leopold's exploitation of the Congo. Men like Morel rarely achieve material prosperity.

(12). 'Obituary'. *Obituary for himself.* This obituary was written by Russell to describe the anticipated reaction of the newspapers, hostile to him, to his death.

Russell's aristocratic birth and early career. Though Russell prefers to regard himself as a commoner the obituary refers to his aristocratic birth. It acknowledges his brilliant academic career and contributions in the field of mathematics, but points out his lack of insight and spiritual depth. The obituary dismisses his pacifist activities during World War I as demonstrations of that very want of spiritual depth, and regards as just the punishments inflicted on him for such activities. It then refers to his visits to Russia and China and goes on to describe his subsequent writings on socialism and reforms as sheer waste of energy. His historical writings of this period, according to the obituary, contain an out-of-date rationalism.

Later life. The obituary admits that though his principles were curious, he always acted upon them. It points out that in private life Russell was a genial, cheerful man, who enjoyed friendship and good health. It concludes saying that his last years were spent in isolation.

3

Philosophy and Politics

I. SUMMARY

Connection between politics and philosophy. The connection between philosophy and politics has been more evident in the Continental countries than in England, where despite the emergence of great philosophers, philosophy has always been looked upon with contempt. On the Continent there has been a tendency to accept or reject a block of doctrines as a whole without going into its details. In many civilized countries the authorities have continued to hold an official opinion on philosophy. In such countries where politics and philosophy are connected there is no room for democracy. The Catholic Church and the Soviet Government are connected to the philosophies of Aquinas and Marx respectively. The Nazis upheld the German idealism advocated by Kant, Fichte and Hegel. Thus the Catholics, Communists, and the Nazis have all blended their views on practical politics with their views on theoretical philosophy. In its early success even democratic Liberalism was connected with Locke's empirical philosophy.

Aims of philosophy. According to many people in modern times, philosophy is a part of the pursuit of knowledge and should have nothing to do with politics or ethics. But the old and historical view, which is quite different, assumes that philosophy has resulted from the attempt to produce a synthesis of science and religion, or to be more precise, to combine a doctrine as to the nature of the universe and man's place in it with a practical ethic inculcating the best way of life. But it differed considerably from both science and religion. The ethical opinions of most philosophers involved political consequences. Some of them admired democracy, others oligarchy; some valued liberty, others discipline.

The basic problem of ethics and politics. The fundamental problem of ethics and politics is to make a compromise between the needs of social life and the urgency of individual desires. It has been achieved, to a certain extent, by means of various devices. For instance, use of criminal law can keep in check anti-social action by individuals, and a dominant priesthood can enforce restrictions on the conduct of individuals including the rulers.

Scepticism and conservatism. Most philosophy, except that of some—including Protagoras in the past and Hume in modern times—has been a reaction against scepticism. Both Protagoras and Hume were sceptics, and, as such, politically conservative. Protagoras believed that philosophy had nothing edifying to teach and that nothing should be done to weaken the popular force of tradition. The same thing may be said about Hume also. Hobbes, though less sceptical than Hume, equally advocated extreme conservatism.

The empiricists. Protagoras and Hume have never been much influential with their brand of scepticism. The most powerful adversaries of Plato and Hegel were the two empiricists, Democritus and Locke respectively.

The philosophy of Democritus. Democritus mainly known as the founder of atomism, was a materialist, a determinist, a free thinker, a utilitarian who disliked all strong passion, a believer in evolution, both astronomical and biological. An ardent democrat, he felt that poverty in democracy is better than prosperity under autocrats.

Plato's views. Acceptance of Plato's *Republic* is a perfect example of literary snobbery. The *Republic*, totalitarian in its preaching, puts forth that the main purpose of education is to produce courage in battle. According to the *Republic*, there has to be a censorship on stories told by mother to children, a ban on Homer and the drama, another kind of censorship on music, and a government practising trickery and lying. Plato succeeded in veiling his absurd thought with a metaphysical mist and has deceived the world for ages. Plato's ideal of static perfection is now considered inapplicable to human affairs. Man, a restless animal, is content only with hope, enterprise and change.

Philosopher's law of progress. Among modern philosophers, the ideal of unending and unchanging bliss has been replaced by that of evolution. This change of outlook accounts for the substitution of dynamics for statics which began with Galileo. Since Laplace no reputable astronomer has agreed with the earlier concept of the unchangeability of the things in the heavens. Everything, including the earth in its present state, is now accepted to have developed gradually. But this scientific concept has not satisfied the philosophers. They try to find a formula of progress showing that the world is becoming more and more to their liking. They persuaded themselves that the universe is governed by a general law leading to a gradual increase of things which please them and a gradual decrease of things they do not like. Hegel was the first to have fully developed this point of view.

Hegel and his views. Russell finds Hegel's philosophy absurd and unacceptable. According to Hegel, real reality is timeless, but there is also an apparent reality consisting of the everyday world in space and time. The character of real reality can be determined through logic alone, since there is only one sort of possible reality that is not self-contradictory. This is what Hegel calls the "Absolute Idea". Russell, rather ironically, defines it thus : "The Absolute Idea is pure thought thinking about pure thought." Hegel has already proved to his satisfaction that all reality is thought, and so it follows that thought cannot think of anything but thought since there is nothing else to think about.

Hegel's views have political implications. They imply that absolute monarchy is good, free speech is an evil, war is beneficial, and that an international organisation for peaceful settlement of disputes is not desirable. Hegel discovered the Nature of reality by a purely logical process called the "dialectic". This consists of discovering contradictions in abstract ideas and correcting them by making them less abstract. Each of these abstract ideas is conceived as a stage in the development of "The Idea", the last stage being the "Absolute Idea".

The successful impact of Hegel's absurd philosophy is surprising. He was widely accepted in Germany, a country considered by him the standard-bearer of the "Absolute Idea", and outside Germany too. During Russell's own youth every teacher of philosophy in England and America was a Hegelian. Marx too came under his influence. He took over some of Hegel's absurd ideas on the basis of which he asserted his concept of history developing according to a logical plan, and advocated an autocratic system.

Locke and Empiricism. The only philosophy that affords a theoretical justification of democracy is Empiricism, founded by John Locke. His philosophy clearly supports liberty and toleration, and opposes absolute monarchy. He has firmly emphasised the uncertainty of our knowledge to make men aware that they may be wrong sometimes and that this awareness should guide them in their dealings with others.

Liberal theory of politics. The Liberal theory of politics is a product of trade and commerce. For instance, it flourished in Athens during the time of Pericles when Athens turned commercial. Trade brings together men with different customs and opinions, encourages free and fair exchange of views, eliminates dogmaticism, and establishes liberalism. The Liberal creed is one of live-and-let-live. It implies toleration, freedom, moderation, and absence of fanaticism in political programme. Even democracy, when it becomes fanatical, ceases to be liberal. The genuine Liberal never holds his opinions with a fanatic finality and is always prepared, like a scientist, to accept new evidence and change his opinions accordingly.

Locke's faith in "order without authority." Locke preached and propagated religious toleration, representative institutions and the limitation of governmental authority by a system of checks and balances. He stood for "order without authority" which means in the intellectual sphere a measure of agreement among experts after adequate discussion, and, in the practical world, submission to the majority after allowing all parties to state their cases.

Necessity of a rational outlook. The world today is going through a war among ideologies. There is a growing tendency to replace liberalism with something more forceful. The world is also facing a grave danger caused by the invention of the atom bomb. The world can survive only if a rational outlook and the liberal tolerance prevail.

The empiricist theory of knowledge. The empiricist theory of knowledge is half-way between dogma and scepticism. It says that all knowledge is, in some degree, doubtful, though it may be negligible in the field of mathematics. Scientific theories are used only as hypotheses for further research and they are always subject to change and modifications. Even Einstein's theory of relativity has not escaped such modifications. In the political sphere this theory of knowledge discourages infliction of 'a comparatively certain present evil for the sake of a comparatively doubtful future good'. If we are certain that abolition of private capitalism will make mankind happy we are at liberty to pursue this end by means of dictatorship, concentration camps, and world war. But if there be the least doubt about the end we should refrain from doing any such thing.

Liberals *versus* fanatics. In the conflicts between the Liberals and the fanatics, the Liberals have always won. The fanatics failed because they adopted wrong and unscientific means, and roused the hostility of a great many people they wanted to oppress. A greater degree of coherence can, no doubt, be produced on the basis of dogma. But it is impractical because it involves persecution of the important sections of the population. Dogmatic beliefs also cannot contribute to a greater political and social unity. Because of their faith in Empiricism and Liberalism the British could demonstrate the greatest solidarity and social coherence during the Second World War.

Plea for empiricism. Empiricism is to be recommended on the grounds of truth, morality and ethics. Dogma requires authority rather than intelligent thought; it requires persecution of those who oppose it. A dogmatic approach fosters hatred, discourages negotiation between the rivals, and considers war the only path to reach a solution. And war in modern times may mean total destruction of the human race. Empiricist Liberalism, on the other hand, is the only acceptable philosophy today. Only this philosophy can be adopted by a sensible person who wants scientific evidence for his beliefs, and places human happiness over everything else. In the prevailing state of chaos and confusion empiricism can play the most important role in saving the world and mankind.

II. ANNOTATIONS

Page 9

Instrumentalism : a form of pragmatism usually associated with John Dewey, the noted philosopher. *Empiricism* : a philosophy that holds observation and experiment, and not theory, to be the basis of knowledge. Locke and Hume were the most important exponents of this philosophy. *Hume* : David Hume (1711-1776), a famous British philosopher and historian.

T.H. Green (1836-1882) : British philosopher and political scientist. He was a follower of Kant and Hegel. *Aquinas* (1226-1274): A prominent Italian theologian whose *Summa Theologica* is a standard authority in the Roman Catholic Church. He was canonised in 1323. *Marx* : Karl Marx (1818-1883), a famous political theorist and the author of *Das Kapital* which laid the foundations of modern communism. *Nazis* : Members of the notorious German National Socialist Party founded by Hitler. The Nazis under Hitler seized power in Germany and committed numerous brutalities. *Kant* : Immanuel Kant (1742-1804), a German philosopher who wrote the *Critique of Pure Reason*. *Fichte* (1762-1814) : Another German philosopher who belonged to the school of Kant. *Hegel* (1770-1831): The most distinguished German philosopher. His philosophy has been discussed, in some detail, by Russell in this essay.

Page 10

Locke : John Locke (1632-1704), is a famous English philosopher, political scientist, and the writer of the well known *Essay Concerning Human Understanding*. His philosophy of empiricism has been discussed in this essay. *Ethics* : code of moral values. *Cosmological* : relating to the universe.

Page 11

Oligarchy : Government or State, governed by the few. *Pre-Socratics* : Those who lived before Socrates (469-399 B.C.), a famous Greek philosopher who advocated justice and truth. *Old Testament* :

The first portion of the Bible. *Scepticism* : Belief that there cannot be any certainty of truth in a particular fact, or theory. *Anarchy*: Absence of government; disorder. *Protagoras* : Famous ancient Greek philosopher who was expelled from Athens for his atheistic views. He figures in Plato's *Dialogues* as an interlocutor.

Page 12

Hobbes : Thomas Hobbes (1588-1679), English philosopher and political thinker. He expounded his philosophy in his well-known work *Leviathan. reactionary* : one opposed to progress. *bugbears* : imagined objects of fear. *Democritus* (460-361 B.C.): an ancient Greek philosopher, known as "the laughing philosopher" for his gaiety; he was one of the founders of the atomic theory of the formation of the universe.

Page 13

Epicurus : Athenian philosopher (300 B.C.) and teacher who founded the school of thought known as Epicureanism. He taught that the highest good was pleasure or practice of virtue. *Lucretius* : Roman poet of the first century B.C. *Vaughan* : Henry Vaughan (1622-1695), one of the metaphysical poets. *Descartes* (1596-1650) : French philosopher, considered to be the father of modern philosophy. *Leibniz* (1648-1716): German philosopher and mathematician. *Peloponnesian War* : a war fought during 431-404 B.C. between Athens and Sparta in which Sparta came out victorious. *Hellenic* : Of Hellene, *i.e.*, Greece. *quisling* : person cooperating with an enemy who has occupied his country; after the name of Vidkun Quisling, a Norwegian army officer who sided with the Nazi Germans against his own country.

Page 14

Utopia : an imaginary state with a perfect social system, described by Sir Thomas More in his book *Utopia*. *exegesis* : exposition. Plato's '*Republic*' : A book by the famous philosopher, Plato, in which he presents his idea of an ideal state. *Rule Britannia* : a patriotic song, written by James Thomson, that glorifies England. *The British Grenadiers* : another patriotic song of Great Britain. *Eugenics* : of the science of production of fine children. *infanticide* : murder of infants. *Status quo* : unchanged position.

Page 15

boa constrictor : a kind of python, usually found in Brazil, that kills its prey by crushing it to death. *Galileo* : Galileo Galilei (1564-1642), a well-known Italian mathematician, physicist and astronomer. He supported the Copernican theory of the universe according to which the earth revolves round the sun. This brought him into conflict with the Church because the scriptures consider the earth to be the centre of the universe. Ultimately Galileo had to repudiate the theory of Copernicus. Galileo's discoveries played a very important role in the development of science. *indubitable* : that cannot be doubted. *Laplace* (1749-1827): French mathematician and astronomer whose contributions to science include the demonstration of the stability of the solar system. *nebulae* : plural of nebula; nebula is a luminous path made by cluster of distant stars. *Sirius* : also known as the Dog Star; it is the brightest star in the heavens. *cataclysm* : violent upheaval. *parochial* : confined to narrow area. *trilobite* : name of an extinct marine animal.

Page 16

Neros : Men like Nero, the Roman emperor in the first century, notorious for his brutalities. It is said that on his order Rome was set on fire and he played on the fiddle when the city was burning. *Genghis Khan* : a tyrant and a Mongol conqueror (1162-1227) who set up a vast kingdom. *Hitler* : German leader (1889-1944) who set up the notorious Nazi party in Germany, committed numerous brutalities on the Jews, and plunged the world into the Second World War.

Page 17

Andromeda : the name of a constellation or group of stars, *lucubrations* : nocturnal studies or meditations; learned discourses.

Page 18

Dialectic : art of investigating and testing of truth by discussion. *terrestrial*: earthy. *farrago* : medley; hotch-potch.

Page 19

Prussia : a state, now a part of Germany. *deification* : Making a God of something. *Heraclitus* : a Greek philosopher who flourished around 500 B.C. In his opinion, all things in the universe are in a state of flux.

Page 20

Ionian cities of Asia Minor : Ionia was the ancient name of a part of Asia Minor. The major Ionian cities were Ephesus, Smyrna, Samoa etc. Asia Minor is a peninsula extending from the Armenian and Kurdistan highlands in Asia. *Pericles* : a Greek statesman belonging to the fifth century B.C. *Lombard cities* : cities such as Milan, Brescia, Pavia and Mantua, that belonged to Lombardy in Italy.

Page 21

Rousseau : Jean Jacques Rousseau (1712-1778), he was a prominent novelist and philosopher. His revolutionary ideas against the existing social order inspired, to a great extent, the French Revolution. *Cromwell* : Oliver Cromwell, who led the Parliamentary Party in the Civil War in England. He was the Lord Protector of England from 1653-1658. *Robespierre* (1758-1794) : He was the leader of the group called the Jacobins in the French Revolution. A fanatical Republican, he was one of the leaders responsible for unleashing the Reign of Terror. He paid for his fanaticism by being beheaded at the guillotine. *The Council of Nicaea* : the first Council of the Christian Chruch held in 325 A.D. in Nicaea, an ancient town in Asia Minor. *geneticists* : persons who specialise in genetics, the study of heredity and variation, including the physiology of reproduction and the art of breeding.

Page 22

Ptolemaic and Copernican systems : views of the nature of the solar system associated with Ptolemy who lived in the second century, and Copernicus who lived from 1473 to 1543. *Swift's war between the Big-endians and Little-endians* : Jonathan Swift in his *Gulliver's Travels* describes a war between the Big-endians and the Little-endians to decide whether an egg should be broken at its big end or at its small end. Swift here satirizes wars and controversies often arising over frivolous matters.

Page 23

Hengist, Horsa : Hengist was the leader of the first Anglo-Saxon invaders of England; Horsa was his brother. According to one view they are only legendary names, and according to another Horsa and Hengist were one and the same person. *Einstein's general theory of relativity* : the theory put forth by Einstein in 1905. The theory states that time and distance as measured by an observer are relative and cannot be absolute. *heretics* : those who hold unorthodox opinions.

Page 24

eschatology : doctrine of death, judgement, heaven and hell. *Auschwitz* : town in Poland where the Nazi Germans set up a concentration camp, and tortured and exterminated thousands of Jews.

Page 25

Edict of Nantes : the edict issued by Henry IV of France in 1598 to grant toleration to the Protestants. The order was revoked by Louis XIV in 1655. *Huguenots* : French Protestants in the 16th and 17th centuries.

III. EXPLANATIONS WITH CRITICAL COMMENTS

1. On the Continent distinctions have been more clearcut, and there has been a greater readiness to accept or reject a block of doctrines as a whole, without critical scrutiny of each separate part. *(Page 9)*

These lines occur in the essay 'Philosophy and Politics' by Bertrand Russell, one of the greatest thinkers of the modern age. Here in his introductory remarks Russell tells us that the connection of philosophy with politics has been less evident in Britain than in the Continental countries (in Europe). According to Russell, the intellectuals of the Continental countries of Europe have a clear idea about the different systems of thought and sets of principles propounded by various philosophers. And, unlike Britain, in these countries there is a tendency and readiness to accept or reject a set of doctrines or principles as a whole, without caring for the details and without a proper critical analysis of the different parts. Thus we find Soviet Russia accepting the principles of Karl Marx and Germany embracing idealism.

2. Among modern philosophers, the ideal of unending and unchanging bliss has been replaced by that of evolution, in which there is supposed to be an orderly progress towards a goal which is never quite attained or at any rate has not been attained at the time of writing. The change of outlook is part of the substitution of dynamics for statics which began with Galileo, and which has increasingly affected all modern thinking , whether scientific or political. *(Page 15)*

These lines have been taken from Bertrand Russell's famous essay, 'Philosophy and Politics'. Here Russell is criticising Plato's ideal of static perfection, and upholding the view of the modern philosophers such as Hobbes and others. Plato in his *Republic* propounded his theory of static perfection. But, according to Russell, man is a restless animal and cannot remain content like a boa constrictor that sleeps for a long period just after taking a good meal. In his support he quotes a famous line from Hobbes : "Felicity consisteth in prospering, and not in having prospered". Modern philosophers are also of the same view as they understand human nature much better. Hence the ideas of eternal bliss without any change have been totally discarded by them. They now believe in evolution, which, according to them, implies a systematic progress towards a goal which can never be fully attained. This new outlook of the modern philosopher is linked with the change that has taken place in the realm of science after substituting statics with dynamics. Galileo was the pioneer to have initiated this change from the study of statics dealing with objects at rest to dynamics that deals with objects in motion. And this sound outlook has profoundly influenced modern thinking both in the realm of science and politics.

These lines also reveal Russell's power of expressing deep thoughts in a very lucid style.

> 3. Even democracy, when it becomes fanatical, as it did among Rousseau's disciples in the French Revolution, ceases to be Liberal; indeed, a fanatical belief in democracy makes democratic institutions impossible, as appeared in England under Cromwell and in France under Robespierre. (*Page 21*)

In these noteworthy lines taken from Russell's 'Philosophy and Politics', Russell is discussing about the significance of the Liberal creed and the evil effects of fanaticism and dogmatism. The most important thing about the Liberal creed is that it implies due toleration, in general, and moderation and absence of fanaticism in political programmes. A liberal man is never dogmatic or fanatical. Liberalism and dogmatism can never go together. A man with a liberal creed holds his opinions tentatively, as he may have to change if fresh evidence proves it to be wrong. And according to Russell even democracy loses its liberal banner if it adopts dogmatical ideas and fanatical ways, although it is generally accepted to be most liberal and the best form of government. Russell then takes up two examples from history to substantiate his point. Firstly, in the Civil War in England, Cromwell : he defeated the Royalist force and then got Charles I executed and founded a republic after abolishing monarchy. But he became so fanatical that people became disgusted and restored monarchy after his death. The same thing happened in France. It was, in fact, the disciples of Rousseau who brought about a great revolution in France. But soon after their unprecedented success the revolutionaries under the leadership of Robespierre threw overboard Rousseau's liberal and democratic ideas and became stark fanatics ushering in the Reign of Terror. Finally the victor had to become the victim of the guillotine.

> 4. For these various reasons, it is not to be expected that, in the long run, nations addicted to dogmatic philosophy will have the advantage over those of a more empirical temper. Nor is it true that dogma is necessary for social coherence when social coherence is called for; no nation could have shown more of it than the British showed in 1940. (*Page 25*)

In these lines from 'Philosophy and Politics,' Russell explodes the false notion that in a war between Liberals and fanatics, the fanatics are sure to win, as they possess a greater unshakable belief in the righteousness of their cause. History shows that in every important war since 1700 the democratic side has been victorious. The main point is that the systems of dogmas have very little rational or empirical foundations. In our times Marxism and Fascism are examples of such dogmatic beliefs. With the help of their irrational beliefs Marxists and Fascists may have the initial advantage of bringing about a great social and political coherence among their followers. But the great drawback is that such dogmatic beliefs involve the persecution of important sections of the population. And the worst case of such a thing was Hitler's Germany. Totally misled by blind and dogmatic political beliefs Hitler persecuted the Jews and expelled them from Germany. And the sad consequence was that with the help of the Jewish scientists Americans first invented the atom bomb. And this was the ultimate cause of Germany's doom and defeat. Thus Russell convincingly establishes the fact that in the long run the nations with Liberal ideas and empirical concepts score over the nations with irrational and dogmatic principles. As regards social coherence he points out that the British without any such dogmatic beliefs displayed wonderful solidarity and striking social coherence during the Second World War, especially during the very hard times of the 1940s.

> 5. Our confused and difficult world needs various things if it is to escape disaster, and among these one of the most necessary is that in the nations which still uphold Liberal beliefs, these beliefs should be wholehearted and profound, not apologetic towards dogmatisms of the right and of the left, but deeply persuaded of the value of liberty, scientific freedom, and mutual forbearance. For without these beliefs life on our politically divided but technically unified planet will hardly continue to be possible. (*Pages 25-26*)

These are the concluding lines of Russell's renowned essay, 'Philosophy and Politics.' Here Russell fervently appeals to all nations, rather the whole of humanity to adopt empiricist Liberalism, which is not incompatible with democratic socialism, as their creed and philosophy. Dogma demands authority in place of intelligent thought to verify the truth of the concepts by evidence. But adherents of Liberalism hold their beliefs in a tentative manner with a readiness to change their opinions if fresh evidence suggests otherwise. Russell is afraid that adherents of rival dogmas may precipitate a world war, as argument is not recognized by them as a means of arriving at truth. So the most urgent need of our times is a whole-hearted recognition of the value of liberty, scientific outlook and mutual tolerance. As regards technological knowledge and progress in the realm of science our world seems to be unified, but politically it is divided into various liberal as well as dogmatic groups bent on crushing one another. And to save the world from the brink of an unprecedented catastrophe we must discard all sorts of dogmatism of the Right and of the Left and stick to the philosophy of Empiricism and Liberalism sincerely and whole-heartedly.

IV. CRITICAL APPRECIATION

Russell as a defender of democracy. Russell, in writing 'Philosophy and Politics' is obviously inspired by his passion for democratic principles and his uncompromising opposition to dictatorship in any form. He attaches great value to mutual toleration and world peace and has an abhorrence of authoritarianism, totalitarianism, dictatorship, and anything that may lead to a war. That is why his main purpose in this essay is to expose the absurdity and the dangerous implications of Hegel's philosophy, to point out the fallacies in Plato's *Republic*, and to advocate Empiricism that has given birth to the concept of Democracy.

Attack on Hegel's philosophy. Russell has taken pains to discuss in detail Hegel's philosophy that should be considered unacceptable and dangerous to mankind. Hegel's theory of the 'Absolute Idea' is absurd and meaningless, because, in Russell's words, this 'Absolute Idea' is merely "pure thought thinking about pure thought". Russell has shown how Hegel has advocated absolute monarchy, a ban on free speech, and war. Russell is surprised that such nonsensical views should have found such wide acceptance. The Nazis, under Hitler, and Marx came under the influence of Hegel's philosophy. Russell implies, in so many words, that we should be aware of the grave implications of such philosophies as Hegel's and discard them at once in the interest of mankind.

Criticism of Plato's 'Republic'. Plato and his well known work have come under severe attack in this essay. According to Russell, the acceptance of Plato's *Republic* is a perfect example of literary snobbery. Plato has advocated war through his concept of education according to which the chief purpose of education is to produce courage in battle. The *Republic* advocates a censorship on stories told by mothers to children, a ban on Homer and the drama, censorship of music, and approves government practising trickery and lying. Plato, according to Russell, veiled his absurd thought with a metaphysical mist, and deceived the world for ages. A man like Russell, who has any regard for the ideas of liberty, equality and fraternity, cannot accept such views.

Defence of Empiricism : Russell's innate respect of democratic ideals makes him turn to the philosophy of empiricism, founded by

Locke. He shows how this philosophy gives rise to the Liberal theory in politics, advocates mutual understanding and toleration, and eliminates fanaticism in political programmes. According to Rousseau, empirical liberalism is the only philosophy acceptable to a man who demands some scientific evidence for his belief, and at the same time, is more concerned with human happiness than anything else. Russell himself is such a man.

Russell's restraint and tolerance. Russell, in this essay, has launched a vigorous attack on Hegel and Plato. He has the ability to expose evil in all its nakedness through unassailable logic and reasoning. He exposes the follies of the philosophies of Hegel and Plato with rare conviction but never gets bitter. His criticism of Hegel is blended with restraint, and shows no signs of emotion. All through the essay he remains the gentleman that he is. This restraint demonstrates Russell's tolerance for others' opinions, his belief that he can also be wrong, and establishes him as a true empiricist.

Russell's scholarship. This essay, like all his works, demonstrates Russell's eruditon. His scholarship allows him to draw at will illustrations from history, astronomy, mathematics and other spheres to establish his points. There is a large number of references to philosophers and writers such as Hume, T.H. Green, Marx, Kant, Fichte, Protagoras, Democritus and others.

Russell's style. Very few can surpass Russell in his mastery of the English language. Anything he writes is characterised by the qualities of lucidity and precision. He can discuss philosophy, metaphysics, or complicated scientific theories in a language that is comprehensible even to a layman. He can give a lucid idea of Empiricist Liberalism, and why it is acceptable, in the simplest way : "I conclude that, in our day as in the time of Locke, Empiricist Liberalism (which is not incompatible with democratic socialism) is the only philosophy that can be adopted by a man who, on the one hand, demands some scientific evidence for his beliefs, and, on the other hand, desires human happiness more than the prevalence of this or that party or creed". The essay abounds in such specimens of lucid, almost transparent writing. The following lines which are meant to show the fundamental difference between change and progress demonstrate the quality of precision : "Change is one thing, progress is another. 'Change' is scientific, 'progress' is ethical ; change is indubitable whereas progress is a matter of controversy."

Though the essay deals with complicated philosophical theories, at no point does it become dull reading. Russell has a tendency to have recourse to irony and humour in order to lend an element of entertainment to his writing. 'Philosophy and Politics' is no exception. His dismissal of Hegel's definition of the Absolute Idea as merely "pure thought thinking about pure thought" is humorously ironical. These recurrent flashes of ironical humour make us feel that he is fond of ridiculing folly by laughing at them.

4

Philosophy for Laymen

I. SUMMARY

Necessity of philosophy. Mankind has always been confronted with two kinds of problems : first, the problem of mastering natural forces and of gaining the knowledge and skill to produce tools and weapons; second, the problem of finding the best way to utilise the acquired command over the forces of nature. The first problem is now dealt with by science and scientific technique. The second problem, which is equally important, includes political and social problems and can be tackled only with a wide survey of human life that philosophy can provide. Acquisition of skill and technique cannot be complete without knowing the proper way to use it. The invention of agriculture, for instance, involved human sacrifice in the beginning. Invention of atomic bombs has become a menace today, only because we do not know how to use our scientific skill.

Philosophy and the layman. 'Philosophy' means 'love of wisdom' and in this sense, has to be cultivated by men. Philosophy as a guide to wisdom should be separated from the philosophy of specialists, and made a part of general education. In fact such distinction has to be made in all branches of academic study. The aim of education should be to attach more importance to things of cultural interest.

Two objects of philosophy. Philosophy, from its earlier days, has had two different aims : firstly, its object has been a theoretical understanding of the structure of the world : secondly, it has tried to discover the best possible way of life. Philosophy has thus been closely associated with science on the one hand and with religion on the other. The view that philosophy is unprogressive is not justified. In fact, many scientific inventions are based on the hypotheses put forth by philosophers. Anaximander in the sixth century B C. had a theory of evolution which was later rejected and substituted by Darwin's theory. As long as a hypothesis cannot be verified by science it remains a part of philosophy, but as soon as science becomes capable of testing the hyphothesis, it becomes a part of science. Philosophy is thus often deprived of its due credit which is appropriated by science.

Utility of philosophy. The utility of philosophy, on the theoretical side, is not confined to speculations that are confirmed or rejected by science later on. We should not attach much importance to what science knows or to what it does not know. We should not think that skill can replace wisdom, and at the same time nor should we refuse to admit that science, if used with wisdom, can open vistas of happiness for mankind. Philosophy can help us to attain the right attitude towards science, by making clear at once the scope and limitations of scientific knowledge. Science cannot explain many things. It cannot tell us anything about the life after death, whether mind dominates matter or *vice versa*, the purpose of the universe, and so on. These questions are of universal interest and have not been adequately answered so far and should, therefore, continue to employ the mind. One function of philosophy is to keep interest in these issues alive.

Dogmatism and scepticism. Philosophy can protect us from two possible evils—dogmatism and scepticism. Passion for quickly achieved certainty often produces silly dogmatic beliefs that succeeds in dividing the human race into rival groups of fanatics, each group convinced that its own brand of nonsense is sacred truth, while the other side's is damnable heresy. Dogmatism is an enemy to peace and a barrier to democracy. The natural demand for certainty is also an intellectual vice. Much of the cruelty that has been committed has been the doing of men who regarded their own opinions as certainties and acted on that basis. Liquidation of capitalists in communist countries and extermination of the Jews in Germany are only a few examples of this. Scepticism cannot be a solution to this problem, because while dogmatism is harmful scepticism is absolutely useless. Dogmatism is certain of knowing, the other is certain of ignorance. The aim of philosophy should be to dissipate *certainty*, whether of knowledge or of ignorance. Therefore, instead of saying, 'I know this' we should say, 'I more or less know something more or less like this'. Similarly, a person who says that democracy is good should always remember that this contention is not so certain as saying two and two make four. However, it is also necessary to learn to act on assumption sometimes. In that case we have to choose the best possible assumption and be careful to avoid such assumptions which may cause harm to others in a significant way. For instance while a person is taking a party to a picnic he may assume that the weather will remain fine and as such carrying mackintoshes would not be necessary. He can act upon this assumption only if the members of his party are of sound health and can endure a little wetting. But if there is a chance of anyone catching pneumonia in case his assumption goes wrong, he is not supposed to act on this assumption.

Philosophy and Religion. If philosophy is expected to play an effective role in the lives of men it must continue to suggest a way of life. In this respect it is trying to do something of what religion has done, but with certain differences. The greatest difference is that there is no appeal to the authority of tradition, or that of a sacred book. The second difference is that a philosopher is not supposed to establish a Church. The third is that more emphasis should be laid on the intellectual virtues than has been customary since the decay of the Greek civilization.

Role of a philosopher today. The role palyed by the modern philosopher differs from that of the ancient philosopher in one important way. The ancient philosopher appealed to the gentlemen of leisure and freedom. The modern philosopher, on the other hand, has to appeal to the immense majority of educated men who lack freedom and have to earn their living within the framework of society. Today a man's ethical convictions have to be expressed more in political advocacy, and less in private behaviour, than was the case in antiquity.

Philosophy and ethics. The pursuit of philosophy is based on the belief that knowledge is good, even if what is known is painful. The philosophic spirit will prompt a person to wish his beliefs to be as true as he can make them. Such a person will love to know, and hate to be in error. The philosophic spirit can also eliminate such beliefs as are caused by fear or self-esteem. It can lend us intellectual sobriety that will make us scrutinize all our beliefs, and put an end to numerous disputes. Philosophy can inculcate another intellectual virtue, namely, generality or impartiality. This virtue helps us get rid of all emotional bias while dealing with a political problem and helps us to look at things objectively. It is not necessary that the study of philosophy has to be allotted as much time as that given to technical studies. But even in the time that can be spared philosophy can help increase the student's value as a human being and as a citizen. It can encourage the habit of exact and careful thinking, provide an impersonal conception of the ends of life, make an individual realise his relation to society and get a clear view of the whole history of man in relation to astronomical cosmos. Philosophy can, among other things, make our vision clear, make us aware of the evils of the world, and help us take steps to eliminate those evils from this tortured world.

II. ANNOTATIONS

Page 27

Cult : system of religious worship. *pillage* : plunder.

Page 28

Cataclysm : political or social upheaval. *Sennacherib* : ruler of Assyria in the 7th century B.C., known for his public works. *Aeschylus* :

(525-456 B.C.) : one of the three great Greek tragedians. He wrote *Agamemnon* and *Prometheus Vinatus*. *Aquinas* : St. Thomas Aquinas (1226-1274), Italian scholar and theologian. He was raised by the church to sainthood. *Duns Scotus* : Joannes Duns Scotus (1265-1308) belonged to the Fransiscan Order. He lectured at Oxford and Paris.

Page 29

Conspectus : general view of subjects, scenes etc.; synopsis. *Anaximander* (611-547 B.C.) : Greek philosopher and astronomer.

Page 30

Empedocles : Greek philosopher and poet who flourished in the 5th century B.C. He believed in the presence of four elements —fire, earth, air and water—and of two opposing forces—love and hate. *pooh-pooh* : express contempt.

Page 31

Parochialism : narrow-mindedness. *Arians* : holders of the doctrine of Arius of Alexandria (4th century) who held that Christ was not equal to God. *Crusaders* : soldiers sent out of Europe in the 11th, 12th and 13th centuries to liberate Palestine for the Christians.

Page 32

Promised Land : the land to which Moses led the Israelites : Canaan. *modicum* : small quantity. *charlatans* : quacks; pretenders to knowledge. *proviso* : stipulation.

Page 33

mackintoshes : water-proof garment. The material was patented by C. Macintosh (1766-1843). *hierarchy* : any graded organisation. *pathological* : of diseases. *Muggletonian* : a member of a sect founded by Lodowicke Muggleton (1609-68). They believed that God possessed a human body and that Eve was the incarnation of the evil spirit.

Page 34

Sophists: Ancient Greek paid teachers of philosophy and rhetoric; persons who indulge in fallacious reasoning. *Auguste Comte* (1798-1857): French philosopher who was the founder of the philosophical system known as positivism. Positivism recognised positive facts and observable phenomena.

Page 36

Millenium : a golden age of happiness and prosperity.

III. EXPLANATIONS WITH CRITICAL COMMENTS

> 1. On the one hand there has been the problem of mastering natural forces, of acquiring the knowledge and the skill required to produce tools and weapons and to encourage Nature in the production of useful animals and plants. *(Page 27)*

Russell observes in his essay 'Philosophy for Laymen' that since the emergence of civilization mankind has been facing two kinds of problems. In the quoted lines he is referring to one of those two kinds. Before and in the beginning of the historic times men were helpless against the violent forces of Nature. The superior intelligence of men made them realise the necessity of mastering those forces for survival against heavy odds. They knew that if they wanted to survive the highly competitive struggle for existence they had to acquire the skill to produce weapons with the help of which they could make up for their physical handicap and protect themselves against ferocious animals. Their intelligence told them that if they could master Nature, they could even use it as an instrument for producing such animals and plants that were useful to men and could make human life much easier and more comfortable. The entire history of civilization has been, therefore, nothing but the history of human endeavour to achieve those ends.

> 2. It will be found that increase of skill has not, of itself, insured any increase of human happiness or well-being. When men first learnt to cultivate the soil, they used their knowledge to establish a cruel cult of human sacrifice. *(Page 27)*

The above extract has been taken from the essay, 'Philosophy for Laymen' by Bertrand Russell. Mankind, according to Russell, has been confronted with two kinds of problems : first, the problem of acquiring skill and technique for controlling the forces of Nature and second, the problem of knowing how best to utilise the acquired command over Nature. With the help of science, we have been able to solve the first problem to a considerable extent, but our negligence of the second has often resulted in misuse of that command over Nature. Russell thinks that the problem of knowing the proper use of our scientific skill and knowledge should be given more attention. Our failure to solve this problem has often brought miseries along with our scientific discoveries. For instance, agriculture is one of the most useful inventions by mankind. It has helped us in using Nature as a permanent supplier of food and has made human life more secure. But even such an invention, because of our ignorance of using knowledge properly, continued to add to human miseries through centuries. It was then believed that unless we appeased the gods by sacrificing human beings, the gods would not ensure a good production of crops. This example amply demonstrates that no invented skill can add to our happiness if we do not learn the best way to utilise it.

> 3. A man might say, with enough truth to justify a joke: "Science is what we know, and philosophy is what we don't know". (*Page 30*)

These lines occur in the essay, 'Philosophy for Laymen' by Bertrand Russell. In this essay Russell has attempted to make the laymen realise the importance of philosophy in human life. The laymen generally have a misconception about the aims of philosophy and dismiss it as an unnecessary abstract thing. By pointing out the close relation between science and philosophy Russell tries to dispel the wrong notions from the minds of the laymen. Philosophy, according to Russell, is closely connected with science. In fact, until the 18th century science was regarded as a part of philosophy. Russell says that philosophy is now unjustifiably dubbed as unprogressive. People tend to forget that many of the scientific inventions were based on the hypotheses put forward by the philosophers. Philosophers possess an unlimited range of speculating power and can speculate upon things that the scientists could never dream of. The speculations remain philosophy until they can be tested scientifically and as soon as they are thus verified they cease to be considered philosophy and become science. Anaximander's theory of evolution for instance, was considered philosophy, whereas Darwin's theory is science. Darwin has been given all the credit for his theory but Anaximander is now totally forgotten. The general contempt for philosophy is summed up in the common joke referred to in the quoted lines implying that science is knowledge while philosophy is mere speculation. Russell says we must not forget the contributions made by philosophy in the field of knowledge.

> 4. Dogmatism and scepticism are both, in a sense, absolute philosophies; one is certain of knowing, the other of not knowing. What philosophy should dissipate is *certainty*, whether of knowledge or of ignorance. (*Page 32*)

In these lines from the essay 'Philosophy for Laymen', Bertrand Russell makes an attempt to remove the misconception about philosophy in the minds of the laymen and tries to make us realize the beneficial role that philosophy can play in ensuring human happiness. Russell shows how philosophy can remove the two dangers that hinder human progress, namely, dogmatism and scepticism. He calls these vices philosophies because they too are based on hypothesis which is also the basis of philosophy. Dogmatism consists in certainty of any knowledge and has always proved harmful. Dogmatism has divided mankind into rival groups of fanatics and has encouraged commitment of cruelty among them. It has been the root of many conflicts, like those between Arians and Catholics, Christians and Muslims, or Communists and Fascists. On the other hand scepticism is the opposite extreme of dogmatism and should also be avoided. Scepticism, which implies certainty of ignorance, leads to inaction and, therefore, is useless to mankind. The fact is, if we want progress we must reject these extreme philosophies and learn to act, very often on hypotheses, with an open, flexible mind. We should never be certain about the hypotheses we act upon, and must always be prepared to modify or reject them when we find them wrong. Philosophy can help our minds get rid of this element of certainty that has very often stood in the way of our progress.

> 5. When you act upon a hypothesis which you know to be uncertain, your action should be such as will not have *very* harmful results if your hypothesis is false. In the matter of the picnic, you may risk a wetting if all your party are robust, but not if one of them is so delicate as to run a risk of pneumonia. (*Page 33*)

Russell, while trying to demonstrate the utility of philosophy, tells us that it can help us get rid of two vices that hinder human progress — dogmatism and scepticism. He says that philosophy can teach us to eliminate the element of certainty and to act upon certain necessary hypotheses that cannot be avoided. He refers to the example of taking a party on a picnic to illustrate his view.

Russell says that there are times when we are forced to act upon hypotheses. In such a case we must be careful to admit that the hypothesis we are acting upon may be false. We must take into account the possible consequences in case of such a happening, and refuse to act upon the hypothesis if there is any chance of dangerous or harmful consequences. When a person takes a party on a picnic he may act upon the hypothesis that the weather will remain fine, and, therefore leave mackintoshes behind. If he acts upon a hypothesis that it will rain, he will decide to take mackintoshes. A dogmatic person will certainly act in one of these ways and will not consider the consequences of his hypothesis proving false. A sensible person will, however, first of all take the health of every member into consideration and then decide on which hypothesis he should act. If all the members of his party are robust, he may choose any of these two. But if there is a single member of the party who is not likely to stand a little wetting he will certainly choose the second hypothesis to act on, and take mackintoshes on the picnic. Philosophy can help us to develop the foresight necessary to choose the acceptable hypotheses.

6. In thinking about political problems this kind of emotional bias is bound to be present and only care and practice can enable you to think as objectively as you do in the algebraic problem.

(*Pages 35-36*)

These lines have been taken from the essay, 'Philosophy for Laymen', in which Russell tries to dispel the general misconception about philosophy and attempts to make his readers understand how philosophy can contribute to human happiness. Philosophy, according to Russell, can help us develop an objective outlook which is necessary while taking decisions, particularly in the political sphere. While taking such decisions we must rid ourselves of every kind of emotional bias; only then we can be impartial and correct in our decisions. In other words, it is of utmost importance to attain an objectivity akin to what we employ while solving arithmetical problems. When we solve a mathematical problem that involves three gentlemen going up a mountain, we replace the gentlemen with symbols such as, A, B and C and forget their real identities. We are not emotionally involved with them. In the political sphere if we can develop this kind of impartial attitude towards other countries we shall be able to solve many of our disputes most of which are based on an emotional bias. Philosophy can, by encouraging this objective outlook among us, ensure peace and happiness for the world.

IV. CRITICAL APPRECIATION

Conception of 'philosophy'. In the essay 'Philosophy for Laymen' Russell has endeavoured to remove the general misconception of philosophy. He offers us a vivid idea of the role philosophy can play in increasing human happiness and well-being. Mankind has made significant progress in the matter of gaining control over the forces of Nature with the help of scientific achievements. But Russell rightly points out that the scientific inventions have not been supplemented with the knowledge of their proper use and as such have hardly been able to contribute to human happiness. He establishes his point by referring to the human sacrifice that agriculture once involved and also the menace of the atomic bombs. We cannot but agree with Russell that the human race is now living a precarious existence and that 'wisdom' has to be acquired by us as soon as possible to save it from disaster. 'Philosophy' that literally implies 'love of wisdom' can naturally provide that necessary wisdom.

Philosophy and science. Philosophy is often dismissed as merely a bunch of speculations that have no basis in reality. Russell refutes this argument saying that until the 18th century science was considered a part of philosophy and that many significant scientific discoveries had their roots in speculations made by philosophers. He points out that as long as a hypothesis cannot be tested and verified it is regarded by us as philosophy; as soon as it is verified it becomes science. Anaximander, for instance, had a theory of evolution as early as the 6th century B . C. But it was considered philosophy because it was not supported by evidence. When Darwin came up with his proven theory we welcomed it and gave all the credit to Darwin. In our disregard for philosophy we tend to ignore the possibility that the very idea of Darwin's theory was derived from Anaximander. It is true that in all such cases the credit that is due to philosophy has been unjustifiably appropriated by science. Moreover, Russell points out very rightly, there have been certain issues of universal interest—the question of life after death for instance—which can never be answered by science. Philosophy must be allowed to continue to explore such issues and to keep the interest in them alive. We agree with the author that if these issues disappear much of the colour of our life will be lost. Such issues also help the growth of a philosophic attitude in us and widen our minds.

Philosophic spirit. Russell, in the course of his essay, has successfully convinced us of the need of developing a philosophic spirit among all men. Any sensible person will admit that dogmatism which implies a 'certainty' of knowledge has caused most of the human miseries by encouraging intolerance and fanaticism. The atrocities committed on the capitalists in communist countries or on the Jews in Nazi Germany were certainly prompted by dogmatic beliefs maintained by the oppressors. Russell, we know, has, all through his life, led a crusade against dogmatism in any form. He is at the same time not in favour of scepticism which is the very opposite of dogmatism. He feels that scepticism, because it implies 'certainty of ignorance', encourages inaction, and is thus, like dogmatism, a hindrance in the way of progress. He believes that only philosophy can eliminate these evils by removing the element of 'certainty' from both of them and by striking the right balance between these two attitudes. Removal of these evils will also teach us to choose the best possible hypothesis, when necessary, to act upon. The philosophic spirit, we agree with Russell, also helps us to develop the intellectual sobriety necessary for being able to look at problems objectively and without bias. It is, indeed, true that if philosophy can rid us of our emotional bias, we shall be free from dogmatism and, as a consequence, many conflicts of the world will come to an end. The world will become a much better place to live in.

Russell's humanism : All of Russell's works are characterised by an essence of humanism. Russell is concerned with the dangers that have been confronting the human race, and has taken much pains to trace the causes of our sufferings and prescribe appropriate remedies for them. In this essay he recommends a study of philosophy as a possible measure against dogmatism and scepticism which are, according to him, the sources of intolerance and inaction, respectively, that may ruin mankind. He sincerely believes that only the growth of a universal philosophic spirit can encourage tolerance and understanding among individuals and nations, and make possible the arrival of a golden age of happiness and prosperity.

Style. Russell, as we know, is well-known for the simplicity and clarity of his prose style and his supreme command over language. He can express the most complex and subtle thoughts in such a lucid and precise way that even an ordinary reader can understand them without any difficulty. Any sentence or paragraph quoted at random, can demonstrate these qualities. Here is an extract as illustration: "Anaximander in the sixth century B.C. had a theory of evolution, and maintained that men are descended from fishes. This was philosophy because it was a speculation unsupported by detailed evidence, but Darwin's theory of evolution was science, because it was based on the succession of forms of life as found in fossils, and upon the distribution of animals and plants in many parts of the world. A man might say, with enough truth to justify a joke, 'Science is what we know, and philosophy is what we don't know'." It is indeed wonderful that in a few simple sentences he has been able to express the connection between science and philosophy and also the present misconception regarding the utility of philosophy. This essay is one of the easiest of his collection *Unpopular Essays*. Perhaps, the absence of ironical humour, which Russell is so fond of using, accounts for the easy understanding of this essay.

Another feature of his prose style is its terseness. Russell, out of his tendency to compress thoughts and ideas, often produces short, simple sentences which are epigrammatic in character. Here are two examples of such statements :

> Dogmatism is an enemy to peace, and an insuperable barrier to democracy.
>
> What philosophy should dissipate is *certainty* whether of knowledge or of ignorance.

5

The Future of Mankind

I. SUMMARY

Three possibilities. One of the following three things may happen before the end of the present century:— (*i*) The end of human life in this world. (*ii*) Return to the primitive barbarism after a catastrophic diminution of the population of the world. (*iii*) A unification of the world under a single government possessing an absolute control over all the important weapons of war.

First possibility : end of human race. This possibility may not materialise in the event of a third world war unless the war is postponed for a longer time. In case war ends without a decision, further technical and scientific developments will follow. The resultant progress in atomic research will provide more destructive weapons which will ultimately wipe out all life on this earth.

Second possibility : return to barbarism. In case the first possibility does not fully materialise, *i.e.*,the human race is not totally wiped out, there can be a return to barbarism which whould leave open the possibility of a gradual return to civilization. The scientific war will destroy the cities, industries, laboratories and libraries; the bacteriological warfare will cause famine and pestilence and will spare only a few survivors. The great states will break up and the survivors, now disillusioned with science, will revert to a primitive village economy.

Third possibility : establishment of a world government. The establishment of a single government with monopoly of the weapons of war may be achieved in various ways : (*a*) by the victory of the United States in the next world war, (*b*) by the victory of the U.S.S.R., (*c*) by agreement, and (*d*) by forming an alliance of nations strong enough to subdue even Russia. The last one is the best because it may not involve a world war at all.

Arguments used against project of world government. One common objection to the project of a world government is that the project is utopian and impossible. This is the view of those who believe that a world government can be set up only by agreement. Russell agrees with this view because he, too, feels that the mutual suspicion between Russia and the West will stand in the way of such an agreement. Russell thinks that a world government can come into existence only through the use of force. The other critics of the project do not consider this necessary. They argue that wars have occurred regularly, but the human race has survived and that there is no reason why it should not survive a few more wars. They even advocate war because it provides an opportunity for heroism and self-sacrifice. Such people are blind to the rapid scientific and technical developments of the weapons that will destroy civilisation even if they do not completely wipe out the human race. Mankind must adopt a system to ensure disappearance of wars. In Russell's opinion, a world government is the only acceptable system in the present situation.

Result of an atomic war. If things are allowed to continue as they are, sooner or later there will be an atomic war between Russia and the western democracies. As a result of this, Western Europe, including Great Britain, will be almost exterminated. If the two warring countries survive as organised states, they will fight again. But if there is victory for one side, that side will rule the world, and thus a unitary government of mankind will come into existence; if not, human civilisation will perish. In Russell's opinion threat of force, and if it fails, actual force has to be employed to establish a world government.

Advantages of a world government. In a world under such a government there will be no successful rebellion as the government will be too strong for it. Occasional assassinations will be there, but mass-killings will stop. There will be peace and material comfort for everybody. These factors will make people good natured and kind. A world government, whether it is formed by Russia, or by America, is, therefore, preferable to the present state of anarchy.

Preference for an American victory. An American victory is preferred because in that country there is greater respect than in Russia for the things that are essential in a civilised way of life. These essential things are the freedom of thought, freedom of inquiry, freedom of discussion, and feelings of humaneness. A world empire of the U.S.S.R. will mean, as we have seen in Poland, a ban on every kind of freedom. There education will be reduced to learning the formulae of communism as formulated by Stalin ; the dissidents and intellectuals will be liquidated or imprisoned ; the middle class will more or less be annihilated, and there will be mass expulsion. Science, philosophy, art and literature, under Russian control, will become narrow and sycophantic adjuncts of the government. No individual will think, or even feel, for himself, but each will become just a unit of the mass. That is why Russell considers a victory for Russia disastrous for mankind.

Favourable consequences of an American victory. An American victory would be much more welcome because, in the first place, it would also mean a victory for an Alliance. In that case the other members of the Alliance would be able to insist upon retaining a large part of their traditional independence. Thus the cultures of France, Great Britain and other countries would remain intact.

Moreover, in the U.S.A., there is no such thing as the all-pervasive Russian orthodoxy. Here there is complete freedom to hold any view and express it whereas in Russia such a thing would invite trouble. In America a professor of philosophy may be an idealist, a materialist, a pragmatist or whatever he wishes to be, in Russia he must be a dialectical materialist always ready to follow the official line of thinking. So in Russia, chances of development in the spheres of intellect and technology are remote whereas it is not so in America.

There is a greater degree of economic inequality in Russia than in America. Economic inequalities, of course, exist in every country. But in a democratic country like America such inequalities tend to decrease whereas in an oligarchy like Russia they always tend to increase.

Three dangers to be guarded against. We have to guard against three dangers to save mankind. They are : (*a*) the extinction of the human race ; (*b*) a return to barbarism ; (*c*) the establishment of a universal slave state involving misery for the vast majority, and stagnation of progress in knowledge and thought.

The first two dangers can be averted only if great wars are brought to an end ; and the only way to do so is to bring about the concentration of armed forces under a single authority. The third danger can be averted by the formation of a firm Alliance. The first step would be to persuade United States and the British Commonwealth to the necessity of a military unification of the world. Then other nations would be persuaded, if necessary by means of inducements, to enter into an alliance. When the Alliance becomes sufficiently powerful, it would challenge any Great Power still refusing to join it. The resultant war is certain to bring victory to the Alliance. But war may not be necessary; the strength of the Alliance itslelf may force Russia to submit to it. There are now only two fully independent states—Russia and America. Russell hopes that in future the two will be reduced to one, bringing to end the organised wars for ever.

Blessings of an era of peace. The abolition of war and the establishment of a world government are bound to be followed by an era of peace and prosperity. It will no longer be necessary to waste human energy and resources on production of weapons. Attention will be diverted to the promotion of human happiness, and scientific techniques will be used to eradicate poverty through out the world.

Liberty and law. Liberty is good only if it is limited by law. There is now the need for effective law to control international relations. Only a single world government possessing full control over armed forces and armaments can keep in check the unlawful and aggressive intentions of any country and ensure peace in the world. There is hope that one day law rather than private force will govern the relations of nations, and then the world will become a far better place.

II. ANNOTATIONS

Page 38

reversion : return to a previous state. *catastrophic* : disastrous. *radioactive* : capable of emitting rays consisting of material particles travelling at high speed.

Page 39

obliteration : complete destruction. *bacteriological warfare* : warfare in which germs of deadly diseases are used. *cohesion* : sticking or remaining together. *extermination* : complete destruction. *millenium* : a period of one thousand years; the golden age of happiness and prosperity. (It is in this sense that the word has been used here.)

Page 40

sham : false pretension.

Page 41

Gallup Poll : a method of assessing the pattern of voting expected in a forthcoming election. The method was invented by G.H. Gallup, an American, in 1935. *altruism* : interest in the well-being of others.

Page 42

Lloyd George (1863-1945) : British statesman. He became famous by opposing Chamberlain and the Boer War. He became Prime Minister in 1916. *Edward I* (1239-1307) : one of the greatest kings of England. He reigned for 35 years, and conquered Wales and Scotland. *Stalinist orthodoxy* : Communist dogma as preached by the great Russian leader, Joseph Stalin (1879-1935). *glib* : fluent . *shibboleths* : test words or principles or behaviour or opinions, the use of or the inability to use which betrays one's party, nationality etc. *annihilated* : blotted out of existence ; completely destroyed. *perjury* : giving false evidence while on oath.

Page 43

sychophantic : parasitic ; servile. *jejune* : barren ; unsatisfying to the mind. *dons* : fellows, or tutors of college. *Mr. Attlee* : Clement Richard Attlee, a British statesman belonging to the Labour Party. He was Prime Minister from 1945-1951. *analogues* : parallel words or things. *Mendelism* : a proven theory of heredity propounded by Abbe Gregor Mendel (1822-1884), an Austrian monk and biologist. This theory states that only the dominant characteristics of the parents from different species are inherited by the hybrids. Mendel's works laid the foundation of the science of Genetics. *Lysenko* (1898-1977) : Well-known Russian horticulturist. According to him the acquired characteristics could be passed on by the parents to their offspring. His theory, considered to be a social theory of biology, became mandatory for all biologists in Russia. However, in 1964 spurious views were discredited. *debunking* : taking away the glory of a celebrity. *Lincoln* : Abraham Lincoln (1809- 1864), American President and one of the greatest men of history. He led the Union to victory in the American Civil War and liberated the Negroes from slavery. *Lenin* (1870-1924): a great Russian leader. After the Revolution of 1917 he established the Soviet regime in Russia.

Page 44

dialectical materialist : one who believes in Marx's philosophy of the material being of society, based on dialectical analysis. *Oligarchy* : Government, state, governed by the few.

Page 45

recalcitrant : refusing compliance.

Page 46

exorcised : expelled; removed. *homo sapiens* : literally means 'intelligent men'. The phrase is used to mean the human race.

III. EXPLANATIONS WITH CRITICAL COMMENTS

1. Although the last survivor may proclaim himself universal Emperor, his reign will be brief and his subjects will all be corpses. With his death the uneasy episode of life will end, and the peaceful rocks will revolve unchanged until the sun explodes. (*Page 38*)

These lines occur in one of the most famous essays of Russell, 'The Future of Mankind'. Here, in the beginning of the essay he has forecast three possibilities for the future of mankind. In these lines he visualises the first catastrophic possibility that may overwhelm mankind. According to Russell the first possibility is the end of human life, perhaps of all life, on our planet, unless something unexpected occurs before the end of this century. His idea is that unless the peoples of the world become wise enough to bring about international harmony and establish a World Government, a third war, or a fourth world war if the third one is undecisive, is bound to take place. Under the existing state of affairs wisdom may not prevail. And then, with more powerful means of utilizing atomic energy being available, the next war would be absolutely devastating and may wipe out the human race and radioactive clouds may afterwards destroy all living tissues everywhere. With grim humour Russell tells us that one person on our planet may survive for some time and declare himself emperor. But he will have no living subjects and he will also pass away soon. Our earth without any sign of life or change will continue to revolve round the sun for a long period till the day the sun itself explodes and vanishes into the great void.

> 2. Even if the dominant nation is completely devoid of altruism, its leading inhabitants, at least, will achieve a very high level of material comfort, and will be freed from the tyranny of fear. They are likely, therefore, to become gradually more good natured and less likely to persecute. *(Page 41)*

Russell would prefer a world government dominated by America, but even a Russian dominated world government, he feels, would be better than the present chaotic state of affairs. Though a world dominated by Russia would initially be impossible to live in, Russell thinks that gradually things would improve. The Communist's tyranny is rooted in the fear of being overthrown from power. But since in a world government successful rebellion would be impossible, the rulers would slowly gain a sense of security which would have a healthy effect on their mentality. The lack of fear of being overthrown and their material luxury would change them for the better and make them less cruel. Russell thinks that in due time the Russian rulers may become humanised and would grant citizenship to the people of the conquered nations.

> 3. An oligarchy which controls all the means of publicity can perpetrate injustices and cruelties which would be scarcely possible if they were widely known. Only democracy and free publicity can prevent the holders of power from establishing a servile state, with luxury for the few and overworked poverty for the many. *(Page 44)*

These lines have been taken from Russell's brilliant essay, 'The Future Mankind'. After stating the reasons for his preference for an American victory over Soviet Russia in the next world war Russell quite logically exposes the drawbacks of oligarchy or dictatorship and expresses his view regarding the superiority of a democratic form of government. Russell tells us that oligarchy or dictatorship generally controls the press and all other means of publicity. It thus becomes capable of hiding all the cruelties and injustices perpetrated on the people. If the press is free to bring all such misdeeds to the knowledge of the public it is not possible for the few to continue to perpetrate injustices for long on the general mass of people. In a democratic state there is freedom of press and publicity. According to Russell, due to the absence of this freedom of press it has been possible for Soviet Russia to establish greater degree of economic inequality than exists in important democratic countries of the world. Only a dictatorial form of government can reduce people to a servile lot with luxury for the few and overworked poverty for the majority. Only democracy with its liberalism can prevent such atrocious things.

4. But such an armed force, like a municipal police force, is not an end in itself; it is a means to the growth of a social system governed by law, where force is not the prerogative of private individuals or nations, but is exercised only by a natural authority in accordance with rules laid down in advance. (*Page 46*)

These lines occur almost at the end of Russell's essay, 'The Future of Mankind". Here Russell is propounding his favourite view regarding the unification of the world under an international government with absolute control over all armed forces. First of all he tells us that liberty is no doubt good, but it cannot be an absolute good. There must be some checks. We all want to restrain murderers; it is even more important to control murderous states. Hence there is the need of law to limit or restrain liberty whenever required. He rightly suggests that the crying need of the hour in our confused present-day world is to introduce some effective laws to control international relations. But simply the creation of such laws will not solve the knotty problem. There must be some supreme agency to enforce these laws so as to have an effective check on different states. Herein comes the need of a world government having complete control over a single armed force in the world and all the principal weapons of war. This international armed force under the control of the world government will have adequate sanctions to enforce laws to prevent nations from coming into violent conflict with one another for any reason whatsoever. According to Russell this and this alone can save mankind from utter doom and destruction by doing away with global wars in future.

Here we find Russell propounding his favourite theory of world government quite forcefully and sincerely. But it seems this great intellectual has more or less overlooked the impediments in the way of establishing a world government in the world of today. Different nations think in different ways, governed by their pride and prejudices. Probably due to his great concern for the future of mankind he could not think of such insurmountable hurdles and impediments.

IV. CRITICAL APPRECIATION

Prophecy of the future. According to Russell, one of three things may happen before the end of this century. The first possibility is that human life will come to an end after the next world war. The second is that very few survivors will remain after that war and that they will be so disgusted with scientific developments that they will return to a primitive village economy. The third possibility is that one of the two super powers, namely Russia or America, will defeat the other and rule the world; as a result of which a single world government possessing the monopoly of all armed forces and armaments will come into existence.

Russell's predictions have come to nought. Any war involving the super powers will inevitably be a nuclear one. Nuclear weapons now have such striking power that any such war will mean the end of the world . As such the super powers will not dare to be involved in direct confrontation. However, wars among others, fought with conventional weapons, have continued, and will continue to happen, but such wars will never bring about the extinction of the entire human race, or even a major portion of it. The possibility of a reversion to barbarism is absurd. Such a prophecy can only be inspired by unfounded pessimism. The devastating impact of another world war may make man disgusted with the wrong or improper use of science and teach him to use it for his own well-being, but he will never discard science. Moreover, Russell has also failed to visualise the emergence of China as the third super power.

Russell's preference for American victory. Russell's preference for an American victory to a victory by Russia is inspired by his deep-rooted love for democratic principles. He is convinced that in America there is a greater respect for freedom of thought, inquiry, discussion and feeling of humaneness—things that are essential in a civilised way of life. In Russia, according to Russell, there is nothing like liberty or freedom. Moreover, in that country education and knowledge are censored, and the dissidents to official policy are either liquidated or expelled from the country.

Russell's portrayal of America and Russia is prejudiced. There may be liberty in America. But that state's imperialist tendencies and atrocities committed in countries like Vietnam, will make every sensible man reluctant to accept an American authority over the world. On the other hand, he has painted an overtly gloomy picture of Soviet Russia, where, in spite of the presence of a totalitarian system, much has been done toward the upliftment of the poor and the downtrodden. Russell perhaps could have been more appropriately described America as "the lesser of the devils."

Russell's idea of a world government. Russell's favourite idea of the formation of a single world government possessing absolute control over all armed forces and weapons is not feasible. He has been over optimistic in expecting all sovereign States to agree to give up their sovereignty and submit to the American or the Russian rule. Even if, for the sake of argument, the western countries including America form an Alliance, they will never be militarily strong enough to force Russia and the upcoming Third World into submission to the Alliance. Wars, in fact, will disappear only when the world leaders begin to see reason, give up mutual distrust and look upon peaceful co-existence was the only way to live.

Russell as a humanisit. Though we find it difficult to agree with Russell's views expressed in this essay we must admit that those views are the product of his intense concern for mankind. He seems genuinely convinced that if the present state of affairs is allowed to continue, the human race will face total disaster. That is why he advocates the formation of a world government, a seemingly utopian project, even, if necessary, by use of force.

Russell's style. Russell has been accepted as an accomplished master of language. All his writings are characterised by the qualities of lucidity and clarity. His main concern in his writings is easy communication to his readers. He often writes long sentences, but they are never vague. He can express profound and difficult ideas in a simple and lucid style. He is a clear thinker and the clarity passes into his style. The following extract from this essay shows these elements of lucidity and clarity :

> There are now only two fully independent states, America and Russia. The next step in this long historical process should reduce the two to one and thus put an end to the period of organised wars, which began in Egypt some six thousand years ago. If war can be prevented without the establishment of a grinding tyranny,a weight will be lifted from the human spirit, deep collective fears will be exorcised, and as fear diminishes, we may hope that cruelty will also grow less.

Another feature of Russell's style is its terseness. Many of his sentences resemble Bacon's in their epigrammatic and pithy quality. Here are two examples: (*a*) "Liberty must be limited by law, and its most valuable forms can only exist within a framework of law." (*b*) "What the world most needs is effective laws to control international relations".

Russell often makes his essays lively and interesting through flashes of wit and humour. He uses irony as his major instrument for creating humour. This feature of his style can be seen in the following example. "In America if you are a geneticist, you may hold whatever view of Mendelism the evidence makes you regard as the most probable;

in Russia, if you are a geneticist who disagrees with Lysenko, you are liable to disappear mysteriously."

Russell has a special fondness for the use of rhetoric to lend force to his arguments. Here is an example from 'The Future of Mankind': "Although the last survivor may proclaim himself universal Emperor, his reign will be brief and his subjects will all be corpses. With his death the uneasy episode of life will end, and the peaceful rocks will revolve unchanged until the sun explodes." Russell's rhetoric, as this example shows, is characterised by simplicity and precision, and is free from the pomp and exaggeration of Carlyle's or Burke's.

6

Philosophy's Ulterior Motives

I. SUMMARY

Views about philosophy. Metaphysics is humorously defined by F.H. Bradley as an attempt to find bad reasons for what we believe as instinct. This dictum is found in the beginning of his long book on metaphysics where he concludes that there cannot be any reality outside the spirit and that the degree of reality of a thing corresponds with that of its spirituality. Bradley is a true philosopher when he is serious. Philosophy has been defined as 'an unusually obstinate attempt to think clearly'. But Russell ironically comments that philosophy has often been interpreted as 'an unusually ingenious attempt to think fallaciously'.

Descartes and Leibniz. The peculiarity of a true philosophic spirit lies in the fact that it combines a desire to believe general propositions with a reluctance to accept anything that is not based on intellectual grounds. Descartes, the father of modern philosophy,illustrates this mental temper. Finding that his teachers disagreed with one another, he came to the conclusion that no existing doctrine was certain. This prompted his quest for certainty, and he decided to disbelieve anything that appeared to be doubtful. He put forth his views that nothing could be accepted as certrain except one's own existence. He also expressed that since he could form an idea of God as a being more perfect than himslf and since this idea must have a cause other than himself, God's existence is certain. Descartes ended by accepting a large number of scholastic maxims. This shows that though he began as a sceptic, his desire for certainty ultimately forced him to throw away intellectual caution and lose his critical faculty. Leibniz was a different kind of man from Descartes. Externally, he was an optimist who invented the phrase that 'this is the best of all possible worlds.' He holds that there are many logically possible worlds, that some of them contain no sin and pain, and that those worlds contain less good than this world which God has chosen to create. However, beneath these superficialities, Leibniz struggled against a deeper problem all his life. He wanted to escape from the rigid necessity that characterised the determinist's world, without diminishing the empire of logic. God could have chosen any other of those possible worlds, but then the choice would have been incompatible with God's goodness, since those worlds are less good. This idea leads to the conclusion that God may not necessarily be good. Unable to solve this problem Leibniz takes refuge in obscurity and ambiguity.

Bishop Berkeley, Hume and Kant. Bishop Berkeley, who attacked the materialists of his day, had a twofold purpose : first, to prove that there is no such thing as matter; secondly, to deduce from this negative proposition the existence of God. He argues when we see a tree, what we really know is not an external object, but a modification of ourselves, a sensation, or an idea. What is real about the tree is the perception of those who are supposed to 'see' it. Later Berkeley advances a paradox by supposing that there must be some permanence about physical objects, and some independence of human beings. So he puts forth the contradictory argument that the tree is really an idea in the mind of God, and as such, continues to exist even when we are not looking at it. All his followers except Hume have shown the same timidity in the face of orthodoxy. Hume finds that if we accept our ideas as the only real thing, then we cannot believe in the existence of anything except our mental states. Hume, as a philosopher, was peculiar in that he had no ulterior motives. However, his activities led to the emergence of two new sets of fallacies, one in England, the other in Germany. The German set aroused more interest.

The German philosopher Kant, initially a follower of the dogmtaic tradition derived from Leibniz, claims to have been awakened from his dogamtic slumber by Hume. After meditation for twelve years, he produced his great work, the *Critique of Pure Reason*. Seven years later, he produced the *Critique of Practical Reason* in which he resumed his dogmatic slumber. Kant possessed the ulterior motive of desiring to prove that the moral maxims he had been taught in his childhood were correct. Pure reason endorsed most of the views held by Hume, but it also helped Kant to prove the credency of the received ideas of morality. Practical reason provided him the excuse needed to establish the correctness of whatever he had believed in before reading Hume, including future life, the existence of God and free will.

Hegel's philosophy. Philosophers are usually timid, and dislike the unexpected. So they tend to invent systems which make the future calculable. Hegel was a supreme practitioner of this art. He believed that the course of logic and that of history were similar in character. He viewed logic as a series of attempts to describe the world. If the first attempt to describe the world provide self-contradictory, one had to try the opposite of the 'thesis' *i.e.*, 'antithesis'. If the 'antithesis' failed, it would require a 'synthesis' of the 'thesis' and the 'antithesis', which would certainly be less contradictory than either the 'thesis' or the 'antithesis. If the synthesis too proved inadequate, it could be considered the 'thesis' and carried through the same process to obtain a new 'synthesis' which would certainly be more adequate than the earlier synthesis. Following this process one could reach a perfect idea, described by Hegel as the 'Absolute Idea', that would describe the real world. Hegel mentioned the Prussian state as an example of his faultless 'Absolute Idea'.

Hegel's philosophy, because of its obscurity and optimism, satisfied the instinct of philosophers. It showed that the philosopher, with the help of his meditations on abstract ideas, can acquire greater knowledge of the real world than the politician or the historian or the scientist. Hegel's system became popular first in Germany, and then in England and America. Now of course his philosophy has come to be regarded as obsolete.

Marxism. Marxism is the last great system that exists. Marx borrowed from Hegel the belief in dialectic *i.e.*, in logical development by thesis, antithesis and synthesis, shown in the course of human history, and not only in abstract thought. Hegel looked upon Germany as the embodiment of the Absolute Idea. To Marx, however, the world was yet to attain perfection and that perfection could be achieved only through a revolution that was sure to come. Marxian doctrine is thus characterised by faith and hope. Most of Marx's theory is independent of Hegel, but the Hegelian element is important, because it contributes to the certainty of victory and the feeling of being on the side of irresistible cosmic forces.

Russell's suggestions. Philosophy is a stage in intellectual development. Two things are essential for its development. We must believe in the traditional doctrines, but must not do so unquestioningly. We must also believe that important truths can be found by mere thinking, without the aid of observation. It is true in mathematics, but not elsewhere because mere thinking cannot establish any non-verbal act. We should cease to believe that a philosopher, by mere thinking, can devise the best possible universe. Philosophy springs from a belief that our purposes have an important relation to those of the universe, and that, in the long run, the course of events is bound to be such as we should wish. Science has rejected this kind of optimism, but is in the process of accepting another: that we, by our intelligence, can make the world such as to satisfy many of our desires. This appears to be practical optimism, though in future this too may prove to be ridiculous.

II. ANNOTATIONS

Page 48

aphorism: maxim; short pithy saying. *acquiescence*: acceptance.

Page 49

quagmire : bog; marsh. *premise* : previous statement from which another is inferred.

Page 50

rhetorical : expressed with a view to obtaining an impressive effect. *slipshod* : unsystematic. *antidote* : something that counteracts an evil. *Voltaire* (1694-1778): French dramatist and philosopher. His works include the plays *Zaire, Merope and Mohamet*, and the stories *Candida* and *Zadig*. *Queen Sophie Charlot* (1666-1726) : Queen of Prussia. She was a patron of literature and philosophy, and was close to Leibniz.

Page 51

determinist : follower of determinism, the theory that human action is not free but determined by motives regarded as external forces acting on the will. *apologetics* : argumentative defence, especially of Christianity. *Bishop Berkeley* (1685-1753) : Irish philosopher and clergyman. *Sir James Jeans* (1877-1946) : English man of science, well-known for his scientific theories contained in *The Universe Around Us*, *The Mysterious Universe* and *The Stars in Their Courses.*

Page 52

limerick : type of nonsense or humorous verse. *quad* : quadrangle; four-sided court. *Ronald Knox* : British writer of fiction.

Page 53

enfant terrible : child who asks awkward questions.

Page 54

Konnisberg : German city, the birth-place of Immanuel Kant. *Euclidean* : of Euclid, the ancient Greek mathematician. He taught at Alexandria around 300 B.C. and is known as the founder of Geometry.

Page 56

contretemps (French): unfortunate accident.

Page 57

empirical : based on observation. *syntax* : sentence construction. *Dr. Pangloss* : a character in Voltaire's *Candida.* He is an optimistic philosopher in the story.

Page 58

Bernard Bosanquet (1848-1923) : British philosopher who observed: 'Logic is the clue to reality, value and freedom'. His works include *Psychology and Moral Self* and *History of Aesthetics.*

III. EXPLANATIONS WITH CRITICAL COMMENTS

1. The typical philosopher finds certain beliefs emotionally indispensable, but intellectually difficult; he therefore goes through long chains of reasoning, in the course of which, sooner or later, a momentary lack of vigilance allows a fallacy to pass undetected. After the one false step, his mental agility quickly takes him far into the quagmire of falsehood. (*Pages 48-49*)

In his essay, 'Philosophy's Ulterior Motives' Bertrand Russell regrets that though philosophy should be taken as an exercise to develop clear thinking, it has been used rather in the sense of an attempt to think fallaciously. He thinks that a philosopher, on the one hand, has a desire to believe in the established doctrine, while on the other, he finds it difficult to accept anything that is not based on intellectual grounds. In these lines Russell continues to explain the philosopher's susceptibility to fallaciousness. General doctrines are of no interest to the completely unintellectual persons. The scientists look upon such doctrines as mere hypotheses on which to base their experiments . To them general doctrines are unimportant until they are tested and verified by scientific experiments. The philosophers view such doctrines as essential mental habits without which life would lose much of its charm. Therefore they consider it necessary to meditate on the doctrines in search of some logical and intellectual reasons to justify them. They adopt various lines of reasoning for doing this. It is possible that in course of a long process of reasoning they may lose concentration for a moment and be derailed from the correct line of reasoning. Such slips can often account for the improper and fallacious reasoning the philosophers are seen to indulge in. Also, as the philosophers possess greater mental alertness than others, they become susceptible to such fallaciousness to a greater degree than all others.

2. Descartes's initial doubt was, I believe, as genuine as that of a man who has lost his way, but was equally intended to be replaced by certainty at the earliest possible moment. (*Page 50*)

This extract has been taken from the essay, 'Philosophy's Ulterior Motives' in which Russell has traced the susceptibility of philosophers to a conflict of contradictory tendencies. The philosopher has a tendency to believe in general doctrine and, at the same time, finds it difficult to accept the general doctrine without intellectual justification.

In the long process of finding such justification he often goes astray and is forced into a false position. Russell presents Descartes as a perfect illustration of the philosopher's peculiar mental temper. The fact that his professors possessed views different from one another led Descartes to conclude that no existing doctrine was certain. He had a passion for certainty and as such began a fervent search for a method to achieve it. He began by rejecting everything that it was possible for him to doubt. He went even to the extent of considering his acquaintances, the heavenly bodies and so on as non-existent on the ground that they might be illusions. He could believe only in his own existence, since if he did not exist, he would not be able to doubt. Upto this point, Russell feels, Descartes's philosophy was based on fairly sound reasoning. But after this Descartes departed from his line of reason and went on to accept a large number of scholastic maxims that he was taught in his schools. His justification of God's existence illustrates this departure from true reasoning. He says that because he can form an idea of God as a being more perfect than himself, and because this idea of God must have a cause other than himself, it is certain that God exists. Though Descartes began as a sceptic, his innate desire to accept existing general doctrines finally got over him and forced him to abandon intellectual caution and his critical faculty.

3. He therefore takes refuge in obscurity and ambiguity. By great dexterity he avoids a sharp contradiction but at the expense of the diffused muddle which pervades his whole system. (*Page 51*)

In the essay, 'Philosophy's Ulterior Motives' by Bertrand Russell, the author attributes the philosopher's susceptibility to fallacious reasoning to the conflict of contradictory elements in his mind. Descartes, Russell shows, was given to false reasoning because, on the one hand, he possessed a passion for certainty and, on the other, a desire to accept the existing doctrines. Russell presents Leibniz's philosophy to further illustrate the philosopher's confusion. Leibniz was a different kind of man from Descartes. He was a professional philosopher and as such possessed greater restraint than Descartes. He was dependent on the patronage of Queen Sophie Charlotte and a few princes and as such had to manufacture such philosophy as would please them. This accounts for the superficial character of his published works, and his reluctance to publish the good philosophy that he was quite capable of. He professed himself to be an optimist and invented the phrase, "This is the best of all possible worlds." Leibniz holds that there are many logically possible worlds some of which contain no sin and pain, that those worlds contain less good than this world created by God, and that God could have created any of those worlds in place of this world. The fact that God created this world shows it is the best. The apparent tone of optimism in this kind of philosophy was enough to satisfy Leibniz's patrons. But under these superficialities Leibniz struggled against a deeper problem all his life. He wanted to escape from the rigid necessity that characterized the determinist's world, without diminishing the empire of logic. The very idea that God could have created any of those worlds that contain less good leads him to believe that such an action on God's part would be incompatible with His goodness, and that, therefore, God may not be necessarily good. The inability to resolve this conflict in his mind explains the obscurity and ambiguity that pervades his system of philosophy.

4. There must, he thinks, be some permanence about physical objects, and some independence of human beings. This he secures by supposing that the tree is really an idea in the mind of God, and therefore continues to exist when no human being is looking at it. (*Page 52*)

In the essay 'Philosophy's Ulterior Motives' Russell says that most of the fallacious reasoning of philosophy is due to the presence of two conflicting tendencies in the philosopher. The philosopher, on the one hand, has a desire to accept the existing doctrines, and, on the other, finds it difficult to accept them without some intellectual justification. In course of the long process of finding such justification the philosopher often goes astray and surrenders to fallacious tendencies. Russell presents Descartes and Leibniz as illustrations of this peculiar mental temper. Bishop Berkeley equally shows such contradictions in his philosophy. Bishop Berkeley, who launched a vigorous attack on the materialists of his time, had a two-fold purpose. Firstly, he wanted to prove there is no such thing as matter; secondly, he wanted to deduce from the earlier proposition that God exists. He points out that when we see a tree, what we really know is not an external object, but a modification of ourselves, a sensation, or an 'idea'. He argues that what is real about the tree is the perception of those who are supposed to 'see' it. However, failing to justify God's existence by this contention, Berkeley jumps to contradictory conclusions. He now takes re-course to a paradoxical statement. He says that there must be some permanence about physical objects, and some independence of human beings. He establishes this contention by fallaciously reasoning that the tree is really an 'idea' in the mind of God, and therefore continues to exist even when we are not watching it. The earlier part of his philosophy is based on sound reasoning. The rest, like the philosophies of Descartes and Leibniz, is paradoxical and fallacious.

5. It was optimistic, since history is a progress in the unfolding of the Absolute Idea. It showed that the philosopher, sitting in his study considering abstract ideas, can know more about the real world than the statesman or the historian or the man of science. (*Page 55*)

In the essay, 'Philosophy's Ulterior Motives', discussing the abundance of fallacy in philosophy Russell traces its origin to certain ulterior motives of the philosopher. Descartes, Leibniz, Bishop Berkeley and others were all overcome by their ulterior motives and produced paradoxcial and fallacious philosophy. The great German philosopher Hegel was no exception. Most of the philosophers dislike the unexpected and, as such, have a tendency to devise ways to make the future calculable. Hegel belonged to this school of philosophers. He viewed logic as a series of self-correcting attempts to describe the world. His theory of 'Absolute Idea' is the culmination of these self-correcting endeavours. If the first atempt to describe proves self-contradictory, one has to try the opposite of the 'thesis'. This will be 'antithesis' and in case this also fails, a 'synthesis' of the 'thesis' and the 'antithesis' will have to be achieved. The 'synthesis' thus will be less self-contradictory than either the 'thesis' or the 'antithesis'. If the 'synthesis' also proves inadequate, it has to be regarded as the new thesis and then a new antithesis and new synthesis may be achieved that will be self-contradictory to a lesser degree. Thus, through repetition of this process it will be possible to reach a perfect idea which has been described by Hegel as 'Absolute Idea'. Hegel had the ulterior motive of pleasing the State of Prussia, which had given him a professorship in Berlin. So he went to the extent of declaring the state as a perfect example of his 'Absolute Idea'. Hegel's philosophy satisfied the instincts of most of the philosophers. They satisfied their self-esteem by consoling themselves that Hegel's obscure philosophy was comprehensible only to them. The optimism underlying the contention that history is a process in the unfolding of the Absolute Idea made them happy. The realization that a philosopher, by going through the process of thesis, antithesis and synthesis, could acquire a better knowledge of the world than the politicians or scientist also served to give the philosophers a feeling of superiority over other human beings.

IV. CRITICAL APPRECIATION.

Philosophy's ulterior motives. Philosophy, according to Russell, is indispensable to us. It helps to develop in us the habit of thinking clearly and objectively. But unfortunately, as Russell regrets, most of the philosophers have abused the object of philosophy by encouraging fallaciousness. He has discovered that those philosophers, in most cases, have been led astray by certain ulterior motives. The typical philosopher has a peculiar mental temper. On the one hand, he has a tendency to accept the traditional doctrines; on the other, he finds it difficult to believe them without finding some intellectual justifications for them. In most cases, the passion for believing those doctrines overpowers the critical faculty and then the philosopher's endeavour is reduced to finding something like an apology for justification through senseless reasoning.

Examples. Russell offers some outstanding examples of philosophers to illustrate how the worth of their philosophy has been marred by the ulterior motives working in their minds. Descartes, the father of modern philosophy began as a sceptic and decided to look for a method to discover certainty of truth. His initial approach followed conventional logic. He rejected everything that he could doubt and believed only in his own existence on the quite logical ground that if he did not exist, he could not doubt. But then his critical faculty gave way to the vehement ulterior motive of believing in the traditional propositions. He went on to justify the common notion of God's existence by arguing that as he could form an idea of God as a more perfect being than himself and that this idea certainly had a cause other than himself, the existence of God was a certainty. Russell then mentions the case of Leibniz who took the stance of an optimist and wrote philosophy in order to please some royal personages on whose patronage he had to depend. He declared that this world was better than other logically possible worlds any one of which the good God could have created. At the same time, inside his heart, he had the doubt that if God could create such a world that contained less good than this world it was possible that God was not necessarily good . Leibniz was a good philosopher, but the conflict between his suspicion about God and the necessity to present God as good confused him and made his philosophy obscure and ambiguous. Kant, the famous German philosopher, produced his great work *Critique of Pure Reason* during the brief period he was under the influence of the liberal philosophy of Hume. But his ulterior motive of justifying the things he had been taught in his school finally overtook him. He now turned dogmatic and produced the Critique of Practical Reason as defence of the things he had learned before reading Hume. Another German philosopher, namely Hegel, also possessed an ulterior motive. He was given a professorship at Berlin and as such he wanted to do something to glorify his state. He invented the process of thesis, antithesis and synthesis by repetitions of which it was possible to reach a perfect idea, described by Hegel as the 'Absolute Idea' of the world. His description of Germany as the embodiment of the 'Absolute Idea'was somewhat responsible for the German's feeling of superiority over others in the racial sphere. Marx's philosophy, that drew inspiration from Hegel's, also possessed the ulterior motive of spreading optimism, and of declaring the imminence and necessity of a revolution that would lead the world to a golden era of happiness and prosperity.

Russell's concern for philosophy. Russell's detailed analysis of the ulterior motives demonstrates his concern for philosophy. Philosophy, if cultivated in the right way, can help to eliminate dogmatism and encourage tolerance among people. Russell rightly points out that there is the necessity of believing in some hypothetical doctrines. But he warns us that we would never be dogmatic in our beliefs and should always be prepared to view everything critically and objectively. If we cannot eliminate our ulterior motives while studying philosophy, it will not be possible for philosophy to flourish.

Style. Russell is accepted as one of the greatest masters of the language. It is his command over his language that has helped to lend his prose the two most noteworthy qualities-lucidity and clarity. He can convey even the most complicated idea in the simplest language. He always finds the right word and the right phrase for an idea's expression, and when we read him, we instantly feel that there could not be a better way of expression. Russell is absolutely clear and logical in his thinking and as such can build up his point gradually and convincingly, and can provide further clarification by drawing examples from every possible source. Here is an extract from this essay that will serve to illustrate the lucidity and clarity of his prose style.

> The typical philosopher finds certain beliefs emotionally indispensable, but intellectually difficult; he therefore goes through long chains of reasoning, in the course of which, sooner or later, a momentary lack of vigilance allows a fallacy to pass undetected. After the one false step, his mental agility quickly takes him far into the quagmire of falsehood.

Russell has a tendency to compress thought into short epigrammatic sentences. In almost all his essays we can trace such sentences :

> In a man whose reasoning powers are good, fallacious arguments are evidence of bias.

> Philosophy is a stage in intellectual development, and is not compatible with mental maturity.

Russell often employs humour in the form of irony to make his essays more absorbing for the readers. The absence of humour in this essay has lent it a tone of seriousness and made it appear somewhat drab as compared to the other essays in this selection.

7

The Superior Virtue of the Oppressed

I. SUMMARY

The superior virtue of the oppressed. The belief that some sections of mankind are morally better or worse than others is not based on reason. It is natural for a man to think well of himself, his sex, his class or his nation. But there are some, especially the moralists, who think ill of their fellow-men and think well of people belonging to other sections. A typical form of such admiration for other sections is the belief in the superior virtue of the oppressed such as the poor, the subject nations, women and children.

The superior virtue of the poor. The eighteenth century witnessed the imposition of abject poverty on the peasantry and the labouring classes. Yet during that century the poor were idealised and described as the 'noble savage'. During the French Revolution the superior virtue of the poor became a party question, and has remained so ever since. The poor became an object of contempt in the eyes of the reactionaries. However, liberals still continued to discover nobility and virtue in the poor, while the socialists and communists began to do the same for the urban proletariat.

The superior virtue of the subject nations. In the nineteenth century the subject nations took the place of the 'noble savage' and were associated with the superior virtue. The Greeks, the Hungarians, the Poles, and the Italians came to be considered poetic and idealistic races. But they were stripped of their nobility as soon as they became independent. Such illusions still persist in case of nations which are still under foreign domination.

The superior virtue of women. The treatment of women has been much more irrational than that of the poor or the subject nations. The Church held two antithetical views of woman. On the one hand, it associated her with Eve and regarded her as the temptress ; on the other hand, it found her a representative of Virgin Mary and viewed her as a saint. In the nineteenth century the idea of the temptress fell into the background and a combination of the Madonna and the lady of chivalry was created to represent an ideal woman. She was considered delicate and dainty, and superior to man in the spiritual sphere. But this attitude made her seem unfit for business and politics. Russell suspects that men adopted this attitude to women deliberately and successfully to keep them inferior to the male sex economically and politically. Today when women have earned equality with men, the so-called male 'reverence' for women has disappeared.

The superior virtue of children. The adult attitude towards children has undergone a similar development. Children used to be considered wicked, unregenerate, limbs of Satan. This often provided the adult a pretext for treating them harshly. In the nineteenth century, when the parental authority began to be threatened, new and subtler methods of bringing children under discipline came into being. They now began to be considered pure and innocent, deserving to be protected from the knowledge of evil. They began to be idealised in literature, and Wordsworth went to the extent of crediting them with "high instincts" which would make every adult aware of his own guilt. This new concept discouraged infliction of punishment on children, and a theory of education, emphasizing the child's welfare grew up.

Subsequently the attitude has changed again. A new child psychology has developed and the children have reverted to being little devils. Freud has now established the concept of children being basically wicked. Children are now supposed to possess a tendency to entertain sinful thoughts and activities. Russell feels that this may only be an adult imaginative compensation for losing the pleasure of thrashing children.

Transience of the stage in which superior virtue is attributed to the oppressed. The stage in which superior virtue is attributed to the oppressed lasts only as long as they remain oppressed. Such idealisation begins only when the oppressors acquire a guilty conscience and the feeling of insecurity. But such idealisation and adoration cannot last long. The oppressed will soon begin to argue that their superior virtue is a reason in favour of their having the power. Thus when power has been equalised at last it becomes clear that all the talk about superior virtue had been baseless and nothing but a means invented by the oppressors to exploit the oppressed classes.

Admiration for the proletariat. The myths about this superior virtue attributed to the poor, women, and children have now been exploded. Today it is the turn of the proletariat to be thus glorified. This admiration is part of the ideology of the machine age; considered in human terms, it will appear as baseless as the admiration for women's spirituality or children's divinity. The idea that bad nourishment, little education, unhealthy living conditions, and overwork can produce better people is absolutely irrational. The socialist and communist intellectuals are still continuing to credit the proletariat with this superior virtue. Children were idealised by Wordsworth just as the proletariat was by Marx. Freud unidealised children, but the person who will unidealise the proletariat is yet to come.

II ANNNOTATIONS

Page 59

delusions : false impressions. *Lao Tze* : Chinese sage and philosopher who was born in the seventh century B.C. He founded Taoism, one of the principal religions of China. *Confucian* : relating to Confucius, the great Chinese sage and philosopher who flourished during the sixth and fifth centuries B.C. Confucius founded the religious system known as Confucianism. *Tacitus* (54-120 A.D.) : a Roman historian. *Madame de Stael* (1766-1817) : a French novelist, an admirer of Rousseau, and a woman gifted with sharp intellect and literary ability. *Cartesian sophistries* : The plausible arguments put forth by the French philosopher Descartes. *pauper* : person without a means of livelihood; extremely poor. *masquerading* : appearing in disguise. *Pope preferred London and his villa at Twickenham* : Alexander Pope expressed admiration for rural life. But he himself preferred to live in a villa in a fashionable area in the vicinity of London. This, according to Russell, is hypocrisy. *French revolution* : The revolution of 1789 which led to the suspension of monarchy in France for some time.

Page 60

proletariat : the labouring classes. *Ausgleich* of 1867 : 'Ausgleich' is a German word that means "agreement". In 1867 an agreement was made between Austria and Hungary which placed the countries under a dual Monarchy and settled the financial and other relations between them. Hungary thus achieved liberation from foreign domination after a long time. After the Second World War it again came under foreign rule, this time that of the U.S.S.R. *St. Augustin* (354- 430 A.D.) : a Christian saint. In his famous work *Confessions* he narrated the follies of his youth. He also wrote a treatise defending the Church. *Madonna* : Virgin Mary.

Page 61

Celts : The people akin to the ancient Gauls. They include Bretons, Cornish, Gaels, Irish, Manx, and Welsh people. *Slavs* : a people spread over most of Eastern Europe including Russians, Bulgarians, Poles and others. *worsted* : defeated. *Evangelicals* : members of the Protestant school which maintains that the doctrine of salvation by faith is the essence of the gospel. It lays less stress on good work. *Dr. Watts* (1674-1748) : an English priest. He wrote many hymns.

Page 62

Holy Spirit : Holy Ghost : the third person of the Trinity, the other two being Father and Son. *Episcopal Church* : The Church which acknowledges superior and inferior orders among the clergy. *heresy* : opinion contrary to the orthodox doctrine of the Christian Church, or to the accepted doctrine on any subject. *Trailing clouds .....infancy* : An extract from Wordsworth's *Ode on Intimations of Immortality.*

Page 63

Freudain : relating to Sigmund Freud (1856-1936), the famous Austrian psychologist. Freud is regarded as the father of modern psychoanalysis. *diatribes* : invectives, pieces of bitter criticism. *St Anthony* (251-351 A.D.) : an ascetic , who is said to have successfully resisted devils from tempting him into sin during his stay in a lonely place for twenty years. *wallop* : thrash, beat. *transient* : not permanent. *Jefferson* : Thomas Jefferson (1743-1826), the President of the United States from 1801-1807. *de rigueur* : a French phrase meaning 'compulsory'.

III. EXPLANATIONS WITH CRITICAL COMMENTS

1. Virtue, it was said, was not to be found in courts : but court ladies could almost secure it by masquerading as shepherdesses.

(*Page 59*)

Russell has ironically pointed out in his essay 'The Superior Virtue of the Oppressed' that it is a fashion to attribute virtue to the poor or otherwise deprived classes. Thus in the eighteenth century the moral attitude was that virtue was not to be found in royal courts but among the lowly classes. The court ladies played the part of shepherdesses as if by playing the part they could imbibe the very virtues associated with those lowly people. According to Russell this attitude was merely a part of the hypocrisy that governed life as a whole.

2. The belief in their ' spiritual' superiority was part and parcel of the determination to keep them inferior economically and politically.

(*Page 61*)

In his essay ' The Superior Virtue of the Oppressed' Russell ridicules the attitude of men towards women. He is firmly of the belief that the habit of attributing superior virtue to the oppressed is partly motivated by the oppressor's need to save his conscience and partly by the desire to perpetuate the oppression. Men wanted to keep women away from the field of employment and politics. So they invented the conception of women as the embodiment of innocence and purity whose 'bloom' would be rubbed off if they worked in the field of mundane realities ; women were compensated by the attribution of virtue superior to the males. However, when men lost the battle, as Russell goes on to say, and women entered the fields of employment and politics, their 'superior' virtue was eroded. Thus as soon as women had to be respected as equals in material terms, men rapidly forgot to "reverence their virtue". There is much truth in what Russell says.

3. They are, it must be said, far more wicked than they were in the diatribes of the monks; they display, in modern text books, an ingenuity and persistence in sinful imaginings to which in the past there was nothing comparable except St. Anthony. (*Page 63*)

In 'The Superior Virtue of the Oppressed', Russell tells us that there are some people, who tend to think well of the sections of mankind to which they themselves do not belong. And a rather strange form of the admiration for other groups is the belief in the superior virtue of the oppressed—subject nations, the poor, women, and children—though this kind of belief is in fact unstable and transient. One of the examples offered by Russell here tells us how men's ideas about children have changed from time to time. At one time, especially in the Middle Ages, children were considered to be very wicked and monks and theologians considered them to be limbs of Satan. Then came the nineteenth century and the educational reformers put forward their theory that children were innocent and pure as angels. According to Wordsworth's poetic vision, "Heaven lies about us in our infancy". Then there was another swing of the pendulum to the other extreme. The adult attitude towards children changed for the worse and they were again considered to be little devils. This time Freud, the great psychologist, came to their aid. Freud's theory of the unconscious established that children were essentially wicked and sinful in their thoughts and imagination. So those who believe in this theory of the unconscious surpass even the monks and theologians as they now consider the erstwhile angels much more detestable than limbs of Satan. But Russell has strongly criticised Freud for putting forward such a theory villifying children.

4. But obvious as this argument is, many socialist and communist intellectuals consider it *de rigueur* to pretend to find the proletariat more amiable than other people, while professing a desire to abolish the conditions which, according to them, alone produce good human beings. Children were idealized by Wordsworth and unidealized by Freud. Marx was the Wordsworth of the proletariat; its Freud is still to come. (*Page 64*)

'The Superior Virtue of the Oppressed' is an interesting and illuminating essay in which Russell has pointed out how some people, especially writers and moralists, very often attribute superior virtue to oppressed classes of people such as subject nations, the poor, women and children. After discussing about this delusion of the people regarding the poor, women and children, in these closing lines Russell has taken up the case of the proletariat or the working class. Formerly, specially in the eighteenth century, when people praised the poor they meant the rural poor. But the admiration of the proletariat, the class of people who have no capital but simply earn wages, is quite modern. It was Karl Marx, the founder of scientific socialism or communism, who first attributed superior qualities to the poor sections of our modern world. Now the followers of Marx, the socialist and communist intellectuals, consider that these sections of people possess superior virtue and more amiable qualities in comparison with other classes of people who are economically and intellectually much better off. The Marxists want to improve their lot by helping them to get better wages and living conditions. Russell argues that, if this be the case, the intellectuals' claim of people living in such poor conditions having superior qualities is dubious. In the end Russell remarks that it was Wordsworth who glorified children in his famous *Ode on the Intimations of Immortality*. But then came Freud with his theory of the unconscious mind and exploded Wordsworth's favourite theory. According to Freud children are really wicked and sinful in thought and imagination. Now Marx has glorified the working class and another Freud to explode Marx's theory is still to come. So let us wait for a future psychologist to explode another delusion of mankind.

IV. CRITICAL APPRECIATION

Russell's contention. Russell's contention is that the oppressors always attribute a superior virtue to the oppressed classes in order to keep those classes under control. The oppressed, in his opinion, include the poor, subject nations, women and children. He then takes up the cases of these oppressed classes to establish his theory. Unfortunately, his theory, and the arguments he offers to establish it, seem forced and unconvincing. We shall go through these cases to examine the validity of his contention.

The case of the poor. According to Russell, superior virtue is attributed to the poor so that the rich can exploit them. He also refers to the present-day glorification of the proletariat, and maintains that little education, unhealthy housing conditions and overwork can never produce better men. According to him, the poor, living in such conditions, cannot acquire the so-called superior virtues. Such an assumption is not universally valid, for numerous examples of persons rising from extreme poverty to all-time greatness can be given. His reference to the Socialist and Communist intellectual "professing a desire to abolish the conditions which according to them, alone produce good human beings" is unjustified and cynical. He has underestimated the sincerity of those intellectuals for whom the upliftment of the poor is a genuine concern.

The case of subject nations. According to Russell, such superior virtue is also attributed to the subject nations by those who rule them and that it is done deliberately to justify the position of the ruler and the ruled. He says that the subject nations are stripped of this virtue as soon as they become independent. His argument in this case would have benefited had he illustrated the change of attitude towards the liberated nations more elaborately. However, at least in case of the colonial aborigines, the "noble savage" was exploited under the guise of idealism.

The cases of women and children. In Russell's opinion, women and children too have suffered because of such attribution of superior virtue to them. He says that in the early days the Church held two antithetical opinions about women; it viewed them as the temptress and also as the saint. In the nineteenth century women were considered spirtually superior to men. But this attribution of superior virtue only served to keep the women out of political and economical progress.

The adult attitude towards children has undergone similar developments. Initially regarded as wicked and degenerate, the children came to be idealised in the nineteeth century, and then reverted to being little devils in the twentieth century. In Russell's opinion, the idealisation of women by men, and of children by adults, was meant to keep women and children under control of the males and the adults respectively. Russell is being somewhat unfair to the nineteenth century poets who developed and expressed in their poetry a genuine admiration for women and children. Interpretation of such spontaneous admiration, as expressed in Wordsworth's poetry, as motivated by evil intentions, amounts to an expression of cynicism. However, Russell's arguments that in many cases the admiration is insincere and motivated by selfish interests is quite convincing.

Russell's style. Russell's mastery of language shows itself in this essay, as in all his works; through the lucid quality of his expression he can communicate to his readers with ease. Russell is fond of using irony as a weaopn of attack. The very title of the essay 'The Superior Virtue of the Oppressed' is ironical. His attack on Pope ironically exposes Pope's hypocrisy. His reference to the change of British attitude towards the Irish is another example of irony : "The Irish were regarded by the English as possessed of a special charm and mystical insight until 1921, when it was found that expense of continuing to oppress them would be prohibitive". His dismissal of Freud's child psychology is done with superb irony :"Is all this the objective truth at last ? Or is it merely an adult imaginative compensation for being no longer allowed to wallop the little pests?" Irony blended with wit and humour never allows his writings to become invective even when he is severely attacking.

8

On Being Modern-Minded

I. SUMMARY

The parochiality of the modern age. In the chronological sense the modern age is the most parochial since Homer's age. This parochiality reveals itself in the general rejection of the past. We, the modern men, have deprived some of the cities of their historic past by renaming them. We rid the prevalent thoughts and ideas of any possible link with the past by inventing new catchwords. We believe that we have reached the peak of intelligence, and therefore find things of the past unworthy of our attention. We find nothing of value in Shakespeare's words unless they are translated into the language of Marx or Freud.

The desire to be contemporary. The desire to remain up-to-date and to ignore the past has continued through all the ages. But the fashion to reject the past *en bloc* has come into existence only after the First World War. The modern belief that fashion should dominate opinions makes further thought unnecessary. By learning the correct use of a few modern catchwords like 'sadism','Oedipus complex', 'bourgeois', or 'left' even an undeserving person can come to be considered a brilliant writer or talker today.

Characteristics of the modern-minded. In spite of his firm belief in the intellectual profundity of his age, the modern-minded man is very modest about his personal abilities. His highest ambition is to think, to say, and to feel ahead of others belonging to his own times : he has no wish to display originality or a deeper insight. He sacrifices his individuality and follows the current fashion so that he can receive universal acceptance and admiration. He is reluctant to follow the examples of Copernicus, Spinoza and Milton, who stood against the opinions of their times and antagonised their contemporaries.

Reasons for suspension of individuality. (*i*) Temptations of money and fame restrain able men from going against the popular fashion. Men, by nature, love to be admired, mentioned in the newspapers, and offered monetary rewards. That is why they prefer to subordinate their judgment to the general opinion.

(*ii*) Various other factors have led the modern man to this state. One of these is the rapidity of progress in every sphere that has led to an apprehension that any individual contribution is going to become obsolete in the near future. Newton's theories became obsolete when Einstein came; Einstein is now already regarded as old-fashioned. Then again, the emotional tone of the modern age is also changing rapidly due to the wars, depressions, and revolutions chasing each other in quick succession. In such a situation a man finds it very difficult to stand out with his individuality. Public events now have more impact on private lives than in the past. Tolerance for unorthodox opinion has now reached an all-time low and anyone expressing such views is likely to be in grave peril.

(*iii*) In the past men regarded themselves as servants of God. The artists, philosophers and the astronomers felt that they were serving God's purpose by following their own convictions. They could, therefore, ignore popular applause. Milton, for instance, considered his poetic talent a gift of God and felt that it was his duty to serve Him with his talent. With the progress of knowledge the firm faith in God began to diminish and in course of time the ideal of God was replaced by the ideals of the True, the Good, and the Beautiful. In the nineteenth century these ideals inspired even the atheists. But soon the pragmatists and the historians of morals came up with explanations that dismissed these ideals. As a consequence of the rejection of God and these lofty ideals the individual was left without any inner defence against social pressure.

(*iv*) The movement towards subjectivity began with Luther and Descartes as an assertion of the individual. But the movemnet has gone too far, resulting in a general disillusionment over such self-assertion. When men lose an illusion, they always fall into another without realizing that one error can never be corrected by another. As a result the earlier fervour of the individual for self-assertion has now ended in his complete subjection.

Value of detachment and objectivity. Detachment and objectivity, both in thought and in feeling, can be, and has to be, preserved. Some amount of isolation, both in space and in time, and finding something more important than the cheap applause of the contemporaries are essential for the creation of an original and individual work.

II. ANNOTATIONS

Page 65

Mudcombe-in-the-Meer : the name of a village. *Praha* : the old name of Prague, the capital city of Czechoslovakia. *Gorki* : the old name of Nijni-Novgorod, situated in Russia. *Peiping* : ancient name for Peking, the capital city of China, now known as Beijing. *catchwords* : repeated words or phrases ; slogans. *Marx* : Karl Marx (1818-1883), a famous political theorist, and the author of Das Kapital which laid the foundations of modern communism. *Freud* : Sigmund Freud (1856-1939), the famous Austrian psychologist. Freud is regarded as the father of modern psycho-analysis. *Santayana* : George Santayana (1863-1952), an American philosopher, poet and essayist. His works include *The Sense of Beauty* and *The Life of Reason. The Renaissance* : The revival of art and learning in Europe during the 15th and 16th centuries. Following the fall of Constantinople in 1453 the Greek scholars moved into Italy and provided a vigorous impetus to the new learning. The term 'Renaissance' refers to the rebirth or renewal of the study of the classical literature of Ancient Greece and Rome. *Gothic centuries* : 12th-16th centuries when Gothic architecture, noted for a pointed-arch style, was prevalent in Western Europe.

Page 66

Lecky : W.E.H. Lecky (1808-1903), an Irish historian and the author of *The History of England During the 18th Century. sadism* : Pleasure derived from inflicting or watching cruelty. *Oedipus* : the legendary king of Thebes, and the son of Laius. Circumstances kept him ignorant of his parentage. He killed his father and married his own mother Jocasta. On discovery of the truth Jocasta hanged herself and Oedipus made himself blind. In psychology 'Oedipus complex' is a sexual complex that influences the child in regard to the parent of the opposite sex. *bourgeois* : the middle class people. The communists regard this class as reactionary and opposed to their ideologies. *Copernicus* : Nicolas Copernicus (1473-1543), the Polish astronomer. He was the first astronomer to demonstrate that the sun is the centre of the solar system and that all planets revolve round the sun. *Spinoza* : Benedict Spinoza (1632-1677), a Dutch philosopher. He was born a Jew, but gave up his Jewish faith and was converted to Christianity. Though unpopular in his time, he is now regarded as one of the greatest philosophers.

Page 67

Cromwell : Oliver Cromwell (1599-1658), who led the Parliamentary Party in the Civil War in England. He was the Lord Protector of England from 1553-1658. At the Restoration of the monarchy King Charles II who held Cromwell's responsible for the execution of his father Charles I, had Cromwell body dug up from the grave and hanged. *Newton* (1642- 1727) : the Great English physicist who is known for his laws of motion, theory of gravitation, etc. *Einstein* : Albert Einstein (1879-1955), the great German scientist who is famous for his theory of relativity. He was Jewish by birth and was forced by circumstances to leave Nazi Germany and settle in the U.S.A. He won the Nobel Prize for Physics in 1921. *antiquated* : rendered out-of-date.

Page 68

'that one.......hide', 'bend to..........Maker' : These lines are from

Milton's famous sonnet *On His Blindness*. *topographical* : geographical; that can be shown on the map. *philistine* : uncultured ; materialistic and commonplace. *Luther* : Matin Luther (1483-1546), the German reformer who revolted against the authority of the Pope and founded Lutheranism, form of Christian religion.The movement initiated by him has come to be known as the Reformation. *Descartes* (1596-1650) : French philosopher, considered to be the father of modern philosophy. His philosophy lays stress on the dominance of the thought expressed as "I think, therefore I am".

III. EXPLANATIONS WITH CRITICAL COMMENTS

1. Some, at least, of such words represented much thought on the part of their inventors, like paper money they were originally convertible into gold. But they have become for most people inconvertible, and in depreciating, have increased nominal wealth in ideas. *(Page 66)*

In his essay 'On Being Modern-Minded', Russell ridicules the superficial knowledge which people pass off as the hallmark of being modern-minded. These people casually use jargon from psychology or politics which originally represented valuable new ideas but have now been rendered thoughtless and mechanical. Russell illustrates the idea picturesquely by saying that these words were originally like paper currency introduced by the government under the pledge that it can be converted into gold. However, for a majority of people, these words have lost their value just as the paper currency has been demonetised by the government. A possessor of large number of such notes may think himself to be rich but his wealth is only nominal, not real. Similarly, people who casually use the current jargon without true depth of thought may think themselves wealthy in ideas and superior to the thinkers of the past, merely on the strength of these borrowed words; in reality they are intellectually poor.

2. Copernicus should have delayed his advocacy of Copernician system until it could be made fasionable; Spinoza should have been either a good Jew or a good Christian; Milton should have moved with the times, like Cromwell's widow, who asked Charles II for a pension on the ground that she did not agree with her husband's politics. *(Page 67)*

In the essay, 'On Being Modern-Minded' Russell, with his sharp wit and sarcasm, has mercilessly exposed modern-minded men's parochial outlook and their pride in intellectual superiority and their foolish belief that fashion alone should dominate opinion. The modern-minded man picks up some current words or phrases like 'Oedipus', 'bourgeois' 'sadism' etc. and, by using them in keeping with the fashion of the day, tries to establish himself as a great talker or writer. For the sake of the admiration of the common crowd he suppresses what is individual in himself. He prefers the doctrine of subjectivity of truth in place of the dispassionate search for knowledge. That is why he is unable to realize the great importance of a mentally solitary life as that of Copernicus, Spinoza or Milton after the Restoration. Russell quite sarcastically remarks that if the ideas and inclinations of modern-minded intellectuals are accepted, then Copernicus ought not to have announced his revolutionary astronomical theories before they became popular and fashionable for the people of his day. And Spinoza, the great Dutch philosopher, should not have gone against the current thinking of his time and propounded his own great philosophical and theological ideas and principles. As a Jew he ought have remained a faithful Jew or accepted Christianity. In the same way Milton should not have gone against the spirit of his times. He could have emulated the example of Cromwell's widow who craved for a pension from Charles II after the Restoration assuring him that she never supported the political views of her husband. So, according to the modern man, all these great men should not have propounded their individual thoughts and ideas before they became fashionable and could easily be accepted by the crowd.

> 3. When with progress of enlightenment this belief began to grow dim, there still remained the True, the Good, and the Beautiful. Non-human standards were still laid up in heaven, even if heaven had no topogragphical existence. (*Page 68*)

In his brilliant essay, 'On Being Modern-Minded' Russell has strongly deplored modern-minded man's changed attitude towards the need of a mentally solitary life and his reluctance to go against the current thinking to create something great and original. Various factors such as money rewards or cheap popularity have contributed to this undesirable attitude. Russell points out a deeper cause for this change and reviews the ideals that inspired the great intellectuals and moral personalities of the past. The most important thing about those great men was that they wished to serve God. So they did what they considered their best, caring very little for the applause of approval of the crowd. One might have been an artist, philosopher or astronomer, but everyone worked with the belief that in following his own conviction he was really an agent to serve God's purpose. But with the progress of knowledge men began to lose this firm faith in serving God's purposes. Then this faith was replaced by an ideal—the ideal of the True, the Good and the Beautiful. Still they looked up to some non-human standard which was accepted to be heavenly, although they had lost their belief in the geographical existence of heaven. But unfortunately, in our age, this ideal has also been exploded by modern historians and pragmatists. And the pity of the situation is that no other noble ideal has replaced it. So the modern-minded man has been left without any inner defence against social pressure.

IV. CRITICAL APPRECIATION

Modern parochialism and the need for detachment and objectivity. Russell has pointed out the modern man's tendency to reject the past and to follow the fashion of the day in the essay 'On Being Modern-Minded'. Modern man thinks he has reached the apex of human intelligence and as such considers the things of the past unworthy of his attention. His main concern is to earn easy money and popular applause. He suppresses his individual thoughts and ideas lest they should offend his contemporaries; his only aim is to echo the prevalent thoughts slightly ahead of the others in point of time. Russell considers temptations of money and fame, the rapid progress in science which renders every individual contribution obsolete with newer inventions, and the decline in the faith in God and the noble ideals reponsible for leading modern man to this state. In his opinion, detachment and objectivity are to be achieved if we want to produce creative and individual works.

This study of the modern mind is the product of a vastly learned and analytical mind. It shows deep thinking on the part of Russell in his attempt to trace the causes of the loss of individuality in the modern age. The logicality of his diagnosis is sound enough to force every sensible reader to agree with him. Russell's suggestion for preserving detachment and objectivity shows his concern for the need of creative and individual works.

Russell as a champion of individual liberty. All through his life Russell advocated individual liberty, not only in the social sphere, but also in the intellectual sphere. In his essay he has referred to the absence of this individual liberty in expressing one's personal thoughts and ideas today. Every individual possesses certain creative faculties of his own; if he cannot express them for some reasons, new creative works will not be produced and 'progress' in the real sense of the term, will come to a stop. Therefore he urges the modern man to ignore the temptations of money and fame and assert his right to express himself.

Russell's style. Russell is one of the most fascinating writers of English prose. His unquestionable command of the language accounts for the unparallelled simplicity, clarity, and lucidity of his style. He is endowed with an original mind and a logical intellect. He can go into the heart of a subject, however complex it is, and can sum up a complex situation in a few clear and simple sentences. In this essay he narrates the temptations that stand in the way of free individual expression thus :

> The money rewards and widespread though ephemeral fame which those agencies have made possible places temptations in the way of able men which are difficult to resist. To be pointed out, admired, mentioned constantly in the press, and offered easy ways of earning much money is highly agreeable; and when all this is open to a man he finds it difficult to go on doing the work that he himself thinks best and is inclined to subordinate his judgment to the general opinion.

The lines here at once show the simplicity and clarity of his style, and the logical thinking of his mind.

Another feature of Russell's style is its terseness. His preference for restraint and economy of words, aided by his mastery of the language, permits him to compress thought into terse, epigrammatic statements. "Our age is the most parochial since Homer", and "We are suffering not from the decay of theological beliefs but from the loss of solitude", are two examples of such epigrammatic sentence.

Russell's essays never become dull even when he is dealing with an abstruse subject. He takes particular care to lend a touch of sprightliness to his writings through occasional flashes of wit and humour. Being a controversialist, he is fond of using irony as the chief instrument for creating humour. This essay, like all others, abounds in irony. Here is one example: "This belief that fashion alone should dominate opinion has great advantages. It makes thought unnecessary and puts highest intelligence within the reach of everyone. It is not difficult to learn the correct use of such words as 'complex', 'sadism', 'Oedipus' 'bourgeous', 'deviation', 'left', and nothing more is needed to make a brilliant writer or talker".

Russell's scholarship. Russell has a tendency to turn to his own encyclopaedic knowledge and use it for establishing his points. He can draw illustrations from every source to make his arguments logical and clear. In order to illustrate the modern man's contempt of the past and subservience to the current fashion, he refers to the modern approach to Shakespeare's *Hamlet*. According to him, a modern man can appreciate *Hamlet* only when it is interpreted by Marx or Freud. To clarify what he means by " mentally solitary life" he refers to the lives of Copernicus, Spinoza and Milton. He gives a clear idea of the unshakable faith in God in former days by quoting two lines from Milton's sonnet, *On His Blindness*. The essay is full of such illustrations and, as such, in spite of the lucidity and clarity of the language, somewhat beyond the comprehension of an ordinary reader.

Feeling of self-importance. People suffer from a feeling of self-importance, individual or generic. If a man is better-off than his neighbour he feels superior to him . Every man has a tendency to take pride in the great men and achievements of his country and consider his country superior to others. This kind of pride is nothing but a false belief because it can lead a Yugoslav to boast of his nation's pigs and a native of Manaco of leading the world in gambling. Again, man thinks that among animals he alone has an immortal soul and is rational. The glorification of Man by man himself took a new form after the theory of evolution was established. People have begun to believe that through millions of years God was preparing the Great Climax, the creation of man. Russell feels that mankind is not a perfect creation because it includes such contemptible specimens like Nero, Caligula, Hitler and Mussolini. Moreover, Russell points out, life on earth is only transient. It is certain that a time will come when the sun will burst and all the planets will be turned into gas leaving no trace of life anywhere. The importance of man thus receives no support from a scientific view of the future of the universe.

Love of the marvellous and rumour. Another source of false belief is the love of the marvellous. People have a tendency to believe anything that strikes them as wonderful. Also, they are prone to believe the worst about their neighbours without asking for evidence. The false belief in these cases is often aided by malice. But even when malice is absent the marvellous is readily believed unless it goes against some strong prejudice. That is why the ancient belief in the supernatural has continued to exist through ages, and still does, in the minds of modern men.

Tendency to make myths. Every powerful emotion creates a tendency to make myths. When the emotion belongs to an individual the myth becomes unconvincing and the individual is considered mad. But when the emotiom is collective, as in war, the myth remains unquestioned, and may often lead to cruelty. The myth that the Jews practised ritual murders offered the Russians and the Nazis an excuse for committing atrocities on them.

Innate cruelty of man. It was believed until the end of the eighteenth century that insanity was due to possession by devils and that the pain suffered by the patient was suffered by the devils. The practice was, therefore, to beat the patient savagely until the devils abandoned him. When anaesthetics were discovered the religious men vehemently opposed their use on the ground that anything to lessen suffering was meant to evade the will of God. Such false beliefs were obviously born of the innate cruelty of man.

Fallacies about race and blood. The fallacies about 'race' and 'blood' are as old as civilization. Even today some modern people say 'blood will tell'. However, the myth that the white man's blood is superior to a black's has been exploded by the physiologists. In the matter of race, Aristotle and Plato considered the Greeks infinitely superior to the barbarians. If the white men feel that they are superior to men of other colours, the Japanese think that yellow people are the best. Hitler thought that Germans were superior to others because they possessed pure Aryan blood. But there is a special absurdity in applying such racial theories to the European races because there is no such thing as a pure race in Europe. The myths about superior 'blood' or 'race' have always been created by the blind self-esteem of the holders of power.

Superstions in the economic sphere. There are many superstitions in the economic sphere also. The most striking among these is the one regarding gold and precious stones. People value gold and gems not for their 'rarity', but for the supposed magical properties they were associated with in the past. It is said that the irrational belief of the ancients still persists among some people, known to be 'practical'.

Superstitions in the political sphere. One of the most popular beliefs is that human nature cannot be changed. There is no truth in this belief. A look into the various ways of life led by different tribes and races will confirm the variability of human nature. Human nature is moulded by circumstances and education. By diet and training, people can be made cruel or kind, dominating or submissive. Adequate governmental action can turn any nonsense into the creed of the majority. The control of governments over men's beliefs has always been great, but now it is greater. Before the last war the Japanese, Russian, and German Governments inculcated false beliefs, which inspired their peoples to fight and kill. It is evident that a government has the power to produce a population either of insane or of reasonable people; depending on its intention. The governments do not wish to have reasonable people because such people would not admire the politicians.

The belief that man by nature wants war is dangerous because it makes wars look inevitable. In fact wars can be totally eliminated if only political organisations lead the people, by proper education, into realizing the unprofitability of war.

Any absurdity, by government action, can come to be generally believed. A powerful government can make people believe two and two make three, that water freezes when it gets hot and boils when it gets cold. Different governments cultivate different dogmas among their peoples and the diversity in dogmas gives rise to hostilities among nations. Peace can be achieved by inculcating common creeds and ideals everywhere.

Some 'advanced thinkers' believe that it is always right to differ from the conventional opinion. This belief is a delusion. Opinions such as 'Julius Caesar is dead' are conventional but based on truth; to differ from them is only a sign of eccentricity.

Abnormality and punishments. The belief that crimes can be prevented through punishment is not rational. Punishment only aggravates trouble, especially in cases of crime which are the outcome of psychological abnormalities. It may reform an ordinary thief, but can never cure a kleptomaniac. The severe punishment meted out to the Germans after their defeat in the Second World War was irrational. There were some plain criminals among the Germans, but most of them were lunatics and homicidal maniacs. The punishment, therefore, would fail to remove the psychological abnormalities of the Germans and cause them to be more contemptuous and vindictive towards other nations. In this regard it has to be remembered that if even a single nation continues to hate the rest of mankind, world peace will remain a dream for ever.

A few more absurd beliefs. Absurd superstitions are still entertained in the most modern and civilised societies. It is still held that people born in March are unlucky and people born in May are liable to corns. Number 13 is considered particularly unlucky and sailors do not like to sail on Fridays.

Belief in 'nature' and what is 'natural' has caused many errors. Treating cuts, colds and diseases with medicines, without allowing nature to cure them, now may seem 'natural', but initially it was looked upon as 'unnatural'. Vaccination, eating cooked food, and every other advance in civilisation, have been denounced as unnatural while they were recent developments. The objection to 'birth control' on the ground that it is against nature, still persists. Some theologians also point out that however large the population may become God will provide for all. They forget that God has exposed mankind to periodical famines in which millions have died.

The treatment of women through the ages has been guided by the same irrationality. In ancient days women were considered harmless but silly; with the coming of Christianity they began to be viewed in the dual role of the temptress and the saint; in the Victorian Age they became saintly and virtuous. There are similar generalisations about national characteristies. Until 1870 the Germans were imagined as a nation of bespectacled professors. Most Americans associate Frenchmen with amorous intrigue. Russell discourages all such generalisations because they rest on paucity of experience or observation.

Russell's suggestions. No superhuman genius is needed to get rid of the foolish notions prevalent among mankind. A person can avoid at least the silly errors, if not all errors, by keeping in mind a few simple rules.

Personal observation. We can avoid some foolish errors if we have recourse to personal observation. Aristotle made a mistake when he declared that women had fewer teeth than men. He could have avoided the mistake by simply counting the teeth of his own wife. We should never pretend to know what in fact we don't know.

A careful analysis of one's own opinions. If an opinion contrary to man's belief makes the man angry it is a sign that his own belief is not based on sound reason. In such a case he has to re-examine the validity of his opinion.

Avoidance of dogmatism. One way to avoid dogmatism is to become acquainted with various opinions held in social circles different from our own. Travelling, or dicussing with people having opinions different from our own, can also help. We may also hold imaginary discussions with people disagreeing with us on some subject, and may very often discover our own mistakes in the process.

Caution against opinions that flatter our self-esteem. A majority of men and women are convinced of the superiority of their own sex. Similarly most men consider their own countries superior to others. No rational man can accept such opinions which are purely based on self-esteem. To deal with the self-esteem of man as being superior to other beings it has to be remembered that man is a brief episode in the life of a small planet in this vast universe and that there may be beings, in other parts of the cosmos, much superior to human beings.

Avoidance of fear. Fear is a major source of rumours, superstitions and cruelty. It has many forms—fear of death, fear of the dark, fear of the unknown, fear of the herd, and so on. Unless we can conquer fear, we cannot hope to think clearly and find out the truth. To conquer fear is, indeed, the beginning of wisdom.

Fear can be avoided in two ways : firstly, by convincing ourselves that we are immune from disaster, and secondly, by the practice of courage; because of the difficulty of the second way, the first has always been popular. Primitive magic, that could secure such sense of safety, was a crude way of avoiding terrors. Newer beliefs, particularly associated with future life, sought more effective ways to dispel fear. Socrates and Plato, for instance,tried to remove the fear of death by offering a cheerful picture of the next world. Orthodox Christianity laid down definite rules of salvation and some modern Christians have professed that everybody will go to heaven after death. In spite of all this the fear of death still remains. Russell now refers to the Stoic doctrine that maintained that the only true good is virtue, which no enemy can take away from us; and therefore there is no need to fear enemies. Spinoza taught that our true good consists indifference to our mundane fortunes. These doctrines dispel fear by pretending that physical suffering is not evil; though based on false belief, they provide a noble way to escape fear.

Disbelief in superstition. Fear often leads to superstitions followed by cruelty. Superstitions encouraged by fear prompted the sailors to throw Jonah overboard, the Japanese to massacre Koreans and Liberals, and the Carthaginians to throw children into fire. We must guard ourselves against such irrational superstitions.

Collective fear and cruelty. Collective fear inspires a herd instinct, and tends to produce a violent antagonism against people outside the herd. During the French Revolution, the fear of foreign armies led to the reign of terror. A similar fear of hostility from enemies made the Soviet government fierce in its first years. Fear generates impulse of cruelty, and that is why cowards are more prone to cruelty than the brave. As such, if fear is not removed no man or crowd or nation can think or act in a sane manner.

The usefulness of superstitions. Superstitions, however, often lend a touch of gaiety to life. During the prohibition in America,. a sect maintained that the communion service ought to be celebrated in whisky and not wine; they were sanctioned the legal right to a supply of hard liquor, and people continued to join the sect to be able to enjoy that right. Many people have been studying the Great Pyramid in order to decipher its mystical lore. Russell has much admiration for a prophetess who told her followers that she possessed the power of walking on water and that she wanted to demonstrate it. On the appointed day, when her followers assembled beside a lake she asked them if they all believed in her power. When they replied in the affirmative, she announced that in that case there was no need for her to demonstrate this power. If such superstitions were all replaced by dull scientific theories, the world would lose much of its charm and colour.

II ANNOTATIONS

Page 70

bombastic : pompous. *old fogey* : old-fashioned person. *Erasmus* (1466-1536) : a well known Dutch humanist. Many European writers were influenced by his writings. His famous work *Encomium Moraei* ("In Praise of Folly") is a satire directed against the Church and the Clergy. He is regarded as the precursor of the Reformation. *Perennial* : perpetual; lasting long. *Aristotle* (384 B.C.-332 B.C.) :

Greek philosopher and one of the greatest thinkers of all times. His *Politics* is regarded as the basis of all political philosophy. His other works include the famous *Poetics*.

Page 71

clergy : priests. *neo-scholastics* : modern followers of the scholastic theology which lays much emphasis on dogmas. *necromancers*: wizards; sorcerers. *antipodes*: places diametrically opposite (to each other).

Page 72

Darwin : Charles Robert Darwin (1809-1882), the famous English naturalist who propounded his sensational theory of evolution in his epoch-making work *The Origin of Species* (1859). *obscurantism* : opposition to inquiry, enlightenment and reform. *Benjamin Franklin* (1706-1790) : American scientist who became famous for his research on electrictiy. *Dr. Price* : American theologian.

Page 73

Toplady : Augustus Montague Toplady (1740-1778), an Irish clergyman who became the Vicar of Broad Hembury, Devonshire, in 1768. He was the author of the hymn *Rock of Ages*. *Borrow*: George Borrow (1803-1881), English traveller and writer. His major contribution is a work entitled *The Bible in Spain* in which he gives an account of his life with the Spanish gypsies. *Copernican* : of Copernicus (1479-1543), who was the first to demonstrate that the sun is the centre of the solar system and that all the planets revolve round the sun.

Page 74

euthanasia : putting a person ailing from an incurable disease to a gentle, easy death. *resurrection*: rising to life after death.

Page 75

St. Thomas Aquinas (1226-1274) : A prominent Italian theologian whose *Summa Theologica* is a standard authority in the Roman Catholic Church. He was canonized in 1323. *Propensities* : tendencies. *Omnipotence* : the quality of being infinitely powerful. *Vesalius* (1514-1565) : Belgian anatomist who pioneered dissection of human corpses for medical research. His book *Fabrica* contains the first complete description of human body. He is now regarded as the Father of Anatomy.

Page 76

Inquisition : an ecclesiastical tribunal set up by the Roman Catholic Church in the 13th century for the suppression of heresy. It became notorious for causing thousands of deaths. *St. Paul* : a Christian saint of the first century. He was condemned to death by the Romans in 67 A.D. *St. Augustin* (354-430 A.D.) : a great Christian saint and theologian. His writings include *Confessions* and *The City of God*. *Columbus*: Christopher Columbus (1447-1506), discovered America in 1492.

Page 77

Reno : An American city in the state of Nevada which permits quick and easy divorce and legalised gambling. *Tolstoy* : Count Leo Tolstoy (1828-1910), Russian author and social reformer. His important works include *War and Peace* and *Anna Karenina*. *Manicheans*: Followers of the religious system founded by a Greek named Manikhaios, who lived in Persia in the third century. The system represented Satan as co-eternal with God. *Samuel Butler* (1612-1618) : English poet whose *Hudibras* became popular for its anti-Puritan sentiments. *petting* : hugging, kissing etc. *taboos* : prohibitions.

Page 78

Nero : Roman emperor belonging to the first century, notorious for his brutalities. It is said that on his order Rome was set on fire and that he played on the fiddle while the city was burning.

Page 79

Gnostics : early Christians who claimed to possess knowledge of spiritual mysteries. *Mr. Homo* : Man. *Rotary Club* : an international society with many branches for service to mankind. *Nelson* : Horatio Nelson (1758-1805), a great British admiral who died on board his ship soon after defeating the Franco-Spanish fleet in the Battle of Trafalgar. *Wellington* : Duke of Wellington (1769-1852), English politician and army commander. He defeated Napoleon in 1815 at Waterloo and became a national hero. *Monaco* : a principality under French protection. Monte Carlo, the most famous gambling centre of the world, is in Monaco.

Page 80

homo sapiens : the human race. *nocturnal hours* : hours of the night. *Holy Ghost* : Holy Spirit ; the third person of the Trinity, the other two being Father and Son.

Page 81

postulate : thing assumed as basis of reasoning. *trilobites* : prehistoric animals, now extinct. *Nero, Caligula, Hitler* and *Mussolini* : the most notorious tyrants and dictators. Caligula was a Roman emperor belonging to the first century. Hitler (1889-1944) was the notorious Nazi dictator of Germany who committed numerous brutalities on the Jews and plunged the world into the Second World War. Benito Mussolini (1883-1945) ruled Italy as a dictator for twenty-one years, and joined Hitler in the Second World War. *Sir James Jeans* (1877-1946) : one of the greatest physicists of modern times. His works include *The Mysterious Universe, The Universe Around Us,* and *The Stars in Their Courses. mundane* : worldly.

Page 82

prohibitionist : one who is in favour of prohibition on consumption of alcoholic drinks. *prodigies* : miracles ; wonders.

Page 83

angels of Mons : town of Belgium where the Allied forces won a victory hours before the Great War came to an end. In 1914, at the beginning of the Great War, the British troops lost a battle here. They were at that time supposed to be inspired by some angels. *King George* III (1738-1820) : King of Great Britain from 1760-1820.

Page 84

God extracted Adam's rib : Eve was created by God from a rib taken out of Adam's body. *Genesis* : The First Book of the Old Testament which describes the creation of man and the world. *Herodotus* : Greek historian of the fifth century. *Cyrus* : ruler of Persia in the sixth century B.C. He founded the Persian Empire.

Page 85

Quisling : a traitorous army officer of Norway. He sided with the Nazi Germans against his own country. *Finns* : inhabitants of Finland. *Lapps* : People of Lapland, a vast region of north Europe.

Page 86

Cain : eldest son of Adam and Eve, and the first murderer. He murdered his brother Abel. *Karl Marx* (1818-1883) : famous political theorist and the author of *Das Kapital* which laid the foundation of modern communism. *Lenin* (1870-1924) : great Russian communist leader. *Proletariat* : the labouring class of people.

Page 87

collectivization : making society capable of collective action. *Transvaal*: a province in South Africa. The province is rich in mineral wealth, especially gold and diamonds.

Page 88

sententious platitudes : commonplace sayings which appear to be proverbial. *Plato* (427-347 B.C.) : a great Greek philosopher. He presents his idea of an ideal state in his *Republic*. *Hobbes* : Thomas Hobbes (1588-1679), English philosopher and political thinker. He expounded his political philosophy in his famous work *Leviathan*.

Page 89

transubstantiation : conversion of the whole substance of Eucharistic bread and wine into body and blood respectively of Christ. *pernicious* : destructive; ruinous.

Page 90

Sunday truth : a truth that is not to be taken seriously.

Page 91

recalcitrant : refusing compliance.

Page 92

exhibitionists : persons with a perverted tendency to expose their bodies in an indecent manner. *Kleptomania* : irresistible tendency to theft in persons not tempted to it by needy circumstances. *sexual aberrations* : strayings from normal sexual behaviour.

Page 93

Versailles Treaty : the treaty of peace signed in Versailles, a town in France. This treaty officially brought the First World War to its end. *Babylonians* : inhabitants of Babylonia, one of the greatest empires of the ancient world. The Babylonians were a highly civilized people. *capricious* : guided by whim.

Page 94

insomnia : habitual sleeplessness. *modicum* : small quantity.

Page 95

Lao-Tze : Chinese sage and philosopher who founded Taoism, one of the principal religions of China. *Malthus* : Thomas Robert Malthus (1766-1834), an English economist. His work *An Essay on the Principle of Population* contained his theory of population which became very controversial. *amelioration* : betterment.

Page 96

objectify : express in concrete form.

Page 97

Walt Whitman (1819-1892) : a famous American poet, and author of *Leaves of Grass*. *Russian Revolution* : the revolution of 1917 that resulted in the end of Czarist rule and capture of power by the Bolsheviks. *unicorns and salamanders*: Both are imaginary creatures. The unicorn is a fabulous animal with a horse's body and a single straight horn in the middle of its forehead. Salamanders are lizard-like creatures believed to live in fire.

Page 98

insular : narrow-minded. *Manchus* : people of Manchuria. They established a dynasty in China in 1644.

Page 100

elixir of life : imaginary liquid that can supposedly change metals into gold or prolong life indefinitely. *talismans* : things which are believed to be capable of working wonders. *spells* : words used as charms or incantation. *Hellenistic* : Greek. *mascot* : person or thing supposed to bring good luck.

Page 101

Hades : In Greek mythology it is the dwelling place of the departed souls. *purgatory* : place where departed souls are believed to be cleansed of their sins before going to heaven. *F.W.H. Myers* (1843-1901) : English poet, essayist and physical researcher. *Marcus Aurelius*: Roman emperor belonging to the first century. He was also a devoted follower of stoic philosophy.

Page 102

Jonah : an ancient Hebrew prophet. He is the subject of Book of Jonah in the Old Testament. *Punic wars* : The three wars between Carthage and Rome over the possession of Sicily. The wars occurred during the third and second centuries B.C. Carthage was conquered by Rome in the last of these wars. *Moloch* : a heathen fire-god to whom children used to be sacrificed. *Carthage*: An ancient African city which became very powerful under Hannibal. It was eventually conquered and destroyed by Rome in 146 B.C. *French Revolution* : the Revolution of 1789 which led to the suspension of monarchy in France for some time.

Page 103

poltroons : cowards. *obloquy* : abuse; being ill-spoken of. *Osiris*: an ancient deity of Egypt. *Messiah* : Christ. *the lost ten tribes* : the ten tribes of Israelites which got lost after their deportation in the eighth century B.C. *Ephraim and Menasseh* : According to the Bible, they were the sons of Joseph. *the Great Pyramid* : The pyramids are tombs where the kings of Egypt were buried. The Great Pyramid is one located outside Cairo. *Armageddon* : according to the Bible the final great battle between the forces of good and evil. *Antichrist* : Great personal enemy of Christ, expected to appear before the end of the world.

Page 104

Abecedarians : members of a religious sect founded in Germany in the sixteenth century. They refused to learn to read because they believed that knowledge severs God's contact with man. *Jesuit* : a member of the Society of Jesus, a religious order founded by Ignatius Loyola in 1533. *sloth* : South American mammal living in trees and capable of very slow movement on ground. *the Flood* : the great flood sent by God to punish the sinners. The flood submerged the world. Noah built an Ark or boat and placed on it a pair of every species to save them from disaster. *Ararat* : It is a mountain where Noah's Ark is believed to have rested. *tardiness* : slowness ; sluggishness.

III. EXPLANATIONS WITH CRITICAL COMMENTS

1. Ousted from one position, they have taken up another. After being worsted in astronomy they did their best to prevent the rise of geology; they fought against Darwin in biology, and at the present time they fight against scientific theories of psychology and education. At each stage they try to make the public forget their earlier obscurantism, in order that their present obscurantism may not be recognized for what it is. (*Page* 72)

These lines occur in Bertrand Russell's illuminating essay, 'An Outline on Intellectual Rubbish'. The great intellectual and man of reason is pained to find cruelty, superstition, and false beliefs without any basis increasing by leaps and bounds, though man is supposed to be a rational animal. First of all, he takes up the irrational attitude of the clergymen and tells us how these men of God have encouraged false and dogmatic beliefs for ages. Russell points out that the great discoveries of science have exposed the irrationality and baselessness of the ideas and beliefs propagated by the clergy one after another. But unfortunately, with a dogmatic faith in their beliefs, they have never accepted the scientific method of inquiry or the truths established by it. When any of their beliefs has been exploded by the new inventions and discoveries, they have sought shelter under some other position. In the field of astronomy their views on the planets and the position of the earth were proved to be totally false by new astronomy. Darwin's theory of evolution proved the Biblical account of the creation of the universe to be absolutely wrong. The clergy, however, did not give up. They continued their fight against the scientifically established recent theories of psychology and education. The pity of the situation is that these men of God try to make the people forget the previous beliefs proved to be wrong, but want them to accept their present irrational beliefs without any scrutiny or question. Thus the priests have always been dogmatic in their views and expect the people to accept their views blindly.

2. Tolstoy thinks tobacco almost as bad as sex, in one of his novels, a man who is contemplating murder smokes a cigarette first in order to generate the necessary homicidal fury. Tobacco, however, is not prohibited in the Scriptures, though as Samuel Butler points out,

St. Paul would no doubt have denounced it if he had known of it.
(*Page 77*)

'An Outline of Intellectual Rubbish' is a devastating essay exposing all sorts of baseless religious and ethical beliefs. Russell does not spare even great men like Tolstoy and Gandhi for propagating some such concepts which have no scientific or rational basis. Both Mahatma Gandhi and Tolstoy preached in their old age the absurd irrational idea that all sexual intercourse was bad, even in the case of married couples. Even the Manicheans, followers of Mani of Persia, preached this doctrine of mortifying the flesh for the sake of the spirit. But Tolstoy went one step farther. He even denounced tobacco-smoking and considered it to be almost as bad as sex. In one of his novels he has tried to show the vicious effect of smoking tobacco. In this novel, a character is found to be smoking tobacco just to excite his passion and rage before committing a murder. Thus Tolstoy wanted to establish that smoking might provide stimulus to commit a heinous crime. Then Russell ironically remarks that tobacco is not prohibited in the religious books. In a vein of sarcasm he adds that Samuel Butler was correct when he pointed out that St. Paul would have definitely denounced this habit if he had known of it.

3. Spinoza wriggles, but does not find any satisfactory answer. If everything happens in accordance with God's will, God must have wanted Nero to murder his mother; therefore, since God is good the murder must have been a good thing. From this argument there is no escape.
(*Page 78*)

In his essay, 'An Outline of Intellectual Rubbish.' Bertrand Russell, one of the greatest intellectuals of our time, is ruthless in demolishing baseless religious beliefs and doctrines. Here he is discussing about the established religious conception of sin and the logical difficulties involved in the notion. According to all the different religions of the world God is all-powerful. But sin consists in disobedience to God's commands. Now, if God is omnipotent, how can He permit people to do something contrary to His will ? So it must be accepted that if a person commits a sinful act, it must be in accordance with the intention of God. If we accept such a conclusion, no act can be sinful, as everything happens according to the will of God. Hence Spinoza's disciples believing in God's omnipotence quite seriously opine that there can be no such thing as sin. But if this be so, great complications crop up. The Roman Emperor Nero brutally murdered his mother. Did he not commit a sin then ? Was not the eating of the apple by Adam a sinful act contrary to the will of God ? From all this it becomes very difficult to reconcile our belief in God's omnipotence to our idea of sin. Even Spinoza, the great German philosopher, and his disciples, staunch believers in God's omnipotence, failed to offer any satisfactory answer to such questions. If we are to accept their contentions, Nero must have done a good act by murdering his mother, as God is good as well as omnipotent. And nothing can be done unless He wills it.

> 4. No one can deny, in face of the evidence, that it is easy, given military power, to produce a population of fanatical lunatics. It would be equally easy to produce a population of sane and reasonable people, but many governments do not seek to do so, since such people would fail to admire the politicians who are at the head of these governments. *(Page 89)*

In his essay,'An Outline of Intellectual Rubbish,' after denouncing and exposing a good number of baseless concepts and false beliefs, religious, political or personal, Russell draws our attention to the power of a government to choose and instil beliefs at their sweet will. In our present-day world, governments have acquired tremendous power over people's beliefs, particularly after the rise of large states. The great majority of Romans embraced Christianity after the conversion of Roman Emperors to Christianity in the distant past. The same thing happened in the case of Protestants and Roman Catholics in the sixteenth century. But the power of governments over beliefs in our times has increased vastly as compared to any earlier times. A government can now mould the minds of men by inculcating wrong ideas and convert them into a race of fanatics to suit its sinister purpose. And a race of fanatics can easily be led to a war and be inspired with an ardent desire to kill one another without mercy. A government can succeed in such an undertaking easily if it is in the possession of full military power. Russell here reminds us of the beliefs inculcated in their peoples before the last war by the German, Japanese and Russian governments. But a government can also mould the minds of the people in such a way that they can become a race of tolerant, reasonable and mentally balanced people. But most of the modern governments are reluctant to do so, as they are afraid that reasonable and mentally balanced people will see through the nasty games of the politicians in power.

IV. CRITICAL APPRECIATION

Russell's aim in the essay. Russell's aim in 'An Outline of Intellectual Rubbish' is to illustrate human irrationality and to stress the immediate need of rationality in thought as well as in action. He has also suggested a few simple ways by which we can shake off at least some superstitions and false belief which have always stood between us and rational thinking.

The case of the clergy. Russell first takes up the case of the clergy, supposedly the best of men, and shows how those men of religion have displayed, through the ages, extreme irrationality by spreading an array of superstitions among mankind. The clergymen interpreted natural calamities as punishments sent by God for our sins, and continued to resist all scientific explanations contrary to their belief. They opposed the researches in astronomy, geology, and anatomy and other branches of science because such researches would only expose the stupidity of their own theories on Man and the Universe. Russell shows the contradictions in the religious concept of sin. The Church considers disobedience to God's will to be sin. At the same time it declares God as omnipotent. Russell argues that if God is omnipotent, no man can act against His will; so if a man disobeys one of His Commandments he does so by the will of God. Therefore, Russell continues, even a murder has to be regarded as good as it can be committed only with the approval of God who is good. Russell's arguments, by their logicality, have put the age-old concept of sin in jeopardy.

Going through the illustrations of the clergy's irrationality given by Russell, any sensible reader will have to endorse Russell's favourite view that religion has always been detrimental to progress.

False beliefs. Russell has also drawn a list of false beliefs and superstitions which have led men into irrational thinking and action. He points out the prevalent feeling of superiority that gives rise to meaningless self-esteem, narrow-minded patriotism, and an unjust aversion to other men and countries. He criticises our tendency to believe in the marvellous and in rumours without bothering about evidence. He then shows the inherent sadism in some people expressed in their attitude towards the insane and in their opposition to the use of anaesthetics. He then proceeds to shatter the fallacies of 'race'and 'blood'. The belief that human nature cannot be changed is also dismissed by him. By offering convincing arguments he shows how governments, if they are guided by reason, can impose reason on their populaces and ensure world peace. Finally he urges us to give up generalizations, such as those about the other sex and the characteristics of other nations. Generalization, he proves with illustrations, is often a source of false beliefs.

Russell's suggestions. Russell suggests adherence to a few simple rules for the avoidance of false beliefs. They are personal observation, careful analysis of opinion, avoidance of dogmatism, caution against self-esteem, avoidance of fear, and disbelief in superstitions. His suggestions, we find, are very sound, and easy to follow if we have the will to do so. Personal observation can remove many silly mistakes that we are prone to commit. Avoidance of dogmatism and self-esteem will teach us to respect others and their opinions, and encourage tolerance on individual as well as international levels. Fear, we are now convinced, is at the root of superstitions and many cruelties, and as such, has to be eliminated.

Russell's analytical mind. The essay is a product of an extraordinarily analytical mind. Russell has observed and analysed human behaviour with utmost precision. He identifies the follies of mankind, and then explores history to trace the origins of those follies. His analysis is always detailed and logical. That is why his arguments always seem reasonable and convincing.

Russell's humanism. Like most of his work, this essay, too, has been inspired by an intense humanism. He is genuinely concerned about the welfare of men. He wants to reform mankind by creating a general awareness of its follies. He is a preacher of tolerance and peace. That is why in this essay he advocates avoidance of dogmatism and self-esteem, the main obstacles in the way of tolerance and peace. He is against war and all kinds of cruelty, and as such, urges us to shed fear which is a major source of conflict and cruelty.

Russell's style. Russell is one of the most accomplished writers of English prose. He has the ability to express complex thoughts and ideas in a language comprehensible even to a layman. He is a man who can think and express himself clearly. All these factors contribute to the two major characteristics of his style—lucidity and clarity. The following lines can be quoted to show these qualities of his language : "A good way of ridding yourself of certain kinds of dogmatism is to become aware of opinions held in social circles different from your own. When I was young, I lived much outside my own country in France, Germany Italy, and the United States. I found this very profitable in diminishing the intensity of insular prejudice. If you cannot travel, seek out people with whom you disagree, and read a newspaper belonging to a party that is not yours. If the people and the newspaper seem mad, perverse, and wicked, remind yourself that you seem so to them. In this opinion both parties may be right, but they cannot both be wrong. This reflection should generate certain caution".

Another characteristic of Russell's style is that he always puts forth an argument and then fortifies the argument with relevant illustrations. He has an encyclopaedic knowledge, and as such, can draw illustrations from philosophy, science, literature, or from anywhere, to establish his point. All his essays, including this one, are full of such illustrations.

Russell has a tendency to moderate the seriousness of his subject by blending it with occasional touches of humour. Irony, to him, is the chief instrument for creating humour, and as such, is found in abundance in all his writings. His summing up of how the nuns—who never take a bath naked—view God, is a superb example of his ironic humour : "Apparently, they conceive of the Deity as a Peeping Tom, whose omnipotence enables Him to see through bathroom walls, but who is foiled by bathrobes". He finds the whole conception of sin puzzling, he explains ironically, "doubtless owing to my sinful nature." He narrates man's tendency to glorify his own country in an ironic vein : "If he is a Yugoslav, he boasts of his nation's pigs; if a native of the principality of Monaco, he boasts of leading the world in the matter of gambling." His account of the glorification of Man himself is another grand example of his ironic humour : "......God was preparing the Great climax. At last in the fullness of time, He produced Man including such specimens as Nero and Caligula, Hitler and Mussolini, whose transcendent glory justified the long painful process". The ample use of irony in Russell's essays does not mean that he is not capable of plain humour. The moment he realises that his essay is " getting too solemn" he gives up all solemnity and has recourse to pure fun. The last three paragraphs of this essay are written in a humorous vein. The story of the prophetess, who claimed to possess the power of walking on water, and her easy method of satisfying her faithful followers is funny. It is this perfect blending of humour with seriousness that makes Russell's essays so interesting and entertaining.

10

The Functions of a Teacher

I. SUMMARY

The teacher in antiquity and modern times. Teaching has a great and honourable tradition. But the position of the teacher has changed considerably. Today the teacher is permitted to teach, not what he thinks, but what his employers want him to teach. In the past, the teacher was usually a man of exceptional wisdom and independent in matters of teaching. Though sometimes the teachers faced execution or imprisonment for their subversive doctrines, their doctrines could never be suppressed. A teacher has to enjoy a feeling of intellectual freedom if he wants to carry out his responsibility of infusing knowledge and reason into his pupils. In antiquity the teacher enjoyed this freedom. But in the Middle Ages teaching became the privilege of the Church and the teacher lost his freedom. The Renaissance brought back a respect for learning and with it considerable independence to the teacher. Institutes of education, however, remained under the control of the dogmatists with the result that most intellectual work was done by independent scholars.

The teacher and state education today. In the modern world education has become the prerogative of the State and the Church. As a result the teacher has become a civil servant obliged to follow propagandist guidelines set by people with little knowledge of education. State education is necessary; but it may also lead to certain evils, such as those seen in Nazi Germany and Russia. In the presence of these evils a teacher is bound to be reduced to the position of a spokesman of the official dogmatic creed. He becomes merely an instrument for infusing into the young, fear, subservience and blind obedience and unquestioned submission to the authority. The result of such education is that the students turn, as they did in Nazi Germany, into fanatical bigots, ignorant of the outside world and unaccustomed to a free exchange of opinions. Furthermore, such preaching of different creeds widens the differences among countries, and stands in the way of the development of an international culture; in many cases it has inspired fanatical nationalism leading to a warlike ferocity among the populaces.

Decay of cultural internationalism. The decay of cultural internationalism has proceeded at a continually increasing pace since the First World War. Fanatical nationalism has affected even the intellectual sphere. The scholars of Russia, for instance, are no longer allowed to go abroad lest they should be compared unfavourably with their counterparts there. Even in England there is a tendency to dispense with Frenchmen and Germans in the teaching of French and German. Such consideration of nationality over competence is harmful to education as well as to the idea of international culture.

Duties of a teacher. These educational evils may become prominent even in democratic countries unless the teachers are protected from intellectual bondage. The first requisite for such protection is a clarification of the functions of a teacher. Imparting definite uncontroversial information is one of his functions. Such information can be used as a basis for building up further information, and is of great utility to the modern communities. Considering the difficulties faced by illiterates, the teacher has to accept the idea of universal compulsory education. There is nothing wrong about a teacher creating among his pupils an urge to defend their country; but he should never try to produce this urge by encouraging obscurantism and irrational feelings. There are silly opinions that nations are made strong by uniformity of opinion and by suppression of liberty, and that democracy weakens a country in war. It will be a misfortune if one set of dogmatists conquer the world and impose a ban on all new ideas; it will be a still greater misfortune if rival dogmatists conquer different regions of the world and spread hatred against each other. The teacher can be the main defence against such misfortunes or spread of dogmatism in any form.

The teacher and politics. Organised party spirit is harmful in that it often leads to wars and civil wars. The teacher should keep away from the strife of parties and try to infuse into his pupils the habit of impartial inquiry. He has to endeavour to investigate opinions in an impartial and scientific manner. In case the results of his investigation seem inconvenient to some people, the teacher must be protected against their resentment. However, the teacher should remember that he is not expected to indulge in dishonest propaganda.

The teacher and civilization. The teachers are the most prominent guardians of civilization. One of their major tasks is to impart a civilized attitude to their pupils. But for this they need to have a clear concept of the meaning of civilization. Civilization, in its true sense, is related to the progress of mind, not of material comforts. A civilized man should be aware of the insignificance of his environment in relation to the world in time and space. He has to develop a broad international outlook and should be able to realise the futility of controversies. An idea of the vast panorama of geological epochs and astronomical abysses helps to enlarge his mind. A truly civilized man can soar above what is purely personal, and can appreciate the love of humanity, intellect and the sense of beauty of the men who have done their best to make human life better. It should be his endeavour to discover and remove the causes of the sufferings of mankind. If all this is in the mind and heart of the teacher, he will certainly convey it in his teaching to his pupils.

The teacher and the propagandist. A good teacher must possess feelings of warm affection towards his pupils, and a sincere desire to impart to them the right type of knowledge. His attitude is not to be that of the propagandist. The propagandist's aim is to thwart the natural growth of minds and to plant in them evil feelings of envy, destructiveness and cruelty. Repressive and cruel passions, which are so universal today, are caused by unhappiness. A good teacher has to show his pupils the possibilities of delightful activities, thereby encouraging their kind impulses and preventing the growth of harmful desires. His aim should be to free adults from psychological misfortunes which give rise to an envy of others thereby leading to an impulse to cruelty.

The difficulties of the teachers. For several reasons, the teachers today are not able to work to the best of their abilities. Firstly, the teachers are mostly overworked and are compelled to prepare the students for examinations rather than give them a liberalising mental training. As a result of overwork, the teachers become nervous, out of touch with the latest works in their subjects, and unable to provide new understanding and new knowledge to their pupils. Secondly, the teachers in most countries have to suppress their own opinions and teach only opinions which are officially recognised as correct. The result is that the inquiring pupils have to go outside the class-room to find out what is being thought by the contemporary great minds.

The teacher and falsehood. A good teacher has to be determined to avoid falsehood in the course of his teaching. He should never conceal truth on the ground that it is 'unedifying'. The pupils can be taught to admire the virtues of the good people but it is of no use to teach them to admire rogues by hiding their vices. Knowledge of such truths, if it comes suddenly, may lead to cynicism. Therefore, the teacher has to prepare his pupils to receive such knowledge by giving them a knowledge of what is good, and then by planting in them a scientifically investigative desire to get at the truth. In any case, telling lies to the young is an unpardonable offence.

Teaching tolerance. The most important function of a teacher is to produce in his pupils a tolerance for opinions which differ from their own. The intolerance that springs from ignorance about other sects, other political parties and other nations, is the antithesis of a civilised outlook. Little is being done towards using the educational system to remove such ignorance. In every country nationalistic feeling is encouraged, and the young are taught that the people living in other countries are inferior to them. Such kind of teaching encourages collective hysteria, the most insane and cruel of human emotions. But, for all this, the teachers are not to blame. They are hardly free to teach what they wish to teach. They know the needs of the students intimately. Yet they are not allowed to decide the subjects and methods of instruction. They ought to be granted more opportunities for self-determination, and more freedom from the interference of bureaucrats and bigots, who know little of education and the needs of the youth.

Freedom for the teacher. A teacher can discharge his duties adequately only when he feels himself to be an individual guided by his own creative impulses, like an artist or philosopher. He can have such a feeling only when he is free from all outside interference. In the modern world an individual finds it very difficult to preserve independence of the great organised forces. It has become necessary, in the interest of the world, to find ways to offer some scope and liberty to its best minds. The Renaissance Popes granted such liberty to the Renaissance artists, but the powerful men of our times hardly share such respect for genius. The turbulence of our times is, in every way, detrimental to the fine flower of culture. In such circumstances, it is necessary that at least some people like the teachers, should be permitted to continue in their search for loop-holes in the present systems. Else, the systems will destroy all that is best in man.

II. ANNOTATIONS

Page 105

instil : infuse into a person. *subversive* : that may lead to overthrow of an authority; that encourages rebellion. *Socrates was put to death* : Socrates (469-399 B.C.), the Greek philosopher, was found guilty of subversive activities against the state of Athens. He was sentenced to death. *spasmodic* : occurring, done, by fits and starts. *prerogative* : privilege; right. *Inquisition* : an ecclesiastical tribunal set up by the Roman Catholic Church in the 13th century for the suppression of heresy. It became notorious for causing thousands of deaths. *Galileo*: Galileo Galilei (1564-1642), the great Italian scientist who was persecuted as a heretic because his theories did not agree with the views of the Church. Ultimately, he had to recant his views.

Page 106

recant : disavow former opinion with public confession of error. *Giordano Bruno* (1548-1600): one of the most original thinkers of his time. He was burned at the stake on charges of heresy. *behests*: commands; orders. *warp* : make perverted. *totalitarian countries* : countries run by a set of people who permit no rival loyalties or parties. *Nazi Germany*: Nazis under Hitler captured power in 1933, and ruled the country until their defeat in the Second World War. *bigots* : those who hold on to some creed or view irrespective of reason.

Page 107

Leningrad : famous city in Russia, named after the Russian communist leader, Lenin.

Page 108

Obscurantism : opposition to inquiry, enlightenment, and reform.

Page 109

ex-parte : made in the interest of one side only. *dissemination* : sowing; scattering. *mitigate* : alleviate, relieve. *adjuncts* : non-essential attributes.

Page 110

epochs : eventful periods in history or life. *abysses* : bottomless chasms. *turbulence* : commotion.

Page 111

topiarian : one who clips shrubs etc. into ornamental shapes. *analogous* : similar.

Page 112

acquiesce : accept. *edifying* : improving morally.

Page 113

antithesis : directly opposite. *hysteria* : morbid excitement.

Page 114

plutocratic magnate : a rich man in a country ruled by the wealthy.

III. EXPLANATIONS WITH CRITICAL COMMENTS

1. **A feeling of intellectual independence is essential to the proper fulfilment of the teacher's functions, since it is his business to instil what he can of knowledge and reasonableness into the process of forming public opinion.** (*Page 105*)

In the very beginning of the essay, 'The Functions of a Teacher' Russell tells us that the profession of teaching has a great and honourable tradition from the very dawn of history till recent times. But this highly skilled profession has now been transformed into a large and important branch of the public service. As a result, unlike the great teachers of the past, honest and inspired teachers of our time cannot teach what they think to be just and necessary, but are compelled to instil such ideas and prejudices as are thought useful by their employers or the governments of their respective countries. Russell asserts that to discharge his duties justly and honestly a teacher would have to maintain his intellectual independence at any cost. He should have a missionary zeal and be inspired by the ideas of his predecessors to teach his pupils what he thinks to be right for the natural development of their mind. Without caring for physical comforts or material possessions a noble and inspired teacher is to wage a tireless battle against all reactionary forces of the world, social, communal or political. Teachers must remember that to uphold the banner of truth and mental independence Socrates drank his cup of poison calmly and Plato had been thrown behind the bars in the ancient past. In a later age Bruno was burnt at the stake and Galileo had to suffer miserably at the hands of bigots and reactionaries. So, in our complex and confused age, teachers should be fully alive to their great and noble mission in life which is to impart the right type of education to their wards so that they may grow into noble and honourable citizens of the world.

2. He desires, like a topiarian artist, that their growth shall be trained and twisted to suit the gardener's purpose. And in thwarting their natural growth he is apt to destroy in them all generous vigour, replacing it by envy, destructiveness and cruelty. (*Page 110*)

In his essay, 'The Functions of a Teacher', Russell opines that to be a good teacher a person must be endowed with feelings of warm affection towards his wards. The right type of teacher should also have a genuine desire to impart to his pupils such knowledge as is deemed by him just and suitable for them. But, unfortunately, in our days, many a teacher has drifted away from the great and noble mission and has become a propagandist under the influence of a reactionary society and wary and ambitious politicians in power. Russell describes the attitude of a teacher turned propagandist, his way of teaching and its evil effects on the tender minds of his growing pupils. The propagandist does not want his students to develop their minds in such a way as to gather the right type of knowledge and to nurture the powers to judge things independently. He would not like them to freely choose an aim or purpose which they consider good for themselves. Here, Russell likens a propagandist teacher to a gardener who trims and twists the shrubs or plants in such a way as to make them grow in particular shapes to suit his purpose. But by working in the same way with the same purpose the teacher is likely to suppress the natural instincts and desire of his pupils and engender in them vicious desires and impulses such as envy, destructiveness, and cruelty. Russell is quite convinced that cruelty is mostly the outcome of suppression of good impulses in early years. In fact there is much cruelty in our world because the noble impulses of the pupils are suppressed in the early stages.

3. Meanwhile, it is important that some at least should continue to realize the limitations of what can be done by organisation. Every system should allow loopholes and exceptions, for if it does not it will in the end crush all that is best in man. (*Page 114*)

In 'The Functions of a Teacher', Russell has given teachers a very high place in society as he considers them to be the real guardians of human civilization and the worthy architects of our society. He has compared them with the artists, the philosophers and the men of letters. So the teachers also should be given full freedom to perform their duties sincerely and adequately as directed by an inner creative impulse. Russell regrets that ours is a confused and disturbed world which is hostile to the growth and development of the fine flowers of culture. Our world is now torn by conflicts and divided into different camps, each with its own party spirit and dogmatic ideas. It is very difficult in this modern world to find a place for the individual with his freedom of thought and judgment. There is very little freedom for teachers to work unfettered in totalitarian states. Ordinary man is cowed down by fear and so does not attach any importance to the need of individual freedom. Russell feels that the time is not yet ripe for such sane conditions but, with his optimism, he fervently expects that soon the propitious time would come when good sense will prevail and the claims of civilization will be again in a position to do away with dogmatism and party spirit. Everyone should realize the limitations of all sorts of human organization, political, social, or religious. So there must be enough room for exceptional people like teachers, artists and philosophers to act and work freely; otherwise human civilization and culture would be doomed forever.

IV. CRITICAL APPRECIATION

Russell's views on the teacher and his duties. The essay 'The Functions of a Teacher' presents a part of Russell's progressive educational philosophy. Here he discusses the position of the teacher in the modern world, the evils of state-owned education, the duties of a teacher, and the necessity of granting the teacher freedom from external interference.

The position of the teacher and state-owned education. According to Russell, the teacher today has lost the independence that he enjoyed in the past. In the present age, the teacher is supposed to teach not what he thinks is right, but what his employers want him to teach. In most of the countries, education is now controlled by the State and, to some extent, by the Church. As a result the teacher has become a civil servant obliged to follow an orthodox and propagandist system of education which is basically designed to teach the young, when they grow up, to remain loyal to the *status quo*. Under such a system the teacher is reduced to an instrument for infusing fear, subservience and blind obedience in his pupils. Russell rightly points out the evils of state-owned educational systems which may often lead to an irrational instillation of negative virtues such as conservatism, militant patriotism, and cruelty. Russell has not been particular about elaborating the positive side of the state-owned education. In a country where the state controls the educational system, education can be imparted in a much more organised, effective way. The state can save a lot of confusion by formulating a uniform education policy for the country. In countries where the state controls education there is more financial security for the teachers and as such some of the best brains are attracted to the teaching profession. The fact is that the state may participate in the sphere of education, but its outlook has to be rational and liberal.

The duties of a teacher. Russell's clarification of the functions of a teacher is again in keeping with his well-known educational philosophy. Russell accepts the utility of the definite uncontroversial information and wants the teacher to impart it to his pupils. In his opinion the teacher may inspire his students to defend their country, but he should not do so by encouraging obscurantism and irrational feelings. Russell was all his life an antagonist to dogmatism in any form. He considers the teacher the main safeguard against the spread of dogmatic creeds. Russell thinks that a teacher should keep away from political parties, and infuse into his pupils the habit of scrutinizing political opinions impartially. Moreover, the teacher is the guardian of civilization and as such it is his duty to convey to his pupils the rational concept of a civilized man. A teacher should not be a propagandist.

He should know that his most important duty is to encourage the growth of the positive virtues, such as kindness and tolerance, in his pupils.

Any sensible person, who is aware of the importance of moral values, would unhesitatingly endorse Russell's views on the duties of a teacher. In today's world, political strifes, power games, and negative virtues, such as greed, envy and cruelty, have destroyed much of true worth and value. Under the circumstances, if we want to regenerate the world, we must forget the present generation that has reached a point beyond rectification and concentrate on building up better generations for the future. So, if we want a better world, we must realise the importance of education in the real sense of the term and free it from political and other evil motivations. We must also accept the fact that the genuine teacher, who understands the needs of the young more intimately than others, can act as the best link between education and the young only if he is permitted to perform his duties without undue outside interference.

Russell's humanism. Russell's concept of education itself is a product of his intense humanism. He is concerned with the demonstration of intolerance and cruelty all around him. He thinks that the only way to create a better world is to evolve a rational educational system and to allow the teacher to teach what he thinks best for the moral upliftment of the pupils. Russell has always been against all kinds of self-esteem, militant nationalism and intolerance; he believes that these vices are the major sources of wars, conflicts, and cruelty in the world. So, he is one of the most ardent advocates of tolerance among individuals and nations. His conviction, that the most important duty of the teacher is to infuse the qualities of kindness and tolerance in his pupils, shows his intense concern for mankind.

Russell's style. Russell's prose is always characterised by the qualities of lucidity and clarity. The thoughts conveyed in the present essay are less complicated than his other 'unpopular essays'. That is why the qualities of lucidity and clarity are more striking in this essay than in the other essays in this collection. Here are a few lines to demonstrate these qualities:

> Clergymen are not expected to preach sermons for several hours everyday, but the analogous effort is demanded of teachers. The result is that many of them become harrassed and nervous, out of touch with recent work in the subjects that they teach, and unable to inspire their students with a sense of the intellectual delights to be obtained from new understanding and new knowledge.

Education has always been a serious subject with Russell. He expects the same kind of seriousness from his readers too. That is why he has not cared to make this essay entertaining with his usual flashes of humour. There are one or two ironical statements, such as, "Something called education is given to everybody, usually by the state, but sometimes by the churches." But in general the element of irony, which Russell is so fond of using is negligible in this essay. The clarity and simplicity of thought and the absence of irony have made it one of the easiest of Russell's essays.

11

Ideas That Have Helped Mankind

I. SUMMARY

Conception of help. Ideas, generally accepted as beneficial to mankind, are those that have helped (*i*) increase in population, (*ii*) becoming less like animals, (*iii*) increase in happiness, (*iv*) diversity of enjoyment, (*v*) greater knowledge, and (*vi*) friendliness to one another.

(*i*) **Increase in population.** Ideas leading to an increase in population have, most certainly, been helpful to mankind. During the pre-historic days men, because of their smallness in number and physical handicaps, were helpless against wild animals. Increase in population compensated for their physical weaknesses and helped them in their struggle for existence.

(*ii*) **Becoming less like animals.** Some ideas that have helped mankind to gain superiority over animals have also been helpful. Unlike animals, men are becoming progressively dependent on cultivated skills. They are also giving more and more importance to forethought which has made them more rational than animals.

(*iii*) **Increase in happiness.** Russell is not certain if ideas have at all helped to increase human happiness. Birds, refusing to learn from experience, continue to die in large numbers in winter; but they are totally free from anxiety. Forethought helps men avert such physical disaster, but it also destroys their happiness by keeping them in a perpetual state of anxiety and insecurity. Animals, which cannot think, are much happier than man.

(*iv*) **Diversity of enjoyment.** As to diversity of enjoyments, however, men are now certainly much more well-placed than animals. With the help of intelligence they have invented enjoyable things like music, poetry, science and games. These things afford no pleasure to animals. This advantage that men enjoy is, however, associated with a much greater liability to boredom.

(*v*) **Greater knowledge.** Most of us believe that man is glorious not because of numerical superiority or other such things but because he possesses intellectual and moral qualities and a vast store of knowledge. Whether greater knowledge is beneficial is, however, doubtful.

(*vi*) **Friendliness to one another.** Some ideas have helped to make human beings friendlier to each other. But such friendship is confined within the limits of herds. Man is still intolerant of people living outside his own herd; in his attitude towards such people he can be, because of his superior intelligence, much more cruel than the most savage animal.

Two kinds of ideas. The ideas discussed in the essay have been broadly divided into two kinds—those that contribute to knowledge and technique, and those that are concerned with morals or politics.

Ideas that have contributed to knowledge and technique

(*i*) *Pre-historic times.* The most important and difficult steps were taken in the pre-historic times. The idea of language materialized in those times. Language has proved to be a convenient medium through which knowledge can be handed from generation to generation. The inventions of fire and the art of cookery were also achieved in those days. Taming of domestic animals for useful purposes started long ago. Invention of agriculture is one of the most important gifts from the pre-historic days. Agriculture, of course, continued to involve a lot of bloodshed in the form of human sacrifice through many centuries. Now we have realised that human sacrifice is not needed for growing crops. The art of writing, which, like speech, developed gradually, was the last of the great pre-historic inventions.

(ii) *Historic times*: Coming to historic times, the earliest important steps were taken in mathematics and astronomy, both of which began in Babylonia and then were developed by the ancient Greeks. Mathematics was, however, used by the Greeks only as a 'gentlemanly' pursuit, valued for its own sake as giving eternal truths. Only Archimedes foreshadowed the modern use of mathematics by inventing engines of war.

The Greeks studied astronomy with no regard for its navigational or such utility until the time when it became associated with astrology. At a very early stage they discovered that the earth was round and found ways to calculate the distance of the sun and the moon. Their works came to be widely known during the Renaissance and that helped the growth of modern science.

The Greeks had the conception of natural law and had the propensity to reduce the natural laws to mathematical terms. However, many of them, including Aristotle, made the mistake of associating natural phenomena with ethical and moral purposes. In the seventeenth century great advances were made in the field of understanding nature, especially through the efforts of Galileo, Descartes, Newton and Leibniz. The concepts of that century were the key to a great many secrets of nature. Modern technique in industry and war, with the exception of the atomic bomb, is still wholly based upon a type of dynamics developed out of the principles of Galileo and Newton. One of the principles, on which the dynamics of Galileo and Newton depended, was the law of inertia which stated that every body, left to itself, will continue to move, as it is moving, in the same straight line, and with the same velocity. Galileo unified the principles governing the earth and the heavens by his law of inertia. This principle also made it possible to develop a science of the motions of matter, free from the ideas of supposed influence of mind and spirit, and thus laid the foundations of the purely materialistic physics.

From the seventeenth century onwards, it has become increasingly clear to us that rejection of every kind of ethical and aesthetical bias is necessary for understanding nature. We must not believe that noble things have noble causes, or that order is impossible without a 'celestial policeman'. The Greeks worshipped celestial bodies as gods. Every bias of this kind was rejected by seventeenth century astronomy. The Copernican system proved that the earth is not the centre of the universe and suggested that man was not the supreme creation of God. In the nineteenth century advancement in the field of geology and Darwin's theory of evolution upset a great many religious ideas. The grand conception of the soul has also been rendered useless with the progress of science.

Ideas that are concerned with moals and politics. The present state of the world and the fear of an atomic war show that scientific progress without a corresponding moral and political progress may only increase the possibility of the destruction of mankind. Those who want to see the human race survive must take stock of moral ideas that great men have put into the world.

(*i*) *Man is a mixture of angel and devil.* From the moral point of view, man is a curious mixture of 'angel' and 'devil'. He has the capacity to feel the splendour of beauty in nature and he can experience tender parental affection. At the same time, man can be greedy and proud, and can surpass even animals in cruelty.

(*ii*) *Brotherhood.* Moral ideas are very often centuries ahead of the times. The brotherhood of man is an ideal that was preached in the antiquity by the Greek Stoics. Christ preached a similar doctrine when he said: 'Thou shalt love thy neighbour as thyself'. Earlier, the Buddhists also had advocated love for fellow beings. Unfortunately, such doctrines have never become widely accepted and practised. However, the ideal of Christian charity remained alive and in every age inspired some notable saints. Modern Liberalism, which is the only hope in the present world, is a product of this idea of charity.

(*iii*) *Equality and liberty.* The watchwords of the French Revolution—Liberty, Equality and Fraternity—have religious origins. Equality was practised by the Orphic societies in Greece. These societies granted women and slaves a status equal to that of citizens. The Orphics believed in transmigration and thought that the same soul could inhabit the bodies of a slave and a king in different lives. Such a view made discrimination between a king and a slave meaningless. The same idea passed over from orphism into stoicism, and subsequently, into Christianity, and whenever circumstances permitted, helped reduce inequalities in the social system.

The term 'Liberty' has two serious meanings. On the one hand, it implies freedom of a nation from foreign domination; on the other hand, it means freedom of a citizen to pursue his legitimate profession. The idea of individual liberty first took shape in the form of religious toleration that followed the failure of the Catholics and the Protestants to wipe out each other in the Thirty Years' War. The greatest exponent of this idea of liberty at that time was John Locke, Free press, free speech and freedom from arbitrary arrest, however, came to be acknowledged only in the nineteenth century, at least among the western democracies.

(*iv*) *Democracy.* Russell is a staunch supporter of a democratic and representative form of Government, which can be workable only if the people are tolerant and self-restrained. Law and government are two political ideas to which mankind owes a lot. Of those two, government is more fundamental because it can exist without law, whereas law cannot exist without government. Government may be defined as a concentration of the collective forces of a community in an organization which, by virtue of this concentration of power, is able to control individuals living in the community and to resist pressures from foreign states. Democracy was invented as a means for reconciling government with liberty. Democracy provides the necessary government and at the same time prevents misuse of power by the government, making it temporary and dependent upon popular approval. The second Triumvirate in Rome, when they needed money to fight Brutus and Cassius, simply declared a few rich men as public enemies, executed them, and seized their properties. Such abuse of power is not possible in a democratic state. Personal liberty can be safeguarded only where individuals are not punished except by legal procedure, and when freedom of speech, press and religion are granted to every citizen.

The present crisis. The human race is today passing through an unprecedented period of crisis. Establishment of an international government is now a must if mankind wants to survive. Such a government may, in the beginning, indulge in oppression. But, like the other governments, it can be expected to shed its vices in course of time and be transformed into a better one. There is now only one alternative to this idea of an international government—to go back to the primitive stage and begin anew. But this step will seem meaningless if we take into account the hazards of the primitive life and man's long and arduous march along the road to civilization. Having recourse to an international government is a more appropriate step also because the present circumstances are conducive to the formation of such a government. At present there are only two really independent states in the world—the United States and the USSR. What is only necessary to save the human race from disaster is the step from two independent states to one—not by war, but by agreement. If this step is accomplished, mankind will be transferred to an era of happiness and well-being. Our scientific skill will then concentrate more on eradication of poverty and disease, will reduce the hours of productive labour, and will offer us more time for leisure and enjoyment. All this is possible only if the men who hold power, and the people who support them, learn to attach more importance to the question of survival of the human race than to the destruction of their enemies. We can only hope that we will be wise enough to avoid the sure ways to disaster and choose the way that can help us achieve a new level of happiness, security, well-being and intelligence.

II. ANNOTATIONS

Page 115

indubitable : certain. *homo sapiens* : the human race. *subsisting* : continuing to exist. *cumulative* : increased by successive additions.

Page 116

Birds of passage : migratory birds. *catastrophe* : disastrous end. *curbing* : checking; restraining. *depredations* : ravages.

Page 117

propitious : favourable.

Page 118

fertility rites : religious celebrations that were expected to ensure good production of crops. These rites often involved sacrifice of children. *Moloch* : a heathen fire-god to whom children used to be sacrificed. *Babylonia* : a great empire of the ancient world which reached the peak of its glory under King Nebuchadnezzar in the 6th century. *Millenia* : plural of millenium which means one thousand years; millenium also means a period of great happiness and prosperity.

Page 119

Xenophanes (576-480 B.C.): Greek poet and philosopher. He founded the Eleatic school of philosophy which believed in the unchangeability of the laws of the universe. *Thracians* : the people of the ancient Thrace, a country in south-eastern Europe. *Archimedes* (287-212 B.C.): Greek mathematician who discovered the principle of specific gravity. *ivory tower* : shelter from the harsh realities of life. *Aristarchus of Samos* : a Greek astronomer belonging to the 3rd century B.C. He was the first to claim that the earth is round and that it revolves on its axis round the sun.

Page 120

quantum mechanics : the quantum theory, advanced by Planck. It states that in radiation the energy of electrons is discharged not continuously but in discrete amounts or quanta.

Page 121

rectilinear : in or forming a straight line. *primum mobile* : outermost sphere added in Middle Ages to Ptolemaic system. The sphere was supposed to revolve round the earth in 24 hours. *projectile* : anything capable of being projected by force.

Page 122

celestial policeman : God. *Plotinus* (203-270 A.D.) : a Greek philosopher who founded the Neo-Platonic school of philosophy. According to his philosophy man should endeavour to be united with God. *Anaxagoras* : a Greek philosopher and scientist belonging to the 5th century B.C. He believed that matter was made of atoms and was the first to explain solar eclipse. *Genesis* : First Book of Old Testament which contains the account of Creation. *amoeba* : a microscopic, unicellular organism which perpetually keeps changing its shape. *pithecanthropus erectus* : an extinct genus of ape which resembled human being. It is hypothetically considered to be the link between ape and man. *homo pekiniensis* : Peking man ; prehistoric type of man represented by remains discovered in 1929 at Peking. *Piltdown man* : Piltdown is the name of a village in Sussex, England. Here in 1913 a skull was discovered which, until 1953, was believed to belong to a prehistoric type of man. *Neanderthal man* : the primeval type of men widely distributed in parts of Europe. Their remains were first found in the Neanderthal valley in Rhine province in Germany.

Page 123

Buchenwald : notorious Nazi concentration camp in Germany. *Tower of Babel* : According to the Bible, a tower was built to enable human beings to reach heaven. God made the builders speak in different languages which led to misunderstanding and chaos among the builders. The work had ultimately to be abandoned.

Page 124

alchemy : chemistry. *Auschwitz* : a town in Poland where the Nazi Germans set up a concentration camp, and tortured and exterminated thousands of Jews.

Page 125

last judgement : final divine judgement. On Doomsday human beings are supposed to be rewarded or punished by God for their actions in this world. *Macedonian* : inhabitant of Macedonia, a small Greek State. Alexander the Great was the King of Macedonia. *Zeno* (342-270 B.C.) : a much respected Greek philosopher who founded the Stoic school of philosophy. *Stoics* : the followers of Stoic philosophy which preached practice of virtue, attention to ethics, control of passions, and indifference to pain and pleasure. *Samaritan* : inhabitant of Samaria, an ancient city of Palestine. The term is usual employed to mean a genuinely charitable person.

Page 126

gladiatorial : of gladiators, men trained to fight with sword or other weapon at ancient Roman show. *Orphic societies* : followers of the mystic doctrines associated with the name of the legendary musician, Orpheus. The Orphics professed the cult of Dionysus, and claimed knowledge of the secret of after-death happiness. *transmigration* : passage or migration of a soul from a body into a different body. *quaker*: colloquial name for a member of the Society of Friends, founded by George Fox in the 17th century. A quaker is peace-loving, observes simplicity in dress and speech, and takes part in peculiar priestless religious meetings.

Page 127

nefarious : wicked. *Cicero* (106-43 B.C.): Marcus Tullius Cicero, a Roman statesman and writer. He was a contemporary of Julius Caesar. *expostulated* : remonstrated. *magnates* : wealthy or eminent men.

vagaries : whimsical or extravagant notions. *avocations* : vocations; professions.

Page 128

John Locke (1632-1704) : a famous English philosopher and political thinker. His philosophy has been discussed in the essay *Philosophy and Politics. Stalin* : Joseph Stalin (1879-1953), a great Russian leader. From 1924 until his death he ruled over Russia as a dictator. *Churchill* : Sir Winston Churchill was Prime Minister of England and is regarded as one of the greatest statesmen. *a Balkan country* : one of the countries in the Peninsula bounded by the Adriatic, Aegean, and Black Seas. Turkey, Greece, Albania, Yugoslavia, Rumania and Bulgaria are the Balkan countries. *Cromwell, Robespierre* : See notes to the essay *Philosophy and Politics.*

Page 129

League of Nations : a world body set up at the end of World War I by the treaty of peace, 1919 to prevent future wars. Now it has been replaced by the United Nations. *Kellogg Pact* : a declaration signed in Paris in 1928 by the major powers. The declaration renounced war, and was named after the then American Secretary of State, F.B. Kellogg. *Xerxes*: King of Persia in the 5th century B.C. He was a despotic and ruthless ruler. *Nero* : See notes to *Philosophy and Politics. Second Triumvirate in Rome* : Mark Antony, Octavian and Lepitus who unitedly ruled Rome.

Page 131

pharaos : Ancient Egyptian kings were called pharaos. *deluge* : Great Flood, described in the Bible.

III. EXPLANATIONS WITH CRITICAL COMMENTS

1. Perhaps—so I sometimes allow myself to fancy—God does not intend us to understand the mechanism by which He regulates the material universe. Perhaps the nuclear physicists have come so near to the ultimate secrets that He thinks it time to bring their activities to a stop. And what simpler method could He devise than to let them carry their ingenuity to the point where they exterminate the human race. (*Page 123*)

In 'Ideas That Have Helped Mankind', Russell tells us how modern scientific inventions and discoveries have exploded myths and wrong ideas and superstitious beliefs and have helped mankind in its march towards progress and prosperity. Then Russell comes to the second kind of idea that has helped or may help mankind in future. This is the moral as opposed to the technical idea. From scientific knowledge man has been able to have a much greater command over the forces of nature and thus made great progress in various fields. But then Russell justly points out that scientific progress without a corresponding moral and political progress may prove disastrous for mankind. In spite of all his scientific and material progress man is now in the grip of fear of an atomic war that may bring about unprecedented disaster on the human civilization. This has happened because there has not been a corresponding moral and political progress along with scientific development. Then, in a humorous, rather flippant manner, Russell refers to the story of the Tower of Babel from the Bible. Just like the men of the Biblical times who started to build a very tall tower to reach heaven by climbing it, men of science have also invented something challenging the power of God, in modern times. God punished those people in a milder way. But this time the punishment may be much more severe, as the nuclear scientists seem to have come very close to the ultimate secrets of the universe which are only known to Him. And God must be resenting it very much and must be thinking of punishing mankind in a terrible manner. By this Russell means that if moral ideas and good sense do not prevail the atom bomb may be the cause of wiping out the human race.

2. Universal love is an emotion which many have felt and which many more could feel if the world made it less difficult. This is one side of the picture. On the other side are cruelty, greed, indifference and overweening pride. *(Page 124)*

These lines have been taken from Russell's 'Ideas That Have Helped Mankind'. Russell divides helpful ideas into two kinds: first the ideas that contribute to scientifc knowledge and technique, secondly those which are concerned with morals and politics. After telling us how the advanced scientific and technical ideas have helped mankind, Russell turns to moral ideas. As regards moral ideas man has undoubtedly made considerable progress. Man is now endowed with fine sensibilities and gifted with aesthetic and artistic qualities. But sadly enough he is still a strange blend of good and evil, retaining as he does some of his savage instincts and impulses. As a result of his progress in moral ideas, man can now appreciate the beauty of quiet nights and the lovely grace of spring flowers. He has also developed the tender emotions of love and affection that a father should have for children. At some rare moments he has visualized a happy and healthy life and how human beings should conduct themselves with one another. Many a person has also been attracted by the great ideas of universal brotherhood and the idea may spread rapidly if there is a favourable atmosphere for its growth. This is one side of the picture. Unfortunately, in spite of developing such finer sensibilities and emotion, man has not yet been able to root out his savage instincts and impulses. So, sometimes the angel in him gives way to the devil and we find him carried away by his primitive impulses and passions like greed, jealousy, cruelty and pride. Hence we are often aghast to find politicians in power in one country torturing inhumanly their opponents in their own country as well as in other countries. The atrocities committed by the Germans on the Jews before and during the Second World War acted as an eye-opener for the whole of mankind.

> 3. Democracy was invented as a device for reconciling government with liberty. It is clear that government is necessary if anything worthy to be called civilization is to exist, but all history shows that any set of men entrusted with power over another set will abuse their power if they can do so with impunity. Democracy is intended to make men's tenure of power temporary and dependent upon popular approval. In so far as it achieves this it prevents the worst abuse of power. *(Page 129)*

In the essay, 'Ideas That Have Helped Mankind,' Russell considers some of the moral ideas that have helped mankind. He is now talking about liberty and democracy. It was John Locke who devoted much thought to the problem of reconciling the maximum of liberty with the indispensable minimum government. It is a fact that law and liberty cannot exist without a government, but often a government, which is really a concentration of the collective forces of a community can deprive citizens of their liberty to a great extent. Russell tells us that when governments have acquired power for resisting foreign forces, it has been found that they have very often used it to further their private interests, curtailing the freedom of citizens. And democracy or the democratic form of government was really invented as a device for reconciling government with freedom of citizens. It is said that power corrupts and a long spell of power corrupts absolutely. History tells us that whenever a group of men have been entrusted with power for long over others, they are sure to abuse their power if they can do it without hindrance. And Russell asserts that only a democratic form of government can prevent this. It is democracy that makes men's tenure of power limited and temporary and dependent upon the approval of majority.

IV. CRITICAL APPRECIATION

Russell's observations on the progress of mankind. In 'The Ideas That Have Helped Mankind' Russell offers a comprehensive and accurate synopsis of the progress made by mankind. He has narrated in brief how ideas leading to increase in population, increase in happiness, diversity of enjoyment, greater knowledge and mutual tolerance can be beneficial to mankind. He refers to the prehistoric achievements like invention of language and fire, domestication of animals, agriculture and the art of writing which helped the human race gain an overwhelming superiority over animals. Coming to the historic times, the Greeks began the study of mathematics and astronomy that were followed up in the 17th century by scientists and philosophers like Galileo, Descartes, Newton and Leibniz. Copernicus showed that the earth was not at the centre of the universe. In the nineteenth century Darwin's theory of evolution further upset the older beliefs and human beings now learned to look upon natural phenomena with more practical wisdom.

Russell regrets that the progress in moral and political spheres has not been in keeping with tremendous progress made in the sphere of science and technology. The concepts of equality, liberty and fraternity originated long ago. But till now they have not been accepted to the degree that they should have been.

Any sensible reader will agree with Russell's view that the progress in science must be accompanied by a corresponding progress in moral and political fields. So far it has not been so and, as such, scientific developments, especially in the sphere of nuclear weapons, have brought forth the danger of disaster to the human race. Now it is absolutely necessary that we must rid ourselves of every kind of irrationality and lay greater emphasis on moral developments until they catch up with our technical progress. We cannot but agree with Russell that if we can develop a sense of toleration for each other, set up a universal brotherhood, ensure equality and liberty to every individual, we shall be able to eliminate the danger of war and open new vistas for mankind towards a golden era of happiness and prosperity. Engines of war will seem meaningless then and we will be able to use our technical skill for more profitable purposes like eradication of poverty and disease, and provision of more leisure and recreation for the individuals.

Russell's liberalism. Russell is a staunch supporter of Locke's liberal empirical philosophy. His repeated advocacy of a democratic form of government is merely a product of his ardent concern for individual liberty. He thinks that a government is necessary to put a kind of restraint on the impulses of individuals without which they become savages. He looks upon democracy as a form of government that can reconcile a government with individual liberty. Only a democratic form of government can enforce law and order and, at the same time, ensure the essential freedoms—freedom of thought, freedom of expression, freedom of press and so on—to individuals living within its territory.

Idea of a world government. A world government is another of Russell's pet ideas. Once again, in this essay, he has prescribed it as the only way to avert total disaster. There are reasons to feel that this is nothing but a utopian project which will ever remain a dream. The ideals of the two states—United States and the U.S.S.R—are so remote in character that it will be too much of optimism to hope that they will ever shed their differences and become united to form such a single government. Moreover, a third super power, namely, China, has already emerged to make things more complicated for the unification of the world. The fact is, wars now can disappear only if the world leaders begin to show more reason and tolerance and look upon peaceful co-existence as the only possible way to live.

Russell's scholarship. Like all his other works, this essay too reveals Russell's great erudition. Going through the essay we cannot help wondering at his store of knowledge that covers almost all the spheres of knowledge—philosophy, mathematics, astronomy, politics, religion, biology, to name just a few. He can easily draw illustrations from any sphere to clarify and give force to his point. In this essay he has alluded to quite a number of persons and their works. They include Aristarchus of Samos, Copernicus, Galileo, Descartes, Newton, Leibniz, Zeno, John Woolmar, Locke, Churchill and others. However, these allusions have not made this essay difficult. The ordinary reader, even without thorough acquaintance with the alluded names, can easily comprehend the main ideas of the essay.

Russell's style. Russell's mastery of language is at its best in this essay. Lucidity and clarity are the two main features of his prose style. These features are always strengthened by his command over the language. He can sum up any idea, simple or complex, and always finds the right words to express it in such a way that it is understood by any reader of average intelligence. For instance we can look at the following extract that narrates how forethought has destroyed our happiness:

> We suffer not only the evils that actually befall us, but all those that our intelligence tells us we have reason to fear. The curbing of impulses to which we are led by forethought averts physical disaster at the cost of worry, and general lack of joy.

Another feature of Russell's style is its terseness. His liking for restraint and economy of words often leads to expression of thought and ideas in short epigrammatic statements. Here is a fine example : "Man, viewed morally, is a strange amalgam of angel and devil". And here is another : "Democracy was invented as a device for reconciling government with liberty".

Russell's essays, even while dealing with sombre topics, never become drab. Russell is ever inclined to keep his readers' interest alive by blending into his writings flashes of wit and humour. But his humour is hardly ever pure fun or frolic. Being a controversialist, he is apt to employ irony as his chief instrument for producing humour. That is why his essays abound in ironical humour. Here are two examples :

> Has civilization taught us to be more friendly towards one another ? The answer is easy. Robins (the English, not the American species) peck an elderly robin to death, whereas men (the English, not the American species) give an elderly man an old-age pension.........
>
> And how about our noble selves? We would not do such deeds, oh no! But we enjoy our juicy steaks and our hot rolls while German children die of hunger......

Metaphors and similes are often used by writers to lend their language an ornamental touch. Russell uses them on rare occasions, but even when he does so, he uses them for their utility rather than their ornamental value. God is thus the "celestial policeman" and after the atom bomb has destroyed all forms of life equally, "the earth will remain for ever a dead clod senselessly whirling about a futile sun."

12

Ideas That Have Harmed Mankind

I. SUMMARY

Human misfortunes. Human misfortunes can be divided into two classes: first, the misfortunes due to non-human agencies; and second, those caused by other people. With the advancement of knowledge and technique, the second class of misfortunes has continually been on the increase. Famine, for instance, was previously known as a natural calamity. Today it is mainly man-made. Now man is the worst enemy of man. The major evils that afflict mankind in the present world are those that have resulted from human stupidity and malevolence.

Sources of evils. The main underlying source of evils inflicted by men on one another is their evil passions which are sometimes cloaked in evil ideas or principles. Burning of heretics and wars and flogging of school children are the products of a sadistic pleasure derived by some people from watching the sufferings of the victims. The initial opposition to the use of anaesthetics, the old method of curing the insane by mercilessly beating them, and beating of wives—all justified by invented false opinions—were only products of such sadistic impulses. Although passions are the main source of human suffering, yet ideas, especially those old and systematic ideas embodied in organizations, have also made considerable contribution to these sufferings. There are many harmful systems of belief.

Religious or superstitious beliefs. Of the ideas that have harmed mankind the religious or superstitious beliefs are the most prominent. In the olden days it was believed that human sacrifice was needed to please the gods, who, in return, would ensure an improvement of crops. The Old Testament declared it a religious duty to destroy the conquered races completely. Christian saints who renounced physical pleasures were not reluctant to derive mental pleasure from the contemplation of the eternal tortures to be inflicted on the pagans and heretics in the next world. In any case, asceticism has not promoted kindliness or tolerance or any other virtues that may be desirable to mankind.

The ascetic form of cruelty has been found in the modern world in new and menacing forms. The Nazi dogmatists pursuaded the

Germans to sacrifice the pleasures of the senses for the mental pleasures of prospective victory. These pleasures were similar to those with which Milton's Satan consoles himself during his suffering in hell. The same attitude of self-denial can be seen among the earnest Communists. Mankind is divided into two classes—saints and sinners. The saints are to achieve bliss in the Nazi or Communist heaven, while the sinners are to be liquidated or sent to concentration camps.

The twin conceptions of sin and vindicative punishment have been at the root of much that is most vigorous, in both religion and politics. The feeling of sin, according to Russell, is a product of early infancy. If this feeling could be removed, there would be a lesser amount of cruelty in the world.

Belief in witchcraft. Our feeling of self-importance leads us to believe that our good or bad fortune is caused by other people's actions. We cannot think that this happens by accident. When we consider ourselves virtuous we cannot dismiss any misfortune that befalls us as a punishment of our sins, and, as such, are led to think that it is due to somebody's malevolence. It was this conviction that resulted in the belief in witchcraft and black magic, and justified the enormous cruelties heaped upon the so-called witches until the middle of the seventeenth century. The Bible also gave approval to this belief since it says : "Thou shalt not suffer a witch to live". Science has dispelled this belief in magic, but has not succeeded in removing the fear and sense of insecurity in men. In modern times, these emotions find an outlet in the fear of foreign nations.

Envy. One of the most powerful sources of false belief is envy. Jealousies are found equally in men and women. In a large office when an official is promoted, others become envious and accuse him of flattering the higher-ups. Envy often causes a misconception of economic self-interest, both individual and national. Some businessmen, out of their envy of their competitors, attempt to eliminate them by having recourse to malpractices. They concentrate their efforts to become monopolist but forget to contribute to the upliftment of the level of prosperity of the customers on which the success of any business depends. In the same way, the entire philosophy of economic nationalism is based on the belief that the economic interest of one nation is necessarily opposed to that of another. This false belief produces international hatreds and rivalries, and has proved to be a major cause of war, starvation and the other evils which may bring our civilization to a disastrous and disgraceful end.

Pride. Another source of false beliefs that are politically harmful is pride—pride of nationality, race, sex, class or creed. When Russell was young, France was still considered an enemy of England, and as such, the young men were taught that one Englishman was capable of defeating three Frenchmen. The English and the Americans usually look upon the national pride of Balkan countries with contempt. But they do not realise that their own national pride is as unjustifiable as that of a little Balkan country.

Racial pride is even more injurious than national pride. This pride of race caused the mutual hatred between the whites and the yellow races, the ancient Greeks and the barbarians, the Jews and the Christians, and Englishmen and Indians in British India. The caste system in India originated from the successive invasions by the so-called 'superior' Northern races, and is equally contemptible.

The belief in male superiority is another form of pride. In fact, males are not superior to females in any sphere, except in having greater physical strength. In the olden days the males demonstrated their superiority by beating their wives whenever it was questioned. The old dogma that men were superior to women in the sphere of intellect has now died out. Male domination made marriage a relationship between a master and a slave, instead of one between equal partners. It forced seclusion on respectable women and consequently made them dull and unattractive. Of course, such notions of male superiority have more or less ended in civilized countries, but it will take quite some time for men and women to adjust completely to the new concept of equality.

Pride of class is fast disappearing everywhere except in Soviet Russia. In Russia, the son of a proletarian is more privileged than the son of a bourgeois. In other countries such concepts of hereditary privileges no longer hold good. However, abolition of class distinction has nowhere been complete. Even in America, that boasts of having achieved social equality, the wealthy men still look down upon the economically inferior people. In England too there is still a large amount of snobbery, though it is more connected with education and speech than with wealth or social status. Pride of creed is also a source of false belief. As a result of this pride the Christians are led to believe that they are superior to the heathens. Throughout the Middle Ages, Christians and Muslims remained entirely convinced of each other's wickedness and of their own superiority.

All these are pleasing ways to feed our self-esteem. To satisfy this self-esteem the Americans claim that America is God's own country, whites think that the black races are cursed by God, men say that women are unreasonable, and women believe that men are all brutes. This feeling also accounts for the mutual contempt existing between the western peoples and the eastern peoples, and between the educated class and the manual labourers.

A delusion. One of the most harmful delusions from which men and nations can suffer, is that of imagining themselves to be special instruments of the Divine Will. The Israelites invaded the Promised Land because they thought they were fulfilling the Divine purpose in doing so. The Romans believed that they were destined by the gods to conquer the world. The Muslims thought that death in battle could take them to a paradise more attractive than that of the Christians. Cromwell was convinced that he was appointed by God as an instrument for suppressing the Catholics. Similarly, today the Marxists feel that they are God's agents for punishing the people who differ from their ideology. For similar reasons Hegel attributed superiority to the Germans, and Marx to the proletariat. This delusion of divine purpose is particularly dangerous in that it provides a justification of cruelty on opponents while carrying out a Divine Will.

Selfishness. There is no need to predict the future even a decade ahead because any belief that a man may hold has a very slender chance of being true. However, significant action in important matters has to be taken with the help of foresight. For instance, it is easy to prophesy the imminence of a world war and action must be taken to avert it. It can be foreseen that selfishness beyond a point, when it meets with failure, precedes terrible consequences. Germany under Bismarck, who encouraged militancy and selfishness among its people, won three wars, but suffered humiliating defeats in the two world wars.

Importance of social science and democracy. Social science can help politicians in making right decisions. New theories can help to avoid slumps and large-scale unemployment. It is also generally known that an international government is badly needed to avert war and that mankind can hardly survive more than another war. This knowledge, however, is yet to penetrate to the masses. Some people have doubts about the usefulness of democracy. But Russell prefers democracy to other forms of government. Belief in democracy, however should never be carried to the point of fanaticism. A democrat need not take the wisdom of the majority or democracy's superiority for granted. He should look upon democracy simply as a government set up by general assent, and not by force. Democracy requires for its success a population that has undergone a certain kind of training.

Need of organization and moral qualities. The present day world needs two things—organization and moral qualities. It needs political organizations for elimination of wars, economic organizations for more productive work, and educational organizations to create internationalism. Moral qualities like charity and tolerance will have to be inculcated in people. These two aims—organizational and ethical—are closely interwoven; the present situation can be bettered only if progress is made simultaneously in both respects. It is now necessary to remove evil passions gradually and increase organizations that are helpful to mankind. Moral defects now stand in the way of clear thinking. Perhaps, the nuclear weapons will soon make people realize their implication and instil sanity and tolerance in them.

II. ANNOTATIONS

Page 134

malevolence : desire of harming others.

Page 135

lynch : execute a person by taking law into one's own hands. *Dr. Arnold, the hero of Tom Brown's Schooldays : Tom Brown's Schooldays* is the title of a book written by Thomas Hughes (1857). The book reveals the life in an English public school, of which Dr. Arnold was the headmaster. The book is now regarded as a children's classic. *cranks*: eccentric persons. *diabolic* : associated with the devil.

Page 136

flagellation ; use of whip. *sadistic impulses* ; impulses which lead a person to derive pleasure from inflicting or watching cruelty.

Page 137

asceticism : practice of severe self-discipline. *Tertullian* (155-230 A.D.) : one of the early Fathers of the Christian Church. He was severely opposed to worldly pleasures. *Nietzche* (1844-1900) : Fredrich Wilhelm Nietzche, a German philosopher and metaphysician. He prescribed attention to the development of vital energy and the cult of superman.

Page 138

Calvinists : Followers of the religious belief put forth by John Calvin in the 16th century. They believed that eternal salvation is bestowed by God on people He chooses, and has nothing to do with deeds. *Marx's father* : Karl Marx's father was born a Jew. *vicarious* : done for another.

Page 139

ruminant : animal that chews cud. *demonology* : belief in evil spirits or demons.

Page 141

Ruhr : The name of an industrial and mining district in Germany.

Page 143

Gentiles : persons not belonging to Jewish race. *Pedigree* : having known line of descent.

Page 145

Jefferson : Thomas Jefferson (1743-1826), an American statesman. He was twice elected President of his country, first in 1801, then in 1809. Jefferson put a ban on trading of slaves. *mesalliance* : French word meaning unsuitable marriage. *Mormons* : members of a religious sect founded in 1830 by Joseph Smith in New York. The sect was based on supposed divine revelations in *Book of Mormon*. The Mormons initially practised polygamy but later refrained from it. *Salt Lake City* : Capital of the state of Utah in the U.S.A. The city is near the Great Salt Lake, the water of which is saline.

Page 146

Ham : a son of Noah who, according to the Bible, is the ancestor of the people of Ethiopia, Egypt, and other parts of North Africa. *woolly* : confused and hazy. *Dutch courage* : courage due to the effects of wine or drugs. *Promised Land* : the land to which Moses led the people of Israel; Canaan. *Hittites........ Jebbusites* : name of tribes living in Canaan when the Israelites invaded it.

Page 147

Cromwell : See notes to *On Being Modern Minded. Andrew Jackson* (1767-1845) : seventh President of the United States. He led the American forces against the British in 1815. *Hegel* : See notes to *Philosophy and Politics. Gott strafe England* : German words meaning 'may God punish England'. *Battle of Dunbar* : battle fought between the forces of Oliver Cromwell and the Scots in 1650. The Scots were defeated in this battle which took place near Dunbar, a town in Scotland. *bowels* : bowels were considered the seat of pity.

Page 148

Bismarck (1815-1898) : a great German general and politician. Under his guidance Germany became a very powerful country.

Page 150

aftermath : consequences ; results.

III. EXPLANATIONS WITH CRITICAL COMMENTS

1. On the contrary, when a man tortures himself he feels that it gives him a right to torture others, and inclines him to accept any system of dogma by which this right is fortified. (*Page 137*)

In the essay 'Ideas That Have Harmed Mankind', Russell has ruthlessly criticized and exposed and exploded many false beliefs and baseless ideas that have harmed mankind. These dogmatic and superstitious ideas have been detrimental to the moral and intellectual development of mankind. Here Russell takes up a Christian dogma and exposes it without mercy. He points out that even the saints of Roman Catholic Church who abstained from pleasures of the senses did not mind deriving great satisfaction from the contemplation of eternal torture which the pagans and heretics are expected to suffer in hell. Russell points out that one of the most vicious and harmful beliefs is the Christian doctrine of ascetism that tells us to abstain from all pleasures of the senses as pleasures of mind were vastly superior to those of the body. The ascetics had also recommended self-torture by refraining from all sorts of sensual pleasures. They saw no harm in any type of mental pleasure. But according to Russell all pleasures are purely mental. However, from the psychological stand point such self-torture and suppression of the pleasures of the senses engender some undesirable impulses and passions. One of the most harmful effects is that by torturing himself a man feels that he has acquired a right to torture others. So asceticism and cruelty seem to go together. And then such a person will accept any system of dogma or false belief that will encourage him to torture other people as a matter of right.

2. This false belief, by producing international hatreds and rivalries is a cause of war, and in this way tends to make itself true, since when war has once broken out the conflict of national interests becomes only too real. (*Page 141*)

In the essay, 'Ideas That Have Harmed Mankind'. Russell calls envy one of the most powerful sources of false belief and harmful ideas. One of the most undesirable results of our proneness to envy or jealousy is that it has caused a complete misconception of economic self-interest both individual and national. Through a parable Russell has illustrated how two merchants in a town, a baker and a butcher, to become monopolists in their trades, ruined themselves by ruining the other businessmen of their own trades. Russell tells us what is true of the two businessmen is truer of the nations of the world. Misguided by envy, every nation thinks that its economic interest is opposed to that of every other nation. And it feels sure that it can prosper and profit only if other nations are reduced to destitution. Now this false conception that economic interest of one nation is opposed to that of another has given rise to the present-day philosophy of economic nationalism. And this is very harmful for the whole of mankind, as it becomes the cause of international rivalry and hatred leading nations to war. Unfortunately, economic rivalry of the nations does not allow them to visualize the stark reality. When war really breaks out only national interest seems to be of importance and the false concept of economic nationalism strikes a deeper root. Hence Russell's wise suggestion is that nations should take a broader and correct view of their mutual relations and discard false conceptions for progress and prosperity of mankind.

3. In our day, the sword of the Lord has been put into the hands of the Marxists. Hegel thought that the Dialectic with fatalistic logic had given supremacy to Germany. 'No', said Marx. 'not to Germany, but to the Proletariat'. *(Page 147)*

These lines occur in Russell's 'Ideas That Have Harmed Mankind' from his renowned book, *Unpopular Essays.* Russell is here referring to a very harmful and false belief that some men and sometimes some nations think themselves to be the chosen people of God. They are under the illusion that they have been chosen by God to fulfil some Divine Mission on this planet of ours. Even in the hoary past when the Israelites, or the Jews, conquered the Promised Land, the land of Canaan, they thought themselves to be carrying out the will of God. Russell tells us that even in later periods some men or nations have taken themselves to be special instruments of the divine will. First he tells about Cromwell, who, after the execution of Charles I became Lord Protector of the British Commonwealth. He imagined himself to be the chosen instrument of God to crush the Roman Catholics and other dangerous adherents of their creed. He suppressed them ruthlessly, causing awful sufferings to them. Then he mentions Andrew Jackson, the seventh President of the United States. He also imagined himself to be an instrument of the divine will. He took up as his mission to liberate North America from the stranglehold of the Spanish people who had very little regard for the sanctity of Sabbath or Sunday meant for rest and religious activities only. Finally he turns his critical eye towards the modern Marxists or communists. Formerly Hegel, the great German philosopher, predicted that the Germans will dominate the world in future. But the communists, followers of another great German philosopher and economist, dogmatically believe that the world belongs to the proletariat or the working class. According to

Russell this idea of the Marxists is as dogmatic as the belief in Divine Will by the Israelites or Cromwell or Andrew Jackson.

IV. CRITICAL APPRECIATION

In the nature of a sequel. *Ideas That Have Harmed Mankind* is the sequel to the preceding essay in this volume *Unpopular Essays*, namely, 'Ideas That Have Helped Mankind'. In the first essay Russell has analysed the ideas that have done good to mankind in certain ways. In the present essay he has tried to trace the cause of the misfortunes of mankind to certain ideas and false beliefs and has suggested ways to avert a possible disaster.

Human misfortunes. Russell has divided human misfortunes into two classes—misfortunes caused by non-human agencies, and misfortunes due to other people. Russell has not dealt with the non-human agencies in this essay; they have already been reduced to a great extent through the increasing dominance of science over nature. He is more concerned with the other class of misfortunes, and rightly so, because most of our misfortunes today are man-made. Stupidity and cruelty has made man, in all centuries, the worst enemy of men.

Russell's analysis of the sources of human misfortunes. Russell thinks that our innate cruelty, often disguised under cover of ideals and principles, is the main source of our misfortunes. He establishes his point by referring to the burning of heretics in the Middle Ages, the old method of curing insanity by beating the so-called 'devils' out of the victims, and the curious opposition to the use of anaesthetic drugs. To admit the existence of sadistic impulses in ourselves is indeed difficult and humiliating. But when we consider seriously the examples Russell has given, we are led to feel that, perhaps, he is not wrong.

Harmful systems of belief. Some harmful systems, according to Russell, have also contributed to human sufferings. He narrates how religious and superstitious beliefs have caused human sacrifice, religious fanaticism, and misunderstanding among the religious sects. He shows how an illogical concept of sin and punishment has encouraged cruelty, and how a stupid belief in witchcraft, endorsed even by the Bible, was responsible for the death of the supposed witches in the Middle Ages. He also holds some of our innate vices—like envy, pride, self-esteem and selfishness—responsible for our own miseries. We cannot but agree with Russell that envy is at the root of a lot of misunderstanding among individuals and nations. Similarly much damage has been done by pride—pride of nationality, race, sex, class or creed. It is national pride which makes us contemptuous of other nations. Racial pride has encouraged divisions among us on the basis of the colour of our skin and has given rise to the caste system in India. Pride of class that still exists in Russia grants more advantages to a proletariat than to a bourgeois. The class distinction is also discernible, though to a lesser degree, even in countries like the U.S.A. and England, particularly in economic or educational spheres. Innate selfishness makes nations indifferent to the interests of other nations and thus causes a feeling of mistrust and enmity among the countries of the world.

Russell as an advocate of democracy and a world government. Being a champion of liberalism, Russell is an ardent supporter of a democratic form of government. Whenever an opportunity occurs he repeats his advocacy of democracy. This essay is no exception. Russell is at the same time against all kinds of fanaticism and dogmatism. So he says in this essay that a democrat should look upon democracy as a government elected by the majority in place of a government set up by force. He should never allow his love of democracy to reach a level of fanaticism and should always believe that there may be better systems of government. World Government is another pet idea of the author that is repeated in this essay. He always dreams of a single government for the world that can unify the nations, eliminate wars, and open up a new era of happiness and prosperity. However, we wonder if his project can ever be feasible. In the present circumstances, with the differences among the super powers steadily increasing; it is, indeed, difficult to foresee a unification of these powers, even in the remote future. Russell's idea of a world government as we find it, will not materialize, at least not in the near future.

Russell as a moralist and social reformer. Russell presents himself in this essay as a moral philosopher as well as social reformer. He was an atheist but like any true Christian he feels the necessity of setting up moral values in this essentially immoral world. We must shake off our innate vices like envy, pride, self-esteem and selfishness if we want to remove the evils that now afflict mankind. He lays stress on inculcating the virtue of tolerance that alone can remove misunderstanding and cruelty existing among us and establish the universal brotherhood that has always been his dream. He feels that more importance has to be attached to the study of social science and then only we can eliminate human problems like slumps and large-scale unemployment. He thinks that it will also lead to a wider recognition of the necessities of democracy and an international government.

Style. The main features of Russell's prose style are its lucidity and clarity. He always intends to convey his ideas in the simplest way, and in this he is aided by his unparallelled command of the language. Being logical and clear-thinking he proceeds to develop his idea step by step, leaving no doubt in the minds of the readers as to what he wants to say. The lines where he tries to show the dismal end of selfishness demonstrates these qualities of simplicity and clarity.

> Bismarck with extreme astuteness won three wars and unified Germany. The long-run result of his policy has been that Germany has suffered two colossal defeats. These resulted because he taught Germans to be indifferent to the interests of all countries except Germany, and generated an aggressive spirit which in the end united the world against his successors. Selfishness beyond a point, whether individual or national, is not wise. It may with luck succeed but if it fails, failure is terrible.

Russell often draws illustrations and stories to give a concrete shape to his ideas. He tells us how a misconception of economic self-interest can harm an individual or a nation through the fable of the butcher and the baker. The fable not only conveys the idea but conveys it with such clarity that we can almost visualise it.

Another feature of Russell's prose style is its terseness. His tendency towards precision and economy of word, helped by his mastery of the language, often produces short, meaningful and epigrammatic sentences. Here are two examples:

> (*i*) One of the most powerful sources of false belief is envy.
>
> (*ii*) Pride of race is even more harmful than national pride.

Russell's writings never become drab because he is always careful to make them entertaining through flashes of humour. But his humour is never pure fun or frolic. Russell considers irony the best instrument for creating humour and as such all his essays abound in irony. Here is an example:

> . . . . . mankind are divided into saints and sinners; the saints are to achieve bliss in the Nazi or Communist heaven, while the sinners are to be liquidated, or to suffer such pains as human being can inflict in concentration camps—inferior, of course, to those which Omnipotence was thought to inflict in hell, but the worst that human beings with their limited powers are able to achieve.

13

Eminent Men I Have Known

I. SUMMARY

Queen Victoria and Browning. The author has come across many eminent persons in his life. Most of those persons have failed to leave a memorable impression on his mind. He met Queen Victoria at the age of two, and does not remember her at all. He met Browning at the same age, and, reportedly, at that time expressed his dislike of the poet. He met Browning frequently afterwards but found nothing in the poet to impress him. Browning appeared to him to be an ordinary, neatly dressed, domesticated person, not much of a poet.

Tennyson, Toller and Brooke. The author met the poet Tennyson frequently in his youth. He did not like Tennyson because he always tried to look like a poet and showed affectation. The poet Earnest Toller, through his capacity for impersonal suffering, seemed unforgettable to the author. He was also well acquainted with Rupert Brooke who, because of his artificiality and flamboyance, failed to impress him.

Philosophers. Russell was really impressed by the eminent philosopher, William James, who was unconscious of his greatness and was a natural aristocrat. Henry Sidgwick, Russell's teacher at Cambridge, is remembered by Russell for his intellectual honesty. In protest against the obligatory signing of the Thirty-nine Articles of the Church of England for a fellowship at Cambridge, Sidgwick resigned. His resignation was followed by the abolition of the custom. Sidgwick's teaching was fruitful because he always took into account the opinions of his students.

Einstein. Russell has particular respect for the men of science who combine in themselves great intellect with the faculty of thinking objectively, and are not bothered by the thought of popular approval or disapproval. Einstein, according to Russell, possessed such qualities.

Politicians—Gladstone and Lenin. Russell has known seven Prime Ministers of whom Gladstone was the most unforgettable. In personal impressiveness only Lenin could come near him. Gladstone was Victorianism incarnate while Lenin was the embodiment of Marxism.

Gladstone had a piercing eye which inspired fear. In the presence of his personality one would feel like a schoolboy facing a disciplinarian schoolmaster. Russell's grandmother, a very formidable woman, was seen to be cowed down by Gladstone's personality. Russell, at the age of seventeen, remained speechless with fear during a brief encounter with Gladstone. The source of Gladstone's political influence was his sound moral conviction. He was a shrewd statesman who believed that all his activities were inspired by noble purposes. He was conscientious and possessed an imposing personality. He was also a controversial character. Half the nation considered him either mad or wicked; to the rest he was a god.

There were similarities and dissimilarities between Lenin and Gladstone. As for the similarities, both of them considered themselves the human agents of a superhuman power. Lenin, like Gladstone, was ruthless and unscrupulous only in his choice of means; not in ends; he would never betray his personal creed or his party to purchase personal power. Both Gladstone and Lenin derived their personal force from strong conviction of their own rectitude. Also, they both ventured into spheres where they could only make themselves ridiculous—Gladstone in Biblical criticism, Lenin in philosophy. As for their differences, Lenin was cruel, which Gladstone was not. Gladstone had great respect of tradition while Lenin had none. Lenin could have recourse to dirty politics to achieve his end; Gladstone thought that politics had to be guided by some principles.

Of these two great persons, Gladstone possessed a more impressive personality. He could impress even a stranger and force him to a speechless semblance of agreement. Lenin, on the contrary, would appear at first sight, to be a narrow-minded fanatic and a cynic. Russell's initial impressions of Lenin were not of his greatness but of his bigotry and cruelty. Unlike Gladstone, Lenin did not possess all the qualities of a political leader. It is doubtful whether he could have become a leader in quieter times. He succeeded because he held out hopes of a victory to a confused and defeated nation. By cold reasoning he could convince the people that pursuit of his preaching was the only possible way to save the nation from disaster.

Persons of no eminence. Russell has often been impressed by some persons of no eminence. These persons displayed a kind of moral quality, selflessness and honesty. Russell remembers an illiterate gardener who was an embodiment of simple goodness. He can never forget a person like E.D. Morel who sacrificed his job as a shipping clerk to publicise the horrors of King Leopold's exploitation of the Congo. Morel fought alone and succeeded in compelling reform by stirring up public opinion. Such men rarely achieve material success, but they gain the love and admiration of those who know them.

II. ANNOTATIONS

Page 151

Queen Victoria (1819-1901) : Queen of England from 1837-1901. *dapper* : neat; smart in appearance or movement. *suave* : polite; refined; cultured. *abstraction* : absence of mind. *Earnest Toller* (1893-1939) : German revolutionary poet. He wrote an autobiography named *I Was a German. Byronic insincerity* : artificiality, characteristic of the poet Byron. *Rupert Brooke* (1888-1915) : the greatest of the English 'war poets'. *William James* (1842-1910) : American philosopher who founded the philosophy of pragmatism.

Page 152

Henry Sidgwick (1839-1900) : English philosopher and professor at Cambridge. His works include the *Principles of Political Economy, Outline of the History of Ethics* and the *Elements of Politics. Thirty-Nine Articles* : creed of the Church of England. The law, requiring clergymen aspiring to receive orders in the Church of England to subscribe to these articles, was passed by Parliament in 1571. *Gladstone* : W.E. Gladstone (1809-1898) became Prime Minister of England four times. He was a Liberal, and a reformer. He was a great orator and administrator.

Page 153

risque : involving suggestions of indecency. *quailed* : flinched; gave way before or to. *tete-a-tete* : together in private; conversation between two persons. *ogre* : man-eating giant.

Page 154

The Vatican : the official residence of the Pope in Rome. *The dialectic* : the principles of thesis, anti-thesis and synthesis, propounded by the German philosopher Hegel. *apostasy* : abandonment of faith, vows, principles, or party.

Page 155

Pacifism : the doctrine that abolition of war is both desirable and possible.

III. EXPLANATIONS WITH CRITICAL COMMENTS

1. I met him frequently in the last years of his life, and found nothing in him to command reverence. He was a pleasant, kindly old gentleman, very much at home at tea-parties of middle-aged ladies, dapper, suave, and thoroughly domesticated, but without the divine power that one expects of a poet. *(Page 151)*

In the essay, 'Eminent Men I Have Known' Bertrand Russell points out how he was disillusioned by the lack of impressive qualities in some eminent men he met personally. In these lines Russell puts forth his impressions of the great Victorian poet, Robert Browning. Even in his childhood, he had an instinctive dislike of the poet. At the age of two he reportedly interrupted Browning's discourse by demanding that he should stop talking. He met Browning quite often during the poet's final years and found no mark of excellence in him. Browning just appeared to be an ordinary man with a kind disposition, refined, smart and quite at home in parties and in domestic atmosphere. Browning's looks never displayed the fiery inspiration associated with poets.

2. He used to stalk about the countryside in a flowing Italian cloak, very emphatically not seeing the people he happened to meet, and displaying the behaviour appropriate to poetic tradition. *(Page 151)*

In the essay 'Eminent Men I Have Known' Bertrand Russell records that he came into personal contact with many eminent persons but was unimpressed by most of them. Browning, the great poet, despite his refinement, culture and neat appearance, looked an ordinary man devoid of poetic fire, and failed to win the author's admiration. Russell here attempts to explain his dislike for Lord Tennyson, the great contemporary of Browning. He disliked Tennyson because he felt that the poet always tried to 'act' the poet. Tennyson, while taking a walk in the countryside, took particular care to pretend absent-minded-ness, a supposed quality of a poet. He wore a long Italian cloak in order to assume the conventional look of a poet. Again, in order to put on the air of abstraction, he would, during these walks, deliberately ignore the people he happened to meet. Russell failed to admire Browning because he did not look like a poet, and hated Tennyson because he endeavoured to look like one.

3. When I say, 'Simplicity', I do not mean anything involving lack of cleverness; I mean the habit of thinking impersonally, without regard for the worldly advantage or disadvantage of an opinion or an action. Among the men of science I have known, Einstein is a supreme example of this quality. *(Page 152)*

In 'Eminent Men I Have Known', Bertrand Russell tells us of

having met a number of eminent men like Browning and Tennyson, but being unimpressed by them. However, some persons such as Earnest Toller, William James, and the less eminent philosopher Henry Sidgwick possessed certain qualities that could win them his admiration. The author has particular respect for the men of science who combine in themselves great intellect with childlike simplicity. Russell explains that by 'simplicity', he does not mean lack of intelligence. The scientists, in fact, possess intelligence to a far greater degree than ordinary men, else they would not be able to establish man's supremacy over Nature. They possess 'simplicity' in the sense that they can look at problems objectively and impersonally, and are concerned with their work without bothering about personal gains. Many scientists, particularly Albert Einstein, have exemplified such wonderful blending of intellect and simplicity.

4. Since then I have faced infuriated mobs, angry judges, and hostile governments, but never again have I felt such terror as in that searing moment. (*Page 153*)

In the essay, 'Eminent Men I Have Known' Bertrand Russell has offered his impressions of many eminent men whom he happened to meet personally. The personality of Gladstone, the former Prime Minister of England, left a permanent impression on his mind. In the quoted lines he narrates his reaction on a meeting with the great statesman. Gladstone, according to Russell, had a quick and piercing eye which inspired terror in the hearts of men who faced him. His personality was so imposing that no one dared to talk nonsense before him. Russell's grandmother, who was a very formidable woman, was seen to remain speechless with awe before that great personality. Russell narrates an incident to give us an idea of the awe-inspiring quality of Gladstone. When Russell was seventeen, Gladstone once came to spend the week-end with Russell's family. Russell was struck with a reverential fear when, after dinner, he was left with the Prime Minister for a *tete-a-tete*. He was so scared that he felt as if he were with a man-eating giant. When Gladstone, in his booming voice, asked him why they had given him wine in a claret glass, Russell was so terrorised that he remained speechless. Russell, in course of his life, has faced the hostility of angry mobs and governments, but he has never experienced the fear he experienced during that brief encounter with Gladstone.

5. In this way the passion of his followers came to appear, to them as to him, to have the sanction of science, and to be the very means by which the world was to be saved. (*Page 155*)

In the essay, 'Eminent Men I Have Known' Bertrand Russell has offered us his impressions of some eminent personalities who include the poets Browning, Tennyson, Ernest Toller and Rupert Brooke, the philosophers William James and Henry Sidgwick, and the politicians Gladstone and Lenin. He puts forth a comparison between Gladstone and Lenin, of whom Gladstone was the more impressive. Russell is here summing up the reasons for Lenin's success as a leader. The qualities which make a great politician were not very obvious in Lenin. He was an unscrupulous and ruthless man. He did not bother to base his political activities on the conventional political ethics accepted by all good statesman like Gladstone. He did not possess the imposing personality of Gladstone—a quality necessary for political success. Instead, he carried the appearance of a narrow-minded fanatic and a cheap cynic. Russell thinks that Lenin succeeded not because he was a good politician, but because he could exploit the confusion of a defeated nation. He raised the morale of his bewildered countrymen by offering them hopes of victory, and convinced them that the pursuit of his philosophy was the only way to save the world from disaster. Lenin himself was certain of the validity of the philosophy of Marx, and therefore, with the help of calculated reasoning and logic, he was able to persuade the masses to follow his gospel. Russell feels that in quieter times people would never accept a leader of Lenin's calibre.

IV. CRITICAL APPRECIATION

Russell's portrayal of personalities. 'Eminent Men I Have Known' offers a valuable record of impressions about certain famous men given by a person who is known for his keen observation. Russell's ideas of those persons deserve attention, because they are not secondhand, but are derived from the author's personal experience.

Browning, the great Victorian poet, failed to impress Russell because he looked an ordinary man rather than a poet. Russell's reference to the kindness and refinement of the poet gives one the feeling that Russell at least did not dislike the poet. His attitude toward Tennyson, however, was one of genuine contempt. Tennyson, according to him, acted the poet and therefore was guilty of insincerity. Russell's impressions help us to get the other side of Tennyson's character and offer us a new angle from which we can judge his poetry. Russell's admiration for the qualities of naturalness and dignity finds expression in his impressions of William James who embodied those virtues. Russell has ever been for intellectual honesty and avoidance of dogmatism. This explains the praises he showers on Henry Sidgwick, his teacher in ethics at Cambridge. Sidgwick resigned from his post in protest against the system of obligatory signing of Thirty-nine Articles of the Church of England before becoming a Fellow of Cambridge. His resignation hastened the change in the law and ended the theological restrictions. As a teacher, he showed respect for the views of his students and became, therefore, a successful teacher.

Russell's impressions of Gladstone are given in some detail, and are highly entertaining. Gladstone had a quick and piercing eye that inspired fear. In his presence, according to Russell, "one felt like a small boy in presence of an old-fashioned schoolmaster, a constant impulse to say, 'please, Sir, it wasn't me'." In order to illustrate further the awe-inspiring aspect of Gladstone's personality he narrates how his very formidable grandmother used to be cowed down in Gladstone's presence, and how once, left with the politician for a *tete-a-tete*, Russell himself remained speechless with fear. Russell liked Gladstone for his moral conviction and also for being a Liberal.

Russell's impressions of Lenin are quite balanced. Lenin appeared to him to be cruel, unscrupulous, a narrow-minded fanatic and a cynic. At the same time he had some virtues for which Russell admired him. Lenin, as Russell feels, possessed profound conviction, and became ruthless and unscrupulous only to attain his goal that he genuinely felt to be good. Lenin would never purchase personal power at the expense of apostasy. However, it is difficult to agree with Russell in his view that Lenin lacked the qualities of a great leader and that he would never be a leader in quieter times. If Russell was right, the universal respect for Lenin would have come to an end soon after the Russian Revolution. In fact, Lenin has continued till today, even through peaceful times, to be accepted as one of the greatest political leaders the world has ever produced.

Russell's emphasis on goodness finds expression in his reference to the rustic gardener who was the embodiment of this virtue. Throughout his life he has advocated honesty and opposition to oppression. That is why he cannot forget E.D. Morel, a shipping clerk of Liverpool, who gave up his job to fight against King Leopold's exploitation of the Congo, and finally succeeded in compelling reforms. Russell is full of admiration for selfless persons like Morel, who rarely attain material prosperity but are loved and admired by people who come to know them. Thus Russell has shown in this essay that being impressive depends not only on eminence but on the basic virtues of men and women.

Style. This is one of the easiest and most entertaining essays in the volume *Unpopular Essays*. Russell's prose style is always lucid and clear. The qualities of lucidity and clarity are more striking in this essay because the content here is simple and devoid of any complicated philosophy or idea. His description of Browning, for instance, is so simple and clear that even a schoolboy will not find it difficult to understand. Here is the description :

I met him frequently in the last years of his life, and found nothing in

> him to command reverence. He was a pleasant, kindly old gentleman, very much at home at tea-parties of middle aged ladies, dapper, suave, and thoroughly domesticated, but without the divine fire that one expects of a poet.

The most striking feature of this essay is the abundance of humour. His impressions of Gladstone are given almost entirely in a humorous vein. His portrayal of Gladstone as resembling a school teacher is hilarious and pure fun. His narration of the so-called *tete-a-tete* with Gladstone, during which he remained speechless with awe, is pure humour again. His reference to Gladstone's conscientiousness is an example of ironical humour:

> Invariably he earnestly consulted his conscience, and invariably his conscience earnestly gave him the convenient answer.

14

Obituary

I. SUMMARY

Death and family background of Russell. The Third Earl Russell passed away at the age of ninety. His grandfather, Lord John Russell, was Prime Minister during the reign of Queen Victoria; his maternal grandmother happened to be a friend of the wife of Charles Edward Stuart, known as the Young Pretender.

Early life. In his youth Russell did some important work in mathematics, but during the First World War showed signs of whimsicality that affected his later writings. The eccentricity was, perhaps, due to his not possessing a public school education. He had been taught at home by tutors before he joined Cambridge and passed the Tripos examination, and subsequently became a Fellow there. He then produced a few books on mathematics on which his reputation is based. However, he always showed a lack of insight and spiritual depth, and a tendency to ignore reasonings which are beyond the reach of logic. His lack of spiritual depth was more evident when he advocated the end of First World War even at the cost of a German victory. He was rightly deprived of his lecturership at Trinity College and sent to prison for a few months. In 1920, he visited Russia, but was not impressed by the government there. He then paid a longer visit to China where he enjoyed the still surviving aroma of the eighteenth century rationalism. In the years to follow, Russell frittered away his energy by advocating socialism, educational reform, and a flexible code of morals as regards marriage. His historical writings of these years contain an out-of-date rationalism hidden beneath his witty style.

Later life. Russell took no public part in World War II when he escaped to a neutral country. Very few share his view that the war was fought by homicidal maniacs. Though much of the civilised world has been destroyed as the result of wars, those who died in the wars did not die for nothing. His life, though perverse, had a kind of consistency so rare these days. He formulated odd principles, but he himself acted upon them. In private life he did not show the bitterness that marks his writings, but was jovial company and a kind man. He had numerous friends, but outlived most of them. Till his end he enjoyed good health and remained cheerful. His last days were spent in isolation like those of Milton. He was the last link of a dead epoch.

II. ANNOTATIONS

Page 157

Third Earl Russell : Bertrand Russell, the grandson of John Russell, the first Earl, was an aristocrat by birth. But he had no respect for titles and as such preferred to call himself just Bertrand Russell. *age of nintey* : In fact Russell died at the age of ninetyseven. *Elba* : An island in the Mediterranean Sea where Napoleon was exiled. *Young Pretender* : Charles Edward Stuart (1720-1788), the son of James Francis Edward Stuart, the Old Pretender, and the grandson of King James II. *Wrangler* : person placed in the first class of mathematical tripos in Cambridge. Russell stood seventh among wranglers in order of merit. *Dr. Whitehead* : Dr. A.N. Whitehead (1861-1947), British philosopher and mathematician *argumentation* : methodical reasoning. *considerations* : meditations; reasonings.

Page 158

perversely : unreasonably. *dissipated* : frittered away; wasted. *antiquated* : obsolete; out-of-date. *Bentham* : Jeremy Bentham (1748-1832), English philosopher, economist and political scientist. The aim of his philosophy was the greatest good of the largest number. His ideas led to many reforms in 19th century. *anachronistic* : out of harmony with contemporary times. *acerbity* : bitterness of speech, manner or temper. *genial* : jovial. *survived* : outlived. *isolated as Milton* : Milton, a Puritan, enjoyed power under Cromwell. After the Restoration he was stripped of his power, and had to spend the rest of his life in complete isolation.

III. EXPLANATIONS WITH CRITICAL COMMENTS

1. Throughout the war, he continued to urge that it should be ended, on no matter what terms. Trinity College, very properly deprived him of his lecturership, and for some months of 1918 he was in prison. *(Page 158)*

In the imaginary obituary written for himself the author tries to point out how he and his ideas have faced hostility in the course of his life. He says that after his death his adversaries will refer to his aristocratic birth (of which he is not proud), his contributions in the field of mathematics, and his lack of insight and spiritual depth. Russell had always been against war and in favour of peace and fraternity. During World War I, he organised rallies and protests against continuing the war. He expressed the view that war should be brought to an end as soon as possible, even if it meant conceding victory to the Germans. Russell's anti-war efforts were misinterpreted as unpatriotic and subversive and as such produced among the people, swayed by heroic notions of war, considerable antagonism for him. As a result, he had to undergo a brief imprisonment, and was also dispossessed of his lecturership at Trinity College.

> 2. His life, for its waywardness, had a certain anachronistic consistency, reminiscent of that of the aristocratic rebels of the early nineteenth century. His principles were curious, but, such as they were, they governed his actions. (*Page 158*)

In 'Obituary' Bertrand Russell refers to the hostility he has faced for his anti-war and other such rationalistic ideas. His advocacy to end World War I even at the cost of a German victory was interpreted as anti-national and led to his imprisonment. The obituary reveals his anticipation of the general reaction to his death. Russell feels that though his ideas have received general condemnation people will at least admit that he has always remained true to those ideas. Though consistency has become a rare thing these days, Russell has always been consistent in the matter of acting upon his principles. Though he has faced severe criticism for his preachings of peace, equality, liberty and fraternity, he has never given up his ideals. In this respect Russell has displayed the characteristics of the nineteenth century rebels of noble birth. However, he points out, that in spite of praising his adherence to 'principles', people will undercut the due credit for it by calling those principles 'curious'.

IV. CRITICAL APPRECIATION

The attitude of the Press to Russell. 'Obituary' offers a distorted portrait of Russell to illustrate how the British Press has looked upon him. Most of the newspapers have been hostile in their attitude to Russell and his views. The imaginary obituary reflects Russell's anticipation of the newspapers' formal evaluation of his life and works after his death.

Russell feels that while writing his obituary the newspapers will, much against his liking, refer to his aristocratic birth. They will, after a brief reference to his brilliant academic career, admit that he has made some contributions in the field of mathematics. But they will try to deprive him of some credit by alleging that his works showed a lack of insight and spiritual depth. They will criticize Russell for his pacifist activities during World War I when he wanted to bring the war to an end even by conceding a victory to Germany. They will defend the action taken by Trinity College to deprive him of his lecturership and his imprisonment as just punishment for taking an unpatriotic stand during the war. They will not recognise the utility of his writings on socialism, educational reforms and morality but will dismiss them as sheer wastage of the writer's energy. They will try to minimise the value of his historical writings by describing the rationalism advocated in them as out-of-date and useless. Russell feels that his being away from England during World War II will be interpreted by the press as an act of cowardice. However, as it is customary to find some virtues in the deceased while writing an obituary, the newspapers will reluctantly admit that he was a man of 'principles' and that he was in his private life, a cheerful and healthy man. Even in doing so, Russell fears, the press will continue in its efforts to discredit him, by describing his 'principles' as curious.

'Obituary' is intended to be a severe attack on the British press. Being a thorough gentleman Russell cannot be expected to write invective. So, instead of resorting to a direct attack, he has to find a means by which he can place his actions and the views of the press on them side by side to enable the readers to see for themselves how the press has been unjust to him. The imaginary obituary provides a subtle and effective means to Russell.

Russell as a pacifist. Even in the distorted portrait in 'Obituary' Russell stands out as an ardent pacifist. He has been, all through his life, an advocate for peace and mutual understanding. During World War I he indulged in countless pacifist activities to arouse public opinion against the continuation of war. He was not swayed by the narrow parochial feeling that a war encourages among participating nations. His urge for peace was so intense that he pleaded for an early end of the war even at the cost of a German victory. He attached no value to the prospect of displaying heroism that a war offers. The men who fought in a war were nothing but homicidal maniacs in his eyes. Russell had to pay dearly for such views during World War I. He was branded unpatriotic, deprived of his lecturership at Trinity College, and sent to prison for a few months.

Style. 'Obituary' is certainly the most entertaining piece in the volume *Unpopular Essays* by Russell. The interest lies in its contents as well as the easy and fluent prose style so characteristic of Russell. The two main features of his style are lucidity and clarity. Any sentence taken at random from this piece can display these characteristics. Here is one example:

> In private life he showed none of the acerbity which marred his writings, but was a genial conversationalist and not devoid of human sympathy. He had many friends, but had survived almost all of them. Nevertheless, to those who remained he appeared, in extreme old age, full of enjoyment, no doubt owing, in large measure, to his invariable

health, for politically, during his last years, he was as isolated as Milton after the Restoration.

'Obituary' is pleasant reading because of the abundance of humour in it. As we have seen in his other essays, Russell's humour is rarely plain humour; it is mostly ironical. Irony is Russell's favourite weapon for attack, and as this obituary is intended to be an attack on the press, the whole of it has been written in an ironic vein. Almost every sentence of the piece can be illustrated as an example of irony. Here are a few examples :

(*a*) In his youth he did work of importance in mathematical logic, but his eccentric attitude during the First World War revealed a lack of balanced judgement which increasingly infected his later writings.

(*b*) Trinity College, very properly, deprived him of his lecturership, and for some months of 1918 he was in prison.

(*c*) True, much of what was once the civilized world lies in ruins; but no right thinking person can admit that those who died for the right in the great struggle have died in vain.

It is such use of ironical humour that has helped Russell to expose the follies of the press and at the same time, kept the piece free of invective.

15

Select University Questions With Answers

I. RUSSELL : ANTI-DOGMATIC CHAMPION OF LIBERALISM

Q. 1. In his preface to *Unpopular Essays* Russell declares that most of the essays "are concerned to combat, in one way or another, the growth of dogmatism". How far has Russell succeeded in achieving his object in these essays ?

Or

Discuss with reference to the *Unpopular Essays*, Russell's opposition to dogmatism.

Or

To what extent does the *Unpopular Essays* present Russell as an adversary of dogmatism and a champion of liberalism?

Ans. **Dogmatism and liberalism.** Dogmatism means the tendency to hold opinions and beliefs in an arrogant and stubborn way. A dogmatic person does not care to verify his opinions, considers them right without any proper reason, and always refuses to take into consideration opinions that differ from his own. Very often such a dogmatic person tends to become intolerant of other opinions and develops an overwhelming desire to suppress them by any means. As a result, dogmatism has been the source of much of the cruelty that has been inflicted on mankind. Being basically rationalistic, Russell all through his life was an adversary of dogmatism in all spheres—political, social, religious and educational. His sympathy lay, on the other hand, with liberalism which advocates a willingness to scrutinise and modify one's own beliefs or opinions and a respect for others' opinions. In this way liberalism encourages tolerance, a virtue which, according to Russell, must be cultivated to save the human race from possible disaster. *Unpopular Essays* indeed establishes Russell as an uncompromising opponent of dogmatism and an ardent champion of liberalism as envisaged by Locke.

Philosophers should not preach dogmatism. Russell makes his anti-dogmatic intentions clear in the opening essay 'Philosophy and Politics'. He condemns the Catholics, Communists and the Nazis for their dogmatic doctrines inherited from the philosophies of Aquinas, Marx and Hegel respectively. Russell launches a severe attack on Plato's *Republic* because it supports dogmatism. He finds Hegel's philosophy unacceptable on similar grounds. Hegel's views have dangerous implications. They imply that absolute monarchy is good, free speech is harmful, war is beneficial, and that an organization for peaceful settlement of disputes is not desirable. Marx took over some Hegel's senseless ideas, on the basis of which he asserted his concept of history developing according to a logical plan, and advocated a despotic system. Both Hegel and Marx are condemned by Russell because they prescribe tyranny and suppression on the basis of certain dogmas.

Advocate of Empiricist Liberalism. Russell mentions John Locke's empiricist philosophy, that has led to Liberalism, as an antidote to the perilous philosophies of Hegel and Marx. He advocates the practice of liberalism because it supports liberty and toleration and opposes absolute monarchy. Liberalism, Russell points out, also implies freedom, moderation, and absence of fanaticism in political programmes. He favours empiricism also because it stands for 'order without authority' and thus affords a theoretical justification of a democratic form of Government. Russell's recommendation of Empiricist Liberalism is based on the questions of truth, morality and ethics. He dismisses dogmatism because it requires absolute authority and persecution of independent opinions, fosters hatred, discourages negotiations and prescribes war. Empiricism, on the other hand, appeals to any sensible person who wants scientific evidence for his beliefs, and places human happiness over everything else. Russell is convinced that in the present state of chaos and confusion Empiricist Liberalism can play the most vital role in saving mankind from total disaster.

Attack on dogmatism of the communists. In the essay 'The Future of Mankind' Russell attacks the political dogmatism of the communists as seen in Soviet Russia and in countries under Soviet domination. In these countries, there is a ban on every kind of freedom, and education has been reduced to learning the formulae of communism as formulated by Stalin. The political dissidents are either liquidated or imprisoned by the Soviet authorities. No individual in Soviet Russia is allowed to disagree with the dogmas prescribed by the authority. Russell, a true Liberal himself, cannot help condemning such suppression of liberty as practised by the Soviet regime.

Against religious dogmatism. In the essay 'An Outline of Intellectual Rubbish' Russell exposes the stupidity of the dogmatic doctrines of the Church. During the ages of faith the clergymen ordered the burning of thousands of persons, declared by them as 'heretics' and 'witches'. They declared pestilence, famine, earthquake and flood as instruments of divine justice, and forced people to agree with such senseless views. Throughout the last four hundred years the clergy have been resisting developments in the sphere of science because these have been exposing the hollowness of their dogmas. Russell finds the dogmas concerning 'sin' contradictory and unconvincing. He can find no logical justification for the clergy's opposition to euthanasia, cremation and dissection of corpses. He also attacks some dogmatic beliefs imposed by the Church such as sexual intercourse being regarded sinful or ill-treatment of animals not being regarded sinful as they have no souls.

Opposition to dogmatism in education. In the essay 'The Functions of a Teacher' Russell exposes the dangers of a dogmatic educational system. In the modern world education has become the prerogative of the State. As a result, the teacher has lost the freedom he enjoyed in the early days and has been reduced to the position of a mere spokesman of the official creed. Under such circumstances, the teacher is likely to be used as an instrument for infusing fear, subservience and blind obedience in his pupils. The result of such education is that the students turn, as they did in Nazi Germany, into fanatical believers in the publicized dogmas, become intolerant of contrary opinions and reluctant to engage in a free exchange of opinions. Russell condemns such a system of education also because it often encourages a kind of fanatical nationalism leading to a mutual hatred and a warlike ferocity among nations. On the contrary, Russell strongly emphasises the need of liberalism in the field of education. He thinks that education should aim at infusing in pupils a habit of impartial inquiry, a scientific and rational outlook and the quality of tolerance. The propagandist system of education thwarts the natural growth of minds and plants in them the evil feelings of envy, destructiveness, and cruelty. Liberal education, on the other hand, encourages kind impulses, and helps the growth of an international culture. He points out that a liberal educational system can develop only if the teacher is granted complete freedom from outside interference.

Harmfulness of dogmatic beliefs. In the essay 'Ideas That Have Harmed Mankind' Russell is seen to continue his attack on dogmatism. He accuses Christian ascetics of cultivating dogmatic doctrines such as those which provide them a sadistic pleasure from the contemplation of pagans and heretics undergoing eternal torture in hell. Russell also points out the evils of another dogma prevalent among all nations, namely, economic nationalism. This economic nationalism, based on the belief that the economic interest of one nation is opposed to that of another, leads to international hatreds and rivalries, and is a major cause of war, starvation and other such misfortunes. Russell also condemns the dogmatic feelings of superiority that have given rise to an irrational pride among mankind in matters of nationality, race, sex, class or creed. Russell points out how these dogmatic beliefs have often led to wars, hatred and cruelty.

Support for liberalism, the idea of fraternity, democracy. In 'Ideas That Have Helped Mankind' Russell is a champion of liberal ideals. Here he traces the origin of the idea of brotherhood and regrets that though this noble idea has been there for a very long time it has never been widely accepted. He recommends a universal acceptance of Locke's idea of liberty which consists in free press, free speech, and freedom from arbitrary arrest. Russell's respect for Liberalism leads him to opt for a democratic form of government that can be the only solution to the problem of reconciling government with individual liberty. Democracy, according to Russell, ensures personal liberty, provides the necessary government and, at the same time, prevents any misuse of power by the government by keeping it dependent on popular approval.

A liberal's optimistic hope for an international government. Russell has discussed his favourite idea of a single international government in quite a few essays in this collection. Since the invention of nuclear weapons, the only way to save mankind, according to Russell, has been to set up a single world government possessing the monopoly of all armed forces and armaments. Such a government, in his opinion, will eliminate wars and encourage toleration and the feeling of brotherhood among mankind. This concept of an international government, however utopian it may seem to us, is no doubt a product of a truly liberal mind.

II. RUSSELL'S ORIGINALITY AS A THINKER—HIS SOCIAL, POLITICAL AND ETHICAL IDEAS

Q. 2. Write a note on Russell as a social and political thinker with reference to *Unpopular Essays*.

Or

Consider in brief, the ideas that Russell puts forward in his *Unpopular Essays* which entitle him to be called an original thinker.

Ans. **Gifted and free thinker.** Russell is "the most gifted of that little band of English scientists and philosophers who in recent years have endeavoured to make the most abstruse problems clear to the general public", says Ceenliffe. He is no ascetic living in a palace of art and deliberately shutting himself out of the life that is lived by ordinary men and women. From the rich family tradition to which he was born he developed even in his early years a sense of instinctive responsibility of the men of intellect. Hence, he throws himself into the life of the age and probes its numerous problems. In his *Unpopular Essays*, Russell explores almost every sphere of life to bring out the evils that afflict mankind and offers his suggestions for the removal of those evils.

Dogmatism *versus* liberalism. Dogmatic beliefs, according to Russell, lead to cruelty, and, as such, constitute the most prominent source of human misfortunes. Therefore, as he declares in the preface to *Unpopular Essays*, most of his essays "are concerned to combat, in one way or another, the growth of dogmatism, whether of the Right or of the Left, which has hitherto characterised our tragic century". He shows in 'Philosophy and Politics' how political dogmatism has led the Soviet regime to take oppressive measures against its opponents. Dogmatism in the field of religion, as shown in 'An Outline of Intellectual Rubbish', led to the commitment of numerous atrocities on so-called 'witches' and 'heretics' and gave rise to countless false beliefs and superstitions. The clergy have, during the last four hundred years, opposed the progress in science because it has been exposing the stupidity of their dogmas. Similarly, dogmatism in the field of education should be condemned because teaching of official dogmas, as Russell points out in the essay 'The Functions of a Teacher', can often produce., as it did in Nazi Germany, a whole lot of fanatical bigots. Dogmatism breeds intolerance, international hatred and rivalries, and often leads to war. Russell presents the concept of Liberalism as an antidote to this prevalent dogmatism. Liberalism encourages toleration, moderation and restraint in political programmes. By inspiring toleration it can help in the growth of a sense of brotherhood and universal respect for the ideals of equality and liberty.

Need of rationalism. One of the major objects of most of the *Unpopular Essays* is to preach the dire necessity of rationalism in the modern world. In 'An Outline of Intellectual Rubbish" Russell sets out to refute, with illustrations, Aristotle's contention that "man is a rational animal". Here he brings out the irrationality displayed by mankind through the ages. The clergy, Russell points out, have displayed extreme irrationality by propagating the belief in black magic and witchcraft, the belief that natural calamities were instruments for divine justice, and foolish conceptions of sin and sex. Despite the success of science in exposing the stupidity of such notions, man[illegible] superstitions and false beliefs still remain in considerable force. [illegible] irrational belief in palmistry or the notions of superiority as reg[illegible] race, nation, sex or creed, for instance, are still th[illegible] if we want to get rid of these evils we must cultivate a rational outlook, points out Russell.

Views on education. Russell is in favour of a rationalistic approach in the matter of formulating educational policies. The essay 'The Functions of a Teacher' tells us, in some detail, about his ideas of what education should aim at. A good teacher, according to Russell, should regard himself as a guardian of civilisation and should try his best to infuse in his pupils a civilised attitude. He has also to encourage kind impulses in his pupils and help them develop an unbiased, investigative curiosity. The most important object of education, according to Russell, is to preach tolerance which is necessary for the growth of democratic ideals. Russell feels that if education is to serve its purpose, the teachers must be granted complete freedom from all outside interference.

Value of liberty and democracy. A true liberal, Russell all through his life stood for the cause of individual liberty. In the essay 'The Future of Mankind' he prefers an American victory to a Russian one because in America there is a greater respect for things such as "freedom of thought, freedom of inquiry, freedom of discussion, and humane feeling". At the same time, Russell believes in the necessity of a government that can maintain law and order by imposing certain restrictions on the individuals. Democracy as he mentions in 'Ideas That Have Helped Mankind' was invented as a means to reconcile government with liberty. Democracy provides the necessary government, and at the same time, safeguards personal liberty by granting freedom of speech, press, and religion. What is more, it prevents any misuse of power by the government by keeping it dependent upon popular approval. Russell is a staunch supporter of a democratic or representative form of government. But he is also aware of the fact that a democracy can be a success only if the people have tolerance and some kind of mental discipline and attitude.

The idea of an international government. Russell's favourite idea of an international government has been mentioned in a number of these essays. Pacificism and establishment of world government are not exactly original ideas, but Russell's expression of these concepts have a sense of urgency and conviction which are fresh and striking. In the essay 'The Future of Mankind' he explains why and how such a government is to be formed. With the nuclear arms race moving fast towards a frightening situation, the human race, Russell fears, is facing the danger of total extinction. This disaster can be averted only if a single world government possessing monopoly of the armed forces and armaments is set up. The present circumstances are ideal for the formation of such a government. Russell explains it thus: "There are now only two fully independent states, America and Russia. The next step in this long historical process should reduce the two to one, and thus put an end to the period of organized wars, which began in Egypt some 6000 years ago." He adds that such a formation of a single government should be achieved by agreement, or, if necessary, by force. In a world under such a government, there will be no successful rebellion as the government will be too strong for it. Also, there will be peace and material comfort. These factors will contribute to the growth of tolerance and other kind impulses among the people and will make the world a much better place to live in. Russell puts forth this idea of an international government again in 'Ideas That Have Helped Mankind' and 'Ideas That Have Harmed Mankind.'

Necessity of the study of philosophy. In the essay 'Philosophy for Laymen' Russell discusses in detail the utility of philosophy in human life. Philosophy, according to him, can teach mankind the best way to use scientific skill. He points out that a distinction should be made between professional philosophy and philosophy as a guide to wisdom, and suggests that the latter should be made an essential part of general education. Philosophy helps us to achieve a theoretical understanding of the structure of the universe, and tries to suggest the best possible ways of life. Moreover, philosophy should not be dismissed as mere speculation because many important scientific inventions have been based on such speculation. Philosophy, Russell points out, can act as a guard against two evils—dogmatism and scepticism. Both of these evils are based on an element of 'certainty'—'certainty' of knowledge in the case of dogmatism and 'certainty' of ignorance in the case of scepticism. Philosophy can help in removing these evils by eliminating 'certainty' in us. It can thus instil in us the kind of intellectual sobriety necessary for being able to view things in an unbiased, objective manner. Above all, philosophy can help us to develop a general awareness of the evils in this world and can lend us the sanity required to deal with these evils effectively.

Russell: an original thinker. As a thinker, Russell is characterised by a fierce originality. He is an intellectual irritant who is not afraid of speaking out what he feels strongly and believes sincerely. Naturally possessed of a keen mind, he refuses to follow the beaten track of human thought and strikes out an altogether new path. He is a practical philosopher who stood by the implications of his philosophy. In the next place, his thoughts are presented with a scientific precision and logical sequence of arguments. Being a logician and scientist by temperament, Russell has applied to his inquiries a keen, cold, calculating method, considering all aspects of a question, seeing it steadily and objectively. His ideas are, therefore, clear and perspicuous, singularly free from vagueness and obscurity. One important point on which Russell differs from all contemporary thinkers is that, while they have pointed out the follies of men without caring to put them right, Russell has explained clearly and succinctly the principles on which reformation can be achieved. His chief suggestion in *Unpopular Essays* is, we find, the adoption of a rational attitude of mind which can tear away the veil that hides truth from us and can bring about the much coveted millenium among men. He was not afraid to debunk accepted philosophers such as Plato and Hegel.

III. RUSSELL'S PROSE STYLE

Q. 3. 'Russell's writing exactly reflects his crystalline, scintillating mind". Discuss with reference to *Unpopular Essays.*

Or

Lucid and effortless, Russell's prose style is enriched by constant flashes of wit and humour. How far is this statement true of *Unpopular Essays* ?

Or

"Russell's best writing is marked by dry wit, intellectual brilliance, and a certain gaiety". Discuss *Unpopular Essays* in the light of the above statement.

Or

Write a note on Russell's prose style with special reference to his *Unpopular Essays.*

Ans. **Magnificence of prose style.** Russell is one of the greatest writers of English prose. He is considered great not only for his contributions to philosophy and mathematics but also for his fascinating command over the English language. His logical and clear thinking helps him produce a style which is readily intelligible to any reader with average intelligence and moderate education. Indeed, as *Unpopular Essays* amply demonstrates, he has the rare gift of clearly summing up any idea, however complex it may be, and always seems to find the right words and phrases to express it in the simplest and yet the most striking way. Therefore, when we go through his ideas as expressed in his writings, we are invariably made to wonder if there could be any better way, or for that matter, any other way at all, to express the ideas without disturbing their meaning.

His style reflects his mind. Russell's style is a true reflection of his mind and temperament. The expression "style is the man" is, in Russell's case, more appropriate than, perhaps, in any other writer's.

He is basically a philosopher, but his approach to philosophy is unconventional. Most philosophers have a tendency to sit in an ivory tower and allow their carefree speculations soar into the realms of fancy without bothering about their utility for the non-philosophers. But to Russell, philosophy is important because it can be of great use to mankind. So, instead of indulging in aimless speculation, Russell endeavours to bring philosophy down to the level of a layman. He is also a mathematician, a logician, and a scientist. So he has no difficulty in achieving his object of simplifying philosophy. His style, therefore, reflects the clear thinking mind of a mathematician, the clear argumentation of a logician, and the precise objective outlook of a true scientific temperament. His main concern in his writings is easy communication with his readers. So he has to base his style on reason rather than on emotion.

Simplicity and clarity of style. Aldous Huxley pays tribute to Russell's prose style : "...what a blessed relief it is to read what Bertrand Russell has to say about politics, or psychology, or the conduct of life, or Nobel Prize Acceptance Speech! No jargon, not a single neologism. Nothing but plain English. There is no hiding behind obscurities, no pretending that the subject is understandable only by specialists and can be talked about only in a private language. Everything is perfectly clear and above-board. Of German scholars Bentley used to say that they dived deeper and came up muddier than any others. Bertrand Russell dives deep, but comes up every time as clear as a whistle". Huxley is obviously referring to the qualities of simplicity and clarity which make Russell's prose style at once grand and fascinating.

Some of the ideas put forth in his *Unpopular Essays* are undoubtedly profound and complicated. But he takes care to expose them in a logical, step-by-step method, garbing them in the simplest possible language to make them comprehensible even to laymen. His explanation of the relation between liberal creed and democracy in his essay 'Philosophy and Politics' may be cited as an example of the simplicity of language and the clarity of thought in his prose style : "The Liberal creed, in practice, is one of live-and-let-live, of toleration and freedom so far as public order permits, of moderation and absence of fanaticism in political programme. Even democracy, when it becomes fanatical, as it did among Rousseau's disciples in the French Revolution, ceases to be liberal; indeed, a fanatical belief in democracy makes democratic institutions impossible, as appeared in England under Cromwell and in France under Robespierre. The genuine Liberal does not say 'this is true', he says, 'I am inclined to think that under the present circumstances this opinion is probably the best'. And it is only in this limited and undogmatic sense that he will advocate democracy."

Ample use of illustrations. Russell has a tendency to add further clarifications to his arguments with illustrations which are relevant to them. In his essay 'Philosophy's Ulterior Motives' he demonstrates how philosophers are led astray by their ulterior motives by referring to and analysing the philosophies of Descartes, Leibniz, Bishop Berkeley, Kant, Hegel and Marx. He tries to establish his contention in his essay 'The Superior Virtue of the Oppressed' by giving a description of the attribution of superior virtue to women and children through the ages. Similarly in the essay 'An Outline of Intellectual Rubbish' he exposes the irrationality of men by amply illustrating their false beliefs and superstitions which have no rational basis. He fortifies all his arguments, even the less important ones, with illustrations drawn from philosophy, history, science, literature, and almost every sphere of life. In 'Philosophy for Laymen' one of his arguments is that increase of skill without a corresponding increase of wisdom cannot ensure human happiness. This is how he illustrates his point; "When men first learned to cultivate the soil, they used their knowledge to establish a cruel cult of human sacrifice. The men who first tamed the horse employed him to pillage and enslave peaceable populations. When, in the infancy of the industrial revolution, men discovered how to make cotton goods by machinery, the results were horrible. Jefferson's movement for the emancipation of slaves in America, which had been on the point of success, was killed dead; child labour in England was developed to a point of appalling cruelty, and ruthless imperialism in Africa was stimulated in the hope that black men could be induced to clothe themselves in cotton goods".

In all the essays in this collection we find illustrations even to describe minor points. In 'On Being Modern-Minded', Russell explains "a mental solitary life", as "that of Copernicus, Spinoza, or Milton after the Restoration". Going through the countless illustrations of this kind in *Unpopular Essays* one feature of Russell's greatness that would come up in any reader's mind is his encyclopaedic store of knowledge. It is the clarity of his mind and knowledge that makes the application of his illustrations always relevant and appropriate.

Terse and epigrammatic. Russell's preference for restraint and economy of words, aided by his mastery of the language, often permits him to compress thoughts into terse epigrammatic statements reminiscent of Bacon. Such statements are often short simple sentences containing deep and profound meanings and, as such, they lend an extra vigour and dignity to his language. Here are a few examples chosen at random from *Unpopular Essays* :

Dogmatism is an enemy to peace but an insuperable barrier to democracy. ('Philosophy for Laymen')

In a man whose reasoning powers are good, fallacious arguments are evidence of bias. ('Philosophy's Ulterior Motives')

We are suffering not from the decay of theological beliefs but from the loss of solitude. ('On Being Modern-Minded')

Politics is largely governed by sententious platitudes which are devoid of truth. ('An Outline of Intellectual Rubbish')

Man, viewed morally, is a strange amalgam of angel and devil. ('Ideas That Have Helped Mankind')

Pride of race is even more harmful than national pride. ('Ideas That Have Harmed Mankind')

Use of similes and metaphors. Russell, whose main object in his writing is easy communication to his readers is least bothered with the employment of decorative devices in his languages. But he is not reluctant to use similes and metaphors, when they can be utilised to lend greater force to his argument. Here are a couple of examples:

. . . . . . that order is impossible without a celestial policeman. ('Ideas That Have Helped Mankind')

But it is to be feared that the dreadful alchemo of the atom bomb will destroy all forms of life equally, and that the earth will remain for ever a dead clod senselessly whirling about a futile sun.... ('Ideas That Have Helped Mankind')

Irony and humour. Russell's essays, even while dealing with abstruse subjects, never become dull and uninteresting. This is because Russell is ever inclined to keep his readers' interest alive by blending his writings with occasional flashes of wit and humour. But it has to be noted that his humour is rarely pure fun or frolic. There is a kind of seriousness in his humour which he often produces to expose and attack the follies and vices of his fellow-man. That is why he employs irony as the chief instrument in his humour. His *Unpopular Essays* abounds in ironical humour. Thus in 'Philosophy and Politics' he ironically dismisses Hegel's definition of the Absolute Idea as "pure thought thinking about pure thought". Here is another superb example from 'The Future of Mankind': "In America if you are a geneticist, you may hold whatever view of Mendelism the evidence makes you regards as the most probable; in Russia, if you are a geneticist who disagrees with Lysenko, you are liable to disappear mysteriously."

Russell employs his ironical humour as a weapon of attack very effectively in 'The Superior Virtue of the Oppressed' the title of which itself is ironical. In this essay Russell's attack on Alexander Pope—"Nevertheless, for himself Pope preferred London and his villa at Twickenham"—ironically exposes the hypocrisy of the poet. His reference to the sudden change of British attitude towards the Irish after they became independent is made in irony : "The Irish were regarded by the English as possessed of a special charm and mystical insight until 1921, when it was found that the expense of continuing to oppress them would be prohibitive." His dismissal of Freud's child psychology is another striking piece of irony : "Is all this the objective truth at last ? Or is it merely an adult imaginative compensation for being no longer allowed to wallop the little pests?" In the essay 'On Being Modern-Minded' Russell criticises the modern tendency to submit to the fashion of the day: "The belief that fashion alone should dominate has great advantages. It makes thought unnecessary and puts the highest intelligence within the reach of everyone."

'An Outline of Intellectual Rubbish', in which Russell attacks the irrational ideas of mankind, abounds in ironical humour. His summing up of how the nuns, who never bathe naked, view God, is one of the most striking examples of his ironic humour : "Apparently, they conceive of the Deity as a Peeping Tom, whose omnipotence enables Him to see through bathroom walls but who is foiled by bathrobes." Again, he narrates the senseless urge in men to glorify their respective countries in an ironic vein : "If he is a Yugoslav, he boasts of his nation's pigs; if a native of the Principality of Monaco, he boasts of leading the world in the matter of gambling." In the same essay he exposes the illogicality of man's self-esteem through another grand example of ironical humour. ; "God was preparing the Great climax. At last, in the fulness of time, He produced Man, including such specimens as Nero and Caligula, Hitler and Mussolini, whose transcendent glory justified the long painful process".

In 'Ideas That Have Helped Mankind' Russell again employs irony to criticise the British indifference to the plight of German children after the World War : "And how about our noble selves? We would not do such deeds, oh no ! But we enjoy our juicy steaks and our hot rolls while German children die of hunger......." Similarly, in 'Ideas That Have Harmed Mankind' Russell ironically condemns the notion of the saint and the sinner '... mankind are divided into saints and sinners; the saints are to achieve bliss in the Nazi or communist heaven, while the sinners are to be liquidated, or to suffer such pains as human beings can inflict in concentration camps—inferior, of course to those which omnipotence was thought to inflict in hell, but the worst that human beings with their limited powers are able to achieve."

One major object of *Unpopular Essays* is to satirize the follies and vices of the human race. But the nature of Russell's satire differs from that of other satirists. Russell is by nature a thorough gentleman. He looks upon human follies not with contempt but with sympathy.

Abundant use of ironical humour helps Russell to satirise without showing any malice or grudge.

Conclusion. Russell's prose style reflects his catholicity, liberalism and urbanity. The richness of illustration does not render his style obscure; the abundance of wit and irony does not detract from the aura of tolerance and gentlemanliness. There is a gaiety in his style which does not prevent him from being irreverent even to Aristotle and Plato.

Q. 4. How far would it be correct to say that Russell's prose style gains in effect because of irony ? Illustrate from *Unpopular Essays*.

Or

What is the purpose of irony in *Unpopular Essays*? Analyse the essays you have read to illustrate Russell's ironic style.

Ans. **Introduction.** Irony involves the use of contrast—contrast between what is said and what is implied, contrast between what is expected and what is given, contrast between the surface meaning of a statement and the real or intended meaning of it, contrast between the levels of knowledge of two or more groups of people. Irony is an instrument of humour.

Russell's purpose in using irony. Bertrand Russell is an accomplished master of the ironic style. The very title of the collection of essays reflects ironical tongue-in-cheek humour. "*Unpopular Essays*" he calls them—because, he informs us, it is just possible that some unusually stupid children of the age of ten may find it difficult to understand some of the sentences. However, if Russell uses irony, it is for a specific purpose, which is to expose the absurdity of certain ideas, attitudes, customs and institutions, and through such exposure induce in his readers greater rationality and balanced attitudes in social and political life. The almost flippant wit that clothes each essay does not quite hide the seriousness of purpose and content.

Irony as a weapon to expose absurdities. Russell uses irony extensively to expose the absurdities that infest the social and political life of the modern times. Russell's logical mind rebelled against the irrational beliefs and convictions of people. He gently ridicules the tendency to blindly accept philosophers' views and feel virtuous in the process—"for reasons, which remain somewhat obscure" as he says in 'Philosophy and Politics'. He makes fun of the "modern-minded" who think they have reached the apex of intelligence illustrated by the casual use of the current jargon. The modern-minded man needs *Hamlet* to be interpreted in terms of Marx or Freud, says Russell ironically in 'On Being Modern-Minded'. The essay is a superb *expose* of the shallowness of the modern-minded persons in language which apparently praises the modern thinker :

> The modern-minded man......must be presumed to be very modest about his personal powers. His highest hope is to think first what is about to be thought....he has no wish to.....have emotions which are not those of some fashionable group, but only to be slightly ahead of others in point of time.

Religious beliefs are also attacked by Russell for their irrationality and illogicality. In his 'An Outline of Intellectual Rubbish' he firmly ridicules the pious men's ideas of God's selective mercies. His illustration of the priest who thanked God for His mercy when his house was burnt down after he vacated it is ironically funny; the concept of Sin is equally the target of Russell's ironic thrusts as is the idea of God. In Russell's essay God comes out to be a Peeping Tom or as not quite so omniscient or omnipotent as He is meant to be, because of the inconsistent and illogical ideas propounded by the clergy and blindly accepted by the laymen.

Irony to expose hypocrisy. Russell uses irony as a weapon to expose hypocrisy. 'The Superior Virtue of the Oppressed' is a consistent exercise in ironic attack on hypocrisy. The very title points at the ironic situation—the attribution of an imaginary quality to the oppressed as a kind of compensation for the exploitation to which they are subjected. Russell satirically traces the different classes of the oppressed through the centuries successively endowed with 'superior virtue'. As and when these oppressed classes have asserted their claim for equality, the tag of superior virtue has been indignantly withdrawn from them. Russell has ironically exposed the selfish motivation behind the attribution of superior virtue to the oppressed. In 'Ideas That Have Harmed Mankind' Russell speaks out strongly against the concept of the kindness of the Christian saints who abstained from physical pleasures but took intense mental pleasure in contemplating the tortures to be suffered by the 'heathen'.

Irony of a devastating kind. Russell is capable of using irony in a devastating manner and not merely in a humorous manner. In 'Ideas That Have Helped Mankind' he speaks strongly against narrow nationalistic ideas which glorify petty things and ignore the possibility that in the process man may be exterminated. He points out that the noble-minded British enjoyed juicy steaks and hot rolls while German children died of hunger after the World War.

Irony for entertainment. It is undeniable that ironic wit lends flavour to a piece of writing and renders it entertaining. Russell's essays have the element of pure fun—as when he points out that Aristotle could easily have counted his wife's teeth before making a dogmatic (and wrong) assertion on the number of teeth females possessed. But mostly the humour in his essays comes from the use of irony. A serious essay like 'Philosophy and Politics', becomes entertaining and easy to read because of the flashes of ironic wit which illumine it. Indeed, it is the ironic style that communicates the serious ideas all the more effectively.

Conclusion. Irony is an indispensable weapon of the satirist. Russell, however, is always urbane in his use of irony. His style never loses its equanimity because of irony. Above all, a genial sense of humour tones down the ironic thrusts and robs them of any bitterness or offence. The crowning comment of the humorous ironist is the last item in *Unpopular Essays*—an obituary written prophetically by the author for himself eight years before he died in which he calls himself "the last survivor of a dead epoch".

IV. RUSSELL'S IDEAS ON POLITICS, HUMANITY, SOCIETY, EDUCATION AND MORALITY

Q. 5. In what ways, according to Russell, is philosophy connected with politics?

Or

How does Russell come to the conclusion that Empiricist Liberalism is the only philosophy acceptable to mankind?

Or

Examine critically Russell's essay 'Philosophy and Politics'.

Ans. **Introduction.** At the very outset of 'Philosophy and Politics' Russell tells us that his main object in this essay is to discuss thoroughly the connection of philosophy with politics. It is a fact that in most civilized countries at most times, philosophy has been a matter in which the rulers or the authorities held an official opinion. Unfortunately where liberal democracy does not prevail this is till the case. Catholics, Communists, and Nazis all hold the opinion that their views on practical politics are firmly bound up with their views on theoretical philosophy. In its early success even democratic liberalism was connected with the empirical philosophy of Locke. Hence Russell feels that prevalent philosophy may have an intimate connection with the happiness or misery of large sections of mankind. That is why his aim in this essay is firstly to consider this relationship between philosophy and political systems and then to enquire how far it is a valid logical relation, and lastly, to consider how far, even if not logical, it has a kind of psychological inevitability.

Old and modern views regarding the aim of philosophy. According to many a teacher of philosophy in modern times the aim of philosophy should be just the pursuit of knowledge. It has nothing to do either with politics or ethics. But the old or historical view of philosophy is quuite different. According to the old view, philosophy has resulted from the attempt to produce a synthesis of science and religion, To be more exact, it is the result of the attempt to combine a doctrine of the nature of the universe and man's place in it with a practical ethic inculcating what is considered the best way of life. Still it differs greatly from both science and religion. It is distinguished from religion as it ordinarily does not appeal to authority or tradition. It is also distinguised from science as the essential part of its purpose is to tell men how to live. But the ethical opinions, with most of the philosophers, involve political consequences. As a result, some of them praise liberty, others discipline. So to find some way of reconciling the needs of social life with the urgency of individual desires is the fundamental problem of both ethics and politics.

Most philosophy a reaction against scepticism. According to Russell most philosophy has been a reaction against scepticism. This is due to the fear, often unconscious, that clear thinking would lead to anarchy. But there have been exceptions. The most notable ones are Protagoras in antiquity and Hume in modern times. Both were, no doubt, sceptics. But unfortunately they were politically conservative. According to Protagoras, as philosophy has nothing edifying to teach, for the survival of morals we must rely upon the thoughtlessness of the majority. The same sort of thing, up to a point, may be said about Hume also. So they were against doing anything to weaken the popular force of tradition. And then Hobbes, though less sceptical than Hume, advocated extreme conservatism. Protagoras and Hume have, however, never been very influential with their brand of scepticism. But the really powerful adversaries against whom Plato and Hegel had to contend were Democritus in the one case and Locke in the other. They were not sceptics but empiricists, that is, those who believe that all knowledge is derived from the senses and experience alone. And in each case empiricism was associated with democracy and with a more or less utilitarian ethic. In each case this new philosophy made itself the champion of injustice, cruelty, and opposition to progress.

Plato with his totalitarianism and static perfection challenges Democritus. Democritus, chiefly famous as founder of atomism, was a materialist, a determinist, a free thinker, a utilitarian who disliked all strong passions, a believer in evolution, both astronomical and biological. As an ardent democrat, Democritus held the view that poverty in democracy should be preferred to prosperity under despots. So naturally Plato, a man of totalitarian views, opposed Democritus vehemently and in fact wanted that all his books should be burnt. Plato's great book, *Republic*, reveals his totalitarian views. At the end of the prolonged Peloponnesian war between Sparta and Athens, the victory of Sparta meant victory of oligarchy over democracy. And Plato was a supporter of oligarchy. So the *Republic*, which is totalitarian in its political teaching, advocates very strongly the ideal of static perfection and this is now generally recognized as inapplicable to human afforts. In his *Republic* Plato tells us that the main purpose of education is to produce courage in battle, that there should be a rigid censorship of the stories told by mothers and nurses to young children, that people should neither read Homer nor drama, that a small oligarchy of the wise should rule, and that their purpose should be to preserve the *status quo*. It is a great surprise for Russell that these ideas deceived the world for ages. In fact, man is a restless animal and needs, for his happiness, hope, enterprise and change. So among the modern philosophers, the ideal of unending and unchanging bliss has been replaced by that of evolution. This change in outlook is a part of the substitution of dynamics for statics which began with Galileo. And this new outlook has increasingly affected all modern thinking, whether scientific or political; for example no astronomer after Galileo believes like the followers of Aristotle that everything in the heavens, from the moon upwards, is unchanging and incorruptible. Even our earth was once too hot to support life, and will in time be too cold to support any life.

Philosophers' endeavour to find a law of progress. But the unpleasant truths of science have not satisfied many philosophers. They want to discover a formula of progress showing that the world is becoming more and more to their liking in course of time. And to establish this, they first decide which are the features of the existing world that give them pleasure, and which are the features that give them pain. And then by a careful selection among facts, they propound that the universe is subject to a general law leading to increase of what they find pleasant and a decrease of what they find unpleasant. Thus, having formulated the law of progress, they turn to the public and assert that it is fated that the world must develop according to their findings and ask them to join their party.

Hegel and his views and their political implications. Hegel was the first man to develop fully and enunciate the above point of view. According to his philosophy real reality is timeless, but there is also an apparent reality, consisting of the everyday world in space and time. And by logic alone we are able to determine the character of real reality, since there is only one sort of possible reality that is not self-contradictory. Hegel uses the term 'Absolute Idea' to convey his notion about real reality. Russell rather ironically defines it thus: "The

Absolute Idea is pure thought thinking about pure thought." Hegel has already proved to his satisfaction that all reality is thought. Hegel's philosophy is absurd and it is surprising to find it exercising so much influence upon the minds of so many intellectuals of different countries. At first sight, the relation of Hegel's philosophy to politics may not be clear. But it follows from his metaphysic that true liberty consists in obedience to an arbitrary authority. So according to him, absolute monarchy is good, free speech is an evil and war is good. And as such, an international organization for the peaceful settlement of disputes would not be desirable at all. Hegel arrived at these conclusions through his dialectic in his own way. He discovered the nature of reality by a purely logical process called the 'dialectic'. This consists of discovering contradiction in abstract ideas and correcting them by making them less abstract.

Curious effect of Hegel's philosophy on Karl Marx. If we accept man to be more or less a rational animal, the success of this odd philosophy is really surprising. And most curious of all was Hegel's effect on Karl Marx. Marx takes over some of Hegel's most fanciful tenets. On the basis of these he propounds that history develops according to a logical plan, and is concerned, like the purely abstract dialectic, with finding ways of avoiding self-contradiction. If we take into account certain very general features of Hegel's practical programme, we will find that his philosophy constrained him to admire order, system, regulation and intensity of government control. According to him, strong government might compel men to act for the best, which democracy could never do. Marx also, to a very great extent, advocated an autocratic system. And such a system is only theoretically justifiable on a basis of unquestioned dogma.

John Locke's empiricism and the liberal theory of politics: Empiricism is the only philosophy that affords a sound theoretical justification of democracy. And so far as the modern world is concerned, Locke may be regarded as the founder of this philosophy. He has made it clear how closely this philosophy is connected with his views on liberty and toleration, and his opposition to absolute monarchy. He has firmly emphasized the uncertainty of most of our knowledge to make men aware that they may be mistaken. So people should be liberal, taking into account the possibility of mistakes in all their dealings with men holding opinions different from their own. So the liberal creed, in practice, is one of live-and-let-live. It means toleration and freedom so far as public order permits, moderation and absence of fanaticism in political programmes. According to him, even democracy, when it becomes fanatical, ceases to be liberal. This is what happened in France during the French Revolution and in England under Cromwell. The genuine liberal always holds his opinions tentatively and not dogmatically. He is always conscious that new evidence may at any moment lead to the abandonment of earlier opinions. This is the scientific outlook, as science is always empirical, tentative, and undogmatic.

Locke and his doctrines. Besides his great contribution to the development of empiricist philosophy, Locke also preached and propagated religious toleration, representative institutions, and the limitation of governmental power by the system of checks and balances. These doctrines might not have been new, but he developed them in a weighty manner. In fact, Locke stood for order without authority both in intellectual and in practical matters. In the intellectual world it means a measure of agreement among experts after adequate discussion. And in the practical world it involves submission to the majority after allowing all parties to state their case freely. Although wars of religion ended long ago, yet we are now again in an epoch of wars of religion; but a religion is now called an ideology. And the world also faces a grave danger due to the invention of the atom bomb. So we should see that a more rational outlook prevails, for our world can survive only through a revival of liberal tentativeness and tolerance.

Importance of rational outlook in the sphere of practical politics. To Russell the empiricist's theory of knowledge is half way between dogma and scepticism. According to empiricists, all knowledge is in some degree doubtful, though the doubt may be negligible as regards pure mathematics. So it must be noted that scientific theories are accepted as useful hypotheses for further research, but no sensible person regards them as immutably perfect. This rational and intellectual attitude has important consequences in the sphere of practical politics. Firstly, it points out that it is nor worthwhile to inflict a comparatively certain present evil for the sake of a comparatively doubtful future good. If, for example, we are sure that by abolishing private capitalism mankind will be happy ever after, then it is right to pursue this end by making people suffer even by means of world wars. But if there be the least doubt about the end, then it is hardly justifiable to go for dictatorship or send men to concentration camps. Thus a rational and an undogmatic attitude is urgently needed in the sphere of politics for the future of mankind.

Liberals have an upper hand over fanatics. There is a wrong notion that the fanatics are sure to win in a war between the liberals and the fanatics. In fact the fanatics have failed over and over again. In all important wars since 1700 the more democratic side has been victorious. And the main causes of the fanatics' failure were that they had attempted the impossible and they were too unscientific to adopt the right means. The fanatics also sensed the hostility of those whom they wished to dominate. But democracy and empiricism, which are intimately connected, never demand a distortion of facts in the interests of theory. Then again, a greater degree of coherence can undoubtedly be produced by systems of dogma among their disciples. But they have their disadvantages too as they involve persecution of important sections of the population. Dogmatic beliefs cannot really lead to a greater political and social unity in a country. No country, for instance, showed a greater solidarity and social coherence than Britain during Second World War, and Britain has a democratic system of government.

Russell's plea for empiricism. Russell asserts with great conviction that empiricism is to be recommended not only on the plea of greater truth, but also on moral or ethical grounds. We have been convinced that dogma demands authority rather than intelligent thought, as the source of opinion. Dogmatic people cannot but persecute those who do not accept their ideas. Dogmas develop and foster systematic hatred leading to war by means of which to reach a decision. And war, in our scientific and atomic age, means total extinction of the human race.

Bertrand Russell has, in this essay, very lucidly and logically established that Empiricist Liberalism is the need of the hour. This is the only philosophy that can be adopted by a man demanding some scientific evidence for his beliefs as well as desiring human happiness irrespective of the ideas of any creed or any party. Russell has firstly exposed the absurdity of Plato's odd political beliefs which duped the world for ages; he does the same regarding Hegel's philosophy that brought about disastrous political consequences. The most important point in this essay is that with same arguments and logical presentation Russell has been able to convince us that men should hold political beliefs as tentatively as a scientist holds his scientific theories. Fanaticism and the tendency to hold on to any kind of belief dogmatically must be discarded, as fanatics and dogmatists would never pay heed to any new evidence which goes against their creed. Our modern world is full of confusion and difficulties, and for its survival and sustenance Empiricist Liberalism is one of the most desired things. We must have faith in liberty, scientific freedom and mutual tolerance so as to save our planet from impending doom and disaster. "For without these beliefs life on our politically divided but technically unified planet will hardly continue to be possible."

Q. 6. Comment on the role that philosophy can play in increasing human happiness or well-being, according to Russell.

Or

"Philosophy can give certain things that will greatly increase the student's value as a human being and as a citizen." Elucidate.

Or

Examine critically the ideas contained in Russell's 'Philosophy for Laymen'.

Ans. **Need of philosophy.** Since the rise of civilization mankind has been facing two kinds of problems—the problem of gaining control over the forces of Nature, and the problem of learning the best way to utilise such control. Men have dealt with the first problem successfully with the help of science. They have gradually acquired knowledge and skill, produced tools and weapons to fight the wild animals and other forces of Nature, and have come out victorious in the grim struggle for existence in this world. As regards the problem of utilizing the acquired skill and technique, the human race has not made much progress. As a result, scientific progress has hardly been able to add to our happiness. The benefits of the invention of agriculture continued to remain neutralised through centuries as a result of the human sacrifice it involved. So, according to Russell, if we want to get the full value of our scientific skill we must solve the problem of utilizing it properly. We can do so only through having a broad knowledge of the human universe, and this only philosophy can provide. When we will learn how to use our scientific skill, the menaces like the atomic bomb will disappear from this world.

Philosophy, a guide to wisdom. 'Philosophy' implies 'love of wisdom', and this sense of 'wisdom' has to be cultivated. A distinction has to be made between professional philosophy and philosophy as a guide to wisdom, and the latter should be made a part of general education.

Two objects of philosophy. Philosophy has always had two different objects which were believed to be closely inter-related. Firstly, it aimed at a theoretical understanding of the structure of the universe; secondly, it tried to devise the best possible way of life. It has thus had a close connection with science on the one hand, and with religion on the other. Until the 18th century, science was considered a part of philosophy. Since then philosophy began to be considered mere speculation and is now dismissed as unprogressive. Russell tries to dispel such general misconceptions about philosophy by pointing out its contribution to the field of science. He thinks that philosophers have put forth hypotheses that have often provided the scientists which clues and have led to significant scientific achievements. Russell regrets that our attitude towards philosophy is biased and as such we tend to ignore its contribution. Anaximander, for instance, had a theory of evolution in sixth century B.C. which could not be verified, and is dismissed by us as mere philosophic speculation. But when Darwin came up with his theory and established it with evidence, we accepted it as science and gave all the credit to him. We tend to ignore the possibility that Anaximander could have encouraged Darwin's theory and thus we deprive him of his due credit.

Usefulness of philosophy. Philosophy should not be looked upon as a mere bunch of speculations that have to be either confirmed or rejected by science. At the same time we need not be much too concerned about what science knows and what it does not know. We should always remember that skill can never be an alternative to wisdom and that science, used with wisdom, can become the greatest blessing to mankind. Philosophy can help the growth of a balanced attitude towards science by showing us the possibilities and limitations of our scientific knowledge. Again, Russell refers to certain questions that have ever continued to disturb and, at the same time, enliven human life. Questions about life after death, the purpose of the universe etc., have remained, and will for a long time remain unanswered by Science. It has to be left to philosophy to keep exploring these universal problems.

Two dangers philosophy may guard against. Philosophy can act as a guard against two possible evils—dogmatism and scepticism. Dogmatism is a product of our passion for a quickly achieved certainty. It is dangerous because it creates rival groups of fanatics, each group convinced that it is right in its convictions, and as such, intolerant of contrary views. Dogmatism can lead to conflicts between individuals and nations, and, as such, is detrimental to peace. Much of the cruelty that has been enacted in this world has been the result of dogmatism. The atrocities committed on the capitalists in communist countries and on the Jews in Nazi Germany can be cited as the consequences of this illogical belief in the certainty of convictions. Scepticism cannot be a solution to dogmatism, for scepticism too is an extreme philosophy that leads to inaction and is, therefore, useless. Dogmatism implies 'certainty' of knowledge whereas scepticism is 'certainty' of ignorance. Philosophy's aim is to eliminate this element of 'certainty' because by doing so it can remove both these evils. Russell feels that the right thing is to associate all our convictions with an element of uncertainty. For instance, a person who is a democrat should never convince himself that democracy is the best system of government, but should be prepared to shift his opinion whenever he comes across a better system. However, it is also necessary to act upon hypothesis sometimes. Philosophy can help us choose the best possible hypothesis to act upon. We must learn to act on such hypotheses, which, even if they prove false, will not cause serious harm to anybody.

Philosophy and religion. Philosophy can play an effective role in human life if it continues to suggest a way of life leading to happiness and prosperity. In this its function is similar to that of religion, with some differences. Philosophy, unlike religion, is not bound by tradition or scriptures, and is not concerned with setting up church-like establishments. Moreover, philosophy lays more emphasis on the development of intellectual virtues whereas to religion moral virtues are more important.

Philosophy and ethics. The philosophic spirit can also eliminate such beliefs which are caused by feelings of fear or self-esteem. Philosophy can instil into us the kind of intellectual sobriety necessary for being able to view beliefs impartially and analytically. Such restraint can rid us of all emotional bias and teach us to look at problems in an objective manner. Russell suggests that even if philosophy is not permitted to encroach into the time for technical studies, every student must study it in his spare hours. Philosophy can provide a person with the faculty of clear thinking and an understanding of his relation to the society. Philosophy can encourage a better understanding of the evils of the world and inculcate the sanity necessary to deal with those evils.

Q. 7. "I come now to the question: what should be our policy in view of the various dangers to which mankind is exposed?" Consider the circumstances that have led Russell to raise the above question. What policy does Russell suggest to avert those dangers ?

Or

Why does Russell, in his essay 'The Future of Mankind', advocate the formation of an international government ? How far do you agree with him ?

Or

Examine critically the ideas contained in Russell's 'The Future of Mankind'.

Ans. **Humanity exposed to three inevitable possibilities.** After the two catastrophic world wars Bertrand Russell foresees another unprecedented war that may bring absolute doom and destruction to humanity. So, according to Russell, humanity is expected to face three possibilities, namely : (*a*) total annihilation or extinction of mankind; (*b*) a reversion to barbarism as there would be very few human beings left alive ; (*c*) establishment of a single world government having a monopoly of all the major weapons of war.

First danger—extinction of human race. According to Russell the next or the third world war may not completely annihilate the human race as it may not continue for a very long period. But if this war is indecisive and if organized states survive it, then with the help of further technical development and with much greater means of utilizing atomic energy the next world war is likely to wipe out the human race and other signs of life. Russell fervently appeals to all men to find out ways and means to prevent such a dire catastrophe.

The second possibility or danger. The second possibility is that the human race may not be completely wiped out after a third world war, but there is the danger of reversion to barbarism, as there will be very few survivors. A scientific world war will completely destroy the chief cities and centres of industry along with all laboratories and libraries. As an aftermath of such a war, vast numbers of people will perish due to famine caused by radioactive spray and due to pestilence caused by bacteriological warfare. The great states will disintegrate and the few survivors would revert to a primitive village economy.

As regards the first possibility Russell seems to have taken a very pessimistic view. Of course it is quite likely that life on our planet may be completely destroyed if two other world wars take place. It is hoped that alert scientists and humanitarian intellectuals will do their utmost to prevent such a dire catastrophe. At least we cannot think with Russell that the end of the human race is likely to happen by the end of this century. But his arguments regarding the reversion to barbarism are quite plausible and convincing.

The third possibility—aversion of danger. The establishment of a single government for the whole world is, according to Russell, the third possibility. And this may be achieved in various ways (*a*) by the victory of the United States in the next world war, (*b*) by the victory of U.S.S.R. (*c*) theoretically by agreement between the two super powers. But Russell feels the best thing would be the formation of an alliance of the nations that desire an international government. Such an alliance would become powerful enough to subdue even Russia and thereby be able to avoid another world war.

Arguments used against the project of a world government.

Russell now takes up the arguments that are used against the project of a world government. Most people think that it is utopian and impossible, as it seems unlikely to come about by agreement. Russell agrees with them as he also feels that the mutual suspicion between Russia and the West will prevent any agreement from taking place. Any pretended universal authority like U.N.O. will not be able to help in any way. So Russell asserts that a world government may have to be imposed by force.

Then again many people think that wars have taken place since men were organized into communities, but the human race has survived. So this race would be able to survive even if wars occur from time to time. But these people miserably fail to visualise that war after the rapid advance of scientific inventions and discoveries will absolutely destroy human civilization, even if it does not wipe out the human race immediately. So mankind must adopt some system to make it impossible for wars to take place. "But the only such system is a single government with a monopoly of armed forces," says Russell.

Dire consequence if things are allowed to drift. If things are allowed to drift, sooner or later there will be an atomic war between Russia and the Western democracies. In such a war Western Europe along with Great Britain is likely to be completely destroyed even if human civilization is not wiped out. In case both America and U.S.S.R. survive they will fight again. But if there is victory for one side, that side will rule the world. And then only a world government will come into existence, otherwise human civilization would perish. Russell feels there is hardly any chance of establishing it by friendly negotiations. Hence the threat of force will be necessary. And if that fails force should be used to establish a single government.

A world government and its advantages. The first important beneficial result after the establishment of a single government will be the impossibility of rebellions being successful, as the victorious nation will have the monopoly of armed forces. In the beginning the victorious nation may be guided only by self-interest. But in a peaceful world its people will soon achieve a very high level of material comfort. And so they are likely to become quite liberal and good-natured and less inclined to persecute the vanquished. Then we will have a true world state. Russell prefers a world empire ruled by either America or Russia to the continuation of the present international anarchy.

Reasons for preferring a victory of America—Russian victory disastrous. Russell's reason for preferring an American victory is that there is in that country more respect than in Russia for the things that are essential in a civilized way of life. In America there is respect for freedom of thought, freedom of enquiry, freedom of discussion, and humane feeling. Russia's victory over Poland is an eye-opener for us. A world empire of the U.S.S.R. will mean the crushing of all the freedoms mentioned earlier. Education will be reduced to learning the formulae of orthodox communism. Dissidents and men of great intellectual eminence will be liquidated or imprisoned if they are unable to escape. The middle class will be, more or less, annihilated or there will be mass expulsions. Science, philosophy, art and literature will be directly under the control of the authorities and so the students will become narrow and stupid and sycophantic adjuncts of the government. No individual will think, or even feel for himself but will become a unit of the mass. A Russian regime would make such a mentality world-wide. That is why Russell feels that a Russian victory will be disastrous for humanity.

A victory by the U.S. and its favourable consequences. A victory by the United States is much more welcome, because in the first place it would not be a victory of the United States alone, but of an Alliance. And in that case the other members of the Alliance would be able to insist upon retaining their traditional independence to a great extent. One can rest assured that the American army would never persecute or banish great intellectuals and free thinkers. So we can justly expect that after a victory of such an Alliance, British culture, French culture or Italian culture will not be disturbed. So there would not be the same dead uniformity as would result from a complete Soviet domination.

Another important thing to be noted is that Soviet orthodoxy is much more all-pervasive than that of America. In U.S.A. whatever may be your subject, genetics, politics or economics, you may hold whatever view you think to be right within the broad principles and express it freely. But in Russia if your view goes against that of the authority, you are liable to be liquidated. In America a professor of Philosophy may be an idealist, a materialist, a pragmatist, or whatever he likes and can express his opinion freely. But in Russia one must be a dialectical materialist and follow the official metaphysic with sufficient nimbleness. So in such a world intellect must stagnate and even technological progress may soon come to an end. Then in Russia there is an oligarchy which controls the publicity media and so can perpetrate injustice and cruelties without the public knowing the truth. "Only democracy and free publicity can prevent the holders of power from establishing a servile state."

To guard against three dangers—formation of alliance against U.S.S.R. Russell then tells us that we have to guard against three dangers to save humanity from utter disaster. The three dangers are; (*a*) the extinction of human race; (*b*) a reversion to barbarism; (*c*) the establishment of a universal slave state by Soviet Russia. The first two dangers can be prevented if great wars are brought to an end. And the only way to prevent great wars is the concentration of armed forces under a single authority. And the third can be prevented by the formation of an alliance against Soviet Russia. And for this purpose the first step would be to persuade United States and the British Commonwealth of the absolute necessity for a military unification of the world without the Soviet Union. Then all other nations should be given the option of entering into a firm Alliance even by offering great inducements. And when this Alliance becomes sufficiently powerful, it would declare war against any dissenting Great Power to bring it to book. In such a war the Alliance is sure to win, enabling it to establish a monopoly of armed forces. In fact there are now only two fully independent states in the world—America and Russia. It is expected that the next step in the long historical process should reduce these two to one after the victory of the Alliance with the U.S. as the leading partner over U.S.S.R. Only this will be able to bring about an end of the period of organized wars which began in Egypt some 6000 years ago.

Blessings of an era of peace without wars. When war is abolished and liberal world government is established, an era of peace and prosperity is bound to ensue. A weight will be lifted from the human spirit and deep collective fears will die out naturally. If there is no fear, cruelty will decrease. If there is no ominous shadow of war, scientific technique, instead of being used for the purpose of war, would at last be used for promoting real progress and happiness for mankind. If there is no real danger of war, men would be able to put an end to depravity and serious poverty throughout the world.

Russell's somewhat unreasonable and unrealistic approach : In this essay Bertrand Russell has tried his best to build up his arguments logically in favour of an American victory over Soviet Russia for creating a democratic and liberal world government to usher in an era of peace and prosperity for the whole of mankind. To him a Russian victory means an appalling disaster. Unfortunately in this very essay the great apostle of reason seems, to some extent, biased, unreasonable and unrealistic. He seems to be prejudiced against the Soviet type of government and places high hopes in a single state under American control. There may be oligarchy or a totalitarian system in Russia, but the people at helm of affairs there stand for the upliftment of the poor and the downtrodden. And is not there in America some sort of oligarchy too? How can we be absolutely sure that a victorious America leading a World Government will really be able to benefit all the people? A victorious America, puffed up with pride, may also become despotic and arrogant.

Russell also argues that a World Government can be established only through another war reducing the two great powers to one. But in the very beginning of the essay he has clearly stated that the next war will be a scientific war and it will mean the end of our civilization, if not the extinction of the human race. Then again in his essay on 'Philosophy and Politics' he has already argued convincingly that if the end is doubtful or the means not sure to achieve it, present misery becomes an irresistible argument against such drastic methods. So, obsessed by his idea of World Government Russell seems to be unreasonable and unrealistic in this essay.

Many changes have taken place in our world after this essay was written. China has become the third great World Power. War machines have become much more destructive. A World War now could easily mean the total extinction of life as we know of it now on our planet. It is difficult to predict anything now. The nuclear deterrent may save us. And the ideal of co-existence with a faith in the principle of live-and-let-live may save our planet from a certain doom and destruction.

Q. 8. Discuss how ulterior motives have made philosophy fallacious. How, according to Russell, should philosophy be cultivated ?

Or

Examine critically the ideas contained in Russell's essay, 'Philosophy's Ulterior Motives.'

Ans. **Ulterior motives of philosophy.** Russell points out that though philosophy should be regarded as a determined attempt to think clearly, it has, in reality, become an attempt to think fallaciously. The philosopher has a curious mental temper. On the one hand, he has a strong desire to accept the general proposition about the universe or human life; on the other, he finds it difficult to accept anything that does not stand on intellectual grounds. The general doctrines are of no significance to the people without intellect; the man of science views them only as hypotheses to be tested by his experiments; to the philosopher they are an essential part of life, needing some kind of justification. So in order to find justification the philosopher often indulges in a long process of reasoning in the course of which there remains every chance of a slip leading to fallacy. His extra mental agility helps only to add to the falsehood.

Descartes as an example. Descartes, the father of modern philosophy, perfectly illustrates this mental inclination. Finding that his teachers possessed views different from one another he became a sceptic and decided that no existing doctrine could be accepted as certain. During his quest for certainty he first decided that he would reject everything that he could doubt. He even rejected his fellow-beings and the heavenly bodies on the ground that they might be only illusions. He believed in only one thing, namely his own existence, because he felt that if he did not exist it would not be possible for him to doubt. Upto this point his arguments were based on a fairly sound footing. But now he began to show signs of losing his critical faculty by accepting a host of existing notions. He tried to justify the existence of God with fallacious arguments. He said that since he could form an idea of God as a being more perfect than himself and because this idea must have a cause other than himself, God's existence was certain. The fact is, Descartes began as a true philosopher, but ultimately gave away to the intense desire to believe in general doctrine and lost his critical acumen.

Leibniz's error. Leibniz was a different kind of man from Descartes. He looked upon philosophy as his profession and as such possessed greater restraint. He wrote philosophy especially to please Queen Sophie Charlotte and a few other royal patrons. He wrote some good philosophy but took care not to publish them lest they should offend his patrons. Leibniz took the stance of an optimist and declared that 'this is the best of all possible worlds'. He held that there were a number of logically possible worlds, some of which contained no sin and suffering, but which contained less good than this world, and that God could have created any one of those worlds instead of this world. But behind these superficialities Leibniz suffered all his life from a more serious problem. The idea that God could have created any of those worlds, which contained less good, could not agree with the concept of God's goodness, and could lead one to conclude that God is not necessarily good. Unable to solve this problem Leibniz resorted to obscurity and ambiguity and produced confusing philosophy.

Berkeley's confusion. Bishop Berkeley, the anti-materialist philosopher, had two objectives. Firstly, he wanted to prove that there can be no such thing as matter; secondly, he wanted to deduce from the earlier proposition the necessary existence of God. He points out that when we think we see a tree what we really know is not an external object, but a modification of ourselves, a sensation, or as he calls it an 'idea'. By his argument the tree ceases to exist as soon as we shut our eyes. Matter, according to Berkeley, is thus a mere hypothesis. Strangely enough, he follows his arguments with a paradox that sets to nought his earlier contention. He now tries to secure some permanence about physical objects by arguing that the tree is really an idea in the mind of God, and therefore continues to exist even when we are not looking at it. Berkeley began well, but was led into confusion by the ulterior motive of establishing God's existence.

Hume: no ulterior motive. Hume was the only follower of Berkeley who did not show timidity in admitting the sceptical consequences of Berkeley's argument. He argues that if we accept 'ideas' as the only real things, we cannot believe in the existence of anything except our own mental states. Hume was one of the few philosophers who did not have any ulterior motive. However, his philosophy in some ways inspired the philosophies of Kant and Hegel.

Kant : too dogmatic. Kant, the German philosopher, was initially a dogmatic philosopher. In the middle of his career he was said to have come under the influence of Hume. During those years he produced his great work, *Critique of Pure Reason.* After this he again turned dogmatic and wrote his *Critique of Practical Reason.* His ulterior motive was to believe in everything that he was taught during his childhood. Hence, he invented practical reason in order to prove the correctness of the things he had known before reading Hume, such as future life, free will and God's existence.

Hegel: attempt to make future calculable. Philosophers are normally physically weak and, as such, they dislike the unexpected. So they have the tendency to invent systems which make the future calculable. Hegel was the supreme practitioner of this art. For him the course of logic was similar to that of history. He viewed logic as a series of self-correcting attempts to describe the world. If the first of these attempts proves self-contradictory one has to try just the opposite, *i.e.*, the 'antithesis' of the 'thesis'. In case of its failure a 'synthesis' of the 'thesis' and the 'antithesis' has to be tried. The result will certainly be less self-contradictory than that of either of the two earlier attempts. If the 'synthesis' too proves inadequate one has to regard it as the new 'thesis' and then the whole process has to be repeated. Repetitions of the same process can ultimately lead to a perfect idea, described by Hegel as the 'Absolute Idea' of the world. Hegel, who had the ulterior motive of pleasing the Germans, used this 'Absolute Idea' to describe Germany.

Hegel's philosophy made philosophers happy for several reasons. It was obscure and, as such, was beyond the comprehension of the amateurs. It also elevated philosophers to a level unattainable by others by showing that philosophers, through meditation, could gather a more perfect knowledge of the world.

Marx: in Hegel's footsteps. Karl Marx took over from Hegel the belief in dialectic, that is to say, in logical development by thesis, antithesis and synthesis, shown in the course of human history and not only in abstract thought. However, he did not share Hegel's view that the 'Absolute Idea' had already been achieved in the shape of Germany.

He believed that a revolution, that was sure to come, was needed by the world to attain perfection. Marx's theory was optimistic because it carried with it hope and faith.

Russell's suggestions. If philosophy has to flourish, we must cultivate it in the most proper way. We cannot ignore the traditional doctrines; but we must be able to view them critically. We must remember that the concept that truth can be achieved by mere thinking and without observation, is true nowhere except in the case of mathematics. Philosophy is inspired by the belief that our purposes have an important relation to the purposes of the universe, and that, in the long run, the course of events is bound to be on the whole such as we should wish it to be. Science has rejected this kind of optimism, but the development of science is creating another kind of optimism: that we, by our intelligence, can make the world such as to satisfy a large proportion of our desires. However, Russell mildly cautions us against being overwhelmed by such optimism, which, in course of time, may prove wrong and make us look ridiculous in the eyes of the future generation.

Q. 9. Why and how is 'superior virtue' attributed to the oppressed classes? Comment on Russell's views.

Or

"Children were idealized by Wordsworth and unidealized by Freud. Marx was the Wordsworth of the proletariat; its Freud is still to come." Describe in detail how Russell comes to this conclusion.

Or

Attempt a critical analysis of Russell's essay 'The Superior Virtue of the Oppressed.'

Ans. **Delusion regarding the superiority of sections of mankind.** It is quite rational and natural for people to think well of themselves and hold a high opinion of their own country and people. But often we find a good number of persons, especially among moralists and some writers, who hold a poor opinion about their friends and fellowmen and think highly of some other sections of mankind. These people argue that some sections of the human race possess certain uncommon qualities and characteristics, though such beliefs have no rational basis. A typical form of this admiration for other sections, according to Russell, is the belief in the superior virtue of the oppressed such as the subject nations, the poor, women and children.

The superior virtue of the poor. The eighteenth century people had a sentimental attitude towards the poor, although they made miserable the condition of totally indigent labourers by introducing many inhuman practices during the early stages of industrialisation. They called the peasants 'noble savages' and thought them to be virtuous and noble. According to Pope, the poor farmers were the really happy people as they were satisfied with 'a few paternal acres'. Then during the French Revolution the superior virtue of the down-trodden poor became a party question. It has remained so ever since. The liberals continue to idealize the rural poor, although the reactionaries look down upon them. And the socialists and communists began to do the same for the urban proletariat or the poor working class.

The superior virtue of the subject nations. In the nineteenth century we find the subject nations becoming a substitute for the 'noble savage' of the past. When the Greeks, the Hungarians, the Poles and the Italians were under the domain of foreigners, they were regarded as gifted poetic races too idealistic to succeed in this selfish and wicked world. Even the English thought that the Irish were endowed with special charm and mystical insight till they were under their thumb. And when these nations became independent one by one, ironically enough all their supposed superior qualities vanished into nothingness in no time. But such illusions persist regarding the nations which are still under foreign domination.

The superior virtue of the weaker sex. Women also have been viewed in the same indulgent manner but much more irrationally than the poor or the subject nations. The Church held two opposite views dividing them into two classes: the temptress and the saint, the former representing Eve, and the latter the Virgin. But in the nineteenth century there came a new attitude. The temptress was pushed into the background and a kind of combination of the Madonna and the lady of Chivalry was created as the ideal for the ordinary married woman. She was supposed to be delicate and dainty and hence too soft to face the blows and buffets of this wicked world. She was endowed with great spiritual virtues and this made her the superior of man. But sadly enough this made her unfit for business, or politics, or for having an independent existence. But gradually a change in the male attitude towards women has taken place. In fact the belief in women's spiritual superiority was due to the men's determination to keep women inferior economically and politically. Now the women have won their equal rights and economic independence. Hence the belief in their superior virtues and spiritual qualities has vanished into nothingness.

The fluctuating virtue of the children. Russell points out that a somewhat similar development has taken place in the adult view of the children. In the Middle Ages children, like women, were considered wicked and were considered to be limbs of Satan. This gave the adults good excuse to treat them harshly for the purpose of saving their souls. But during the nineteenth century the pendulum swung to the other end. Children now began to be regarded as wise, pure and innocent and deserving to be protected from knowledge of evil. This view was made popular by Wordsworth. In his great poem *Ode on the Intimations of Immortality* he tells us:

> Heaven lies about us in our infancy.

This led to a rather unusual development. Parents and schoolmasters found that the pleasures they had derived from inflicting punishment were being curtailed, especially when a theory of education grew up, which made it necessary to give priority to the child's welfare.

Unfortunately another change regarding the attitude of adults towards children took place. They invented a new child psychology and children were considered to be little devils once again. According to Freud's theory of the unconscious, children were far more wicked than they were in the theological sense in the past. The new child psychology propounds that in their unconscious minds children display a subtle tendency to entertain sinful thoughts and activities. Russell with his great love for children is rather reluctant to accept this Freudian abomination. He feels this may be an adult imaginative compensation for their loss of pleasure derived from inflicting corporal punishment on their wards.

Irrational admiration for the proletariat. Russell has shown how one by one the concepts and myths about the superior virtue of the oppressed nations, the poor, women and children have been proved to be entirely irrational and false. But in our present age it is the turn of the working classes or the proletariat to be credited with superior virtue. This admiration is but natural in this machine age with its dams, power-stations and aeroplanes. A careful scrutiny will convince us that this admiration is also as baseless as was the admiration for women's spirituality or children's innocence and divinity. It is atrocious to believe that bad nourishment, little education and unhealthy housing conditions can produce better people than are produced by healthy surroundings and environment. But the Socialists and Communists now find the proletariat amiable and credit them with superior virtue. Russell then remarks with sarcasm that children were idealized by Wordsworth and individualized by Freud, whereas Marx was the Wordsworth of the Proletariat and another Freud to undo him is still to come.

Transience of delusions of superior virtue. Russell finally tells us that our attribution of some sort of superior virtue to the oppressed is short-lived as well as unstable. The pity of the situation is that it is the oppressors who try to idealize their victims when they have a guilty conscience and when they feel insecure about their power. But there is no logic in their attitude—to have some virtue is really praiseworthy, and if they are virtuous when they are in subjection, that state must be continued to preserve their virtue. But this state of affairs cannot last long. Sooner or later the oppressed will turn the table against the oppressors by turning their own weapon against them. They will rightly argue that their superior virtue is a strong enough reason to give them an equal status with the ruling class. Russell rightly points out that when power has been equalized, it becomes absolutely clear to everybody that all the talk about superior virtue was baseless and was just an excuse by the ruling class to maintain its sway over the oppressed and the downtrodden.

Q. 10. Describe the prominent features of a modern-minded man as put forward by Russell.

Or

"Our age is the most parochial since Homer." How does Russell elucidate this remark?

Or

"A certain degree of isolation both in space and time is essential to generate the independence required for the most important work." Discuss, in detail, how Russell comes to this conclusion.

Or

Examine critically the ideas contained in Russell's essay 'On Being Modern-Minded.'

Ans. **Introduction: ours is the most parochial age.** At the very beginning of his essay 'On Being Modern-Minded' Russell tells us that ours is the most parochial or narrow-minded age in the history of mankind. But he adds that it is in the chronological sense that we are parochial, not in the geographical sense. The new and fashionable catchwords have cast such a spell on modern men that they have severed all their links with the past. And so we find that old Praha is now Prague and Nijni-Novgorod has become Gorky. People want to translate everything into the language of Marx and of Freud to make it interesting. And then they hold a very high opinion about their intellectual acumen and originality and so ideas and achievements of the past are of very little importance to them. This desire to be modern and progressive is not new to our age only. It has existed to a fairly good extent in all periods. The Renaissance had a contempt for the achievements of the Gothic centuries and the Romantic Movement despised the age of heroic couples, that is the age of Pope and Dryden. But the intellectuals of these periods had cherished some regard for the achievements of our forefathers in the realm of art and literature. Indeed the Romantic Movement revived the Middle Ages. But the contempt for the past seems to be complete now. Since the 1914-18 war especially it has become fashionable to ignore the past *en bloc*. Then the belief that fashion alone should dominate thought makes thought unnecessary. By learning the correct use of such words as Oedipus complex, sadism, bourgeois, etc. one can become a brilliant writer or talker in our age. So there is no need to bother about the intellectual achievements of the past.

Main characteristics of modern-minded men. Firstly the modern-minded man has a profound belief in the intellectual superiority of his age. But then he is very modest about his own personal powers. His highest ambition is to think and to say and to feel ahead of others, just to be slightly ahead of others in point of time. Hence he does not like to think better or say something which reveals more insight. For the sake of popular admiration he suppresses his own individuality or originality. A mentally solitary life, like that of Copernicus, or Spinoza, or Milton is of no significance to modern man. He alsways avoids setting himself up as an independent judge and evades offering any independent opinion, as the powerful agencies of publicity will go against him.

The reasons for suspension of independent thinking and judgement. The modern man's keen desire to earn name and fame through the powerful agencies of publicity and the prospect of earning easy money turn him away from the right path. So he subordinates his judgement to the general opinion. Another important factor contributing to this result is rapid progress in almost every realm of science and knowledge. Now everyone apprehends that the independent results achieved by an individual due to his original ideas are likely to be superseded in no time. Newton was superseded by Einstein and Einstein is also now regarded by many as antiquated. Then again the emotional tone of our present-day world is also changing rapidly due to wars, depressions, and revolutions pursuing each other in quick succession. So a man is unable to stand alone with his independent ideas. Public events overshadow his private life more forcibly than in the past. Only a man with very firm and extraordinary personal convictions can stand against the current of his times these days.

A deeper cause—loss of faith in God and in established ideals. This change of attitude of modern man has a deep cause. This is the loss of faith in God and in some other great ideals. In the past the artists, philosophers and even the scientists worked, feeling themselves to be in the service of God. They all felt that they were serving God's purpose by following their own convictions. Hence they had a very good reason for doing what they considered to be their best without caring in the least for any popular applause. Milton's ideal was to exercise 'that one talent which is death to hide.' But with the progress of knowledge this firm faith in God began to dwindle at a great pace. In the nineteenth century however this belief was happily replaced by the great ideas of the True, the Good and the Beautiful by those who had lost faith in God. But unfortunately in our age these great concepts have been demolished by the modern pragmatists and historians of morals. The former explains that Truth is what it pays to believe and the latter have reduced the good to a matter of tribal custom. The modern artists abolished the ideal of beauty in a revolt against the sugary insipidity of a philistine epoch. The sad consequence of all this is that the individual is now left without any inner defence against social pressure.

Russell's suggestions. According to Russell, the movement towards subjectivity has completely dominated modern man and it has now gone too far. This movement began with Luther and Descartes as an assertion of the individual. It is also to be noted that subjectivity of truth is a hasty doctrine. Men lived by one kind of illusion, and when they lost it they fell prey to another. We are to remember that it is not by old errors that a new error can be combated. Russell recommends detachment and objectivity, both in thought and feeling, even if we give up our traditional beliefs. According to him, a certain degree of isolation both in space and time is very much needed to generate the independence required for the most important work. And he concludes by asserting : "We are suffering not from the decay of theological beliefs but from the loss of solitude."

Conclusion. In this fine essay Russell has correctly pointed out that the modern age is the most parochial or narrow-minded age in the history of mankind. He has logically analysed the main characteristics of the modern-minded man. He has told us quite convincingly in his own critical way how the lure of flimsy fashion, easily earned money, cheap popularity and rapidity of progress have deprived the modern man of his originality of thought and independence of judgement, leaving him without any inner defence against social pressure. Finally the modern man must accept his just and correct recommendation : "A certain degree of isolation both in space and time is essential to generate the independence required for the most important work; there must be something which is felt to be of more importance than the admiration of the contemporary crowd."

Q. 11. "Man is a rational animal." What arguments does Russell offer against this contention in his essay 'An Outline of Intellectual Rubbish'?

Or

Give a critical analysis of the ideas that Russell has put forth in his essay 'An Outline of Intellectual Rubbish'.

Ans. **Man is in fact not rational :** Man is almost universally accepted to be a rational animal. Probably Aristotle was the first great man to proclaim it explicitly. According to him, man has intellect, and it is by virtue of the intellect that man is a rational animal. But unfortunately after the lapse of so many centuries after Aristotle, Bertrand Russell can hardly gather any evidence in favour of this statement. Even in this advanced modern age of ours Russell finds superstition, cruelty and persecution increasing by leaps and bounds. Even great nations are found to be led astray by preachers of bombastic nonsense in this age of science. People are still carried away by superstitions and follow ideas and customs without caring for any rational basis for them. And the irrational ideas, beliefs and superstitions constitute the intellectual rubbish of human beings. Then Russell takes up one by one the great statesmen, philosophers, men of letters and men of religion of all ages and points out how they too have failed to be rational in their outlook and ideas which are nothing but intellectual rubbish.

Irrationality of men of religion or clergymen. First of all Russell takes up the clergymen and exposes their superstitious beliefs and most irrational ideas in the Ages of Faith when they had everything their own way. People were taught to believe in miracles performed by saints and in wizardry perpetrated by devils and black magicians. They encouraged men to burn thousands of witches at the stake. Very little was known scientifically about the world. And people were made to believe that earthquakes, floods and pestilence took place just to punish men for their sins. They also propagated many other irrational beliefs, one of them being that the devil would take possession of the body of a person who forgot to make the sign of the cross before each mouthful.

Irrationality of the clergy even after the rise of science. Strangely enough during the first four centuries when the growth of science gradually taught men how to acquire knowledge of the ways of nature, the clergy were caught in a losing battle against scientific knowledge and theories and inventions. When Benjamin Franklin invented the lightning-rod, clergymen from almost all parts of the world condemned it as an impious attempt to defeat the will of God who sent lightning to punish the sinners for their sins. And when there was a severe earthquake in Massachussets, it was perceived to be due to God's wrath for erecting those iron rods. Even a great man like Mahatma Gandhi propagated the same view when there were some severe earthquakes in India.

Some other irrational views and ideas of the clergy. We can discover such intellectual rubbish in many views and ideas of the clergy-men. Even today many people continue to believe in such irrational ideas. For example during the 1914-18 War when England was not faring well, a Scottish clergyman opined that it was so because potatoes had been planted on the Sabbath. Then according to these men of the church even God's mercy seems to be selective. He protects some and destroys some others according to some plan best known to the clergymen. Then again the conception of sin as upheld by the clergy is strange and puzzling. A bill for legalizing euthanasia or mercy killing in cases of painful and incurable diseases could not be passed due to the objection of the Archbishop of Canterbury. According to him if the patient's consent is taken, as of course it should be, it will mean desire to commit suicide which is a sin. The Pope once opined that ill-treating animals is not sinful as they have no soul. The belief in the resurrection of the body, the curious objection to cremation, the opposition to the dissection of dead bodies—all are absolutely irrational. Not very long ago when a French surgeon in China wanted corpses for dissection, they were shocked, but wanted to supply live criminals for the purpose. Finally the views of these men of Church regarding marriage, women and sexual intercourse are unrealistic and irrational. Persons who divorce and remarry are guilty of adultery in the sight of God. Unfortunately two great men of modern times, Tolstoy and Gandhi, also laid down that all sexual intercourse is wicked. Then there are logical difficulties in the notion of sin based on religion that tells us that disobedience to God's commands is sin. But religion also tells us that God is all-powerful. If He is really omnipotent then how can one commit any sin against His will? So the notion of sin and punishment becomes quite confusing.

Basis of modern morals—Russell is correct in his criticism. Russell finds that modern morals are a mixture of elements. On the one hand, they follow rational percepts as how to live together peaceably in a society. On the other hand, they are also guided by superstitions and taboos derived from religious and sacred books. Modern man is aware of what science has done in the way of bringing new knowledge and altering conditions of social life. But it is odd and sad that he continues to believe in the most irrational taboos and ancient superstitions which have been proved to be wrong scientifically.

We can now safely assert that Russell's criticism of clergymen and people's blind faith in most of their preachings is correct and fully justified. His rational arguments based on scientific truths fully convince us that the control of men of religion has been harmful. Even modern men are not free from blind and superstitious ideas. Russell is justified when he asserts that as soon as men abandon their own reason, and are content to rely upon authority, there is no end to their troubles.

Other irrational beliefs from various causes. There are many other irrational beliefs whose causes cannot be defended reasonably. First we have self-importance, individual or generic. A man better-off than his neighbour feels superior. If a man lives in a city with better amenities than in another, he considers his city much superior to the other. Then comes the country. An Englishman with pride in his Shakespeare, Milton or Newton or Darwin thinks how immeasurably his country surpasses all others. A Frenchman has similar pride in his country that has led the world in culture, fashion, and cookery. Then comes the glorification of Man himself. Man considers himself to be superior to all other animals and creatures, considering himself to be the climax of creation and of the greatest importance in the universe of created beings. This vain idea took a new form after the theory of evolution was scientifically established. People have started believing that God was preparing for the great climax through millions of years and at last, in the fulness of time, He produced man and in all probablity in His own image. But the question is whether God also created such specimens as Nero, Caligula, Hitler and Mussolini in His own image. Russell quite ironically points out that, in spite of this glorification of Man by man, we forget that this planet is almost certainly temporary and, as James Jeans prophesies, a time will come when the sun will burst and all the planets will be turned into gas leaving no trace of these so-called glorious beings. Hence this glorification can never get any support from a rational scientific view of the universe.

Love of the marvellous—another source of false belief. Another source of false belief is love of the marvellous. This leads to exaggeration and falsification of facts. Falsification is still more true of rumours. The news about some exciting incident gets exaggerated when it passes from one to another. Even during the 1914-18 Great War people of England believed in the rumours that 'angels of Mons', a Belgian town, encouraged the British troops and that the Russian troops had passed through England on the way to the Western Front. Every powerful emotion has its own myth-making tendency. This myth-making faculty leads to cruelty. For example, ever since the Middle Ages Jews have been accused of practising ritual murders without an iota of evidence and they have been cruelly tortured. In modern times the Nazis accepted this myth without question. Then there is a theory that insanity is due to possession by the devil; so to beat the madman black and blue was considered the best way to make the devil fly away from him in pain. There were and still are many futile treatments based purely on the myths and false beliefs.

Fallacies about race and blood. Even in modern times there are so many absolutely irrational beliefs regarding superiority of race and blood. Unfortunately such beliefs are as old as civilization in some form or other. In our present day civilization, Nazis embodied such theories in their official creed. The white man's idea that his blood is superior to that of a Negro is just a myth that physiologists have exploded scientifically. In the matter of race too there are several false beliefs in different societies. In the past, men like Aristotle and Plato considered Greeks infinitely superior to Barbarians who were fit only to be their slaves. A white man's idea is that by nature he is superior to men of other colours. But in Japan men think that yellow is the best colour. Until very recently, it was universally believed that men are born with more intelligence than women. There is also a special absurdity in applying racial theories to the various populations of Europe, as there is not any such thing as a pure race in Europe. Russell is absolutely correct in his criticism of all such theories which have been proved false. The whole conception of superior blood or race is nothing but a myth. And such myths have been created by the blind self-esteem of the holders of power.

Superstitions in economic sphere—importance of gold and precious stones. Russell then points out that there are many superstitions in the economic spheres too. People do not value gold simply for its rarity, but because gold and gems were originally valued on account of their supposed magical properties. Sadly enough this belief still exists among the sort of men who are called practical. The mistakes of governments in modern times seem to prove it—for example, the Allies after their victory over Germany in the 1914-18. War demanded to be paid in money rather than in goods. This superstition is slowly dying out, but we note that in India even educated people believe that special stones like ruby, diamond or emerald may bring good luck to the wearer of these stones.

Intellectual rubbish in the sphere of politics—inevitability of war. In the sphere of politics we find another irrational belief that says that human nature cannot be changed. It means that all men everywhere will always continue to behave as they do in their home town. But a little anthropology will prove this to be false. Truly speaking, adult human nature is extremely variable. It can be moulded by education. By diet and training, people can be made cruel or kind, masterful or slavish.

And ever since the rise of large states the power of government over men's ideas and beliefs has become very great. It is vastly greater in the present day. Before the last great World War some nations inculcated such false beliefs in their people that they became fanatical lunatics. Now Russell argues that if a nation by their own method of education can produce a population of fanatical lunatics, then a powerful and good government can surely educate its people in such a way that they turn out to be sane and reasonable. So the doctrine—that human nature cannot be changed and hence there will always be wars—absolutely falls flat. Modern psychology has also established the truth of the above point of view.

Wrong notion of punishments for abnormalities. There has always been a false belief that wrong-doing can be remedied through punishments. We do not understand that punishment generally aggravates troubles, specially in abnormal cases. It is likely to prevent crimes that are sane in origin. It cannot prevent crimes which are the outcome of some psychological abnormality. The irrationality of such a belief in punishment for all sorts of crime has been proved by medical men and psychologists. Punishment may reform an ordinary thief, but it can never reform a kleptomaniac, that is one who steals due to some psychological abnormality and not due to needs or other ordinary reason. Hence Russell points out that it was really unwise on the part of the Allies to be so vindictive and severe towards the Germans after the First World War for their aggressiveness. We ought to have regarded the rank and file of the Nazis as we regard lunatics. It must be remembered that so long as the Germans hate the rest of mankind it will be hardly possible to establish peace in our world.

A few more absurd beliefs. Russell then mentions a few more absurd beliefs held by modern men. To men of our age the beliefs of savages, or the ancient Babylonians and Egyptians seem to be absurd, but certain beliefs entertained by modern men are equally foolish and absurd. People still have beliefs about lucky and unlucky days and unlucky numbers. They still raise strange objections against birth control. The absolute belief in nature and what is natural is a source of many errors for many people. They won't understand that often aids to nature are desirable. Thus vaccination was objected to as unnatural. The most common objection to birth control is that it is against nature. Women too have been the victims of our irrational beliefs through ages. Almost everybody allows himself or herself some unjustifiable generalisation on the subject of women. Sometimes, they are considered to be silly, sometimes saints and often temptresses. But Russell distrusts all generalisations about women, favourable and unfavourable. Lastly he speaks of generalisations about national characteristics without any rational basis, for example, Germans until 1870 were thought of as a nation of spectacled professors and most Americans thought of Frenchmen as perpetually engaged in amorous intrigue.

Conclusion. Bertrand Russell has very clearly shown us how modern men still entertain strange and irrational ideas which may be called intellectual rubbish. These can never be explained with any logic or scientific reasoning. With his vast knowledge and sound reasoning Russell convinces us that there is neither sense nor substance in such false ideas and superstitious beliefs and that, on the other hand, most of such ideas and beliefs lead to unjustifiable cruelty and persecution.

Q. 12. What remedies for avoidance of false and foolish opinions does Russell prescribe in his essay 'An Outline of Intellectual Rubbish'?

Or

"To avoid the various foolish operations to which mankind are prone, no superhuman genius is required. A few simple rules will keep you, not from all error, but from silly error." What does Russell mean here? Analyse and comment on the simple rules suggested by him.

Ans. **Introduction.** In his essay 'An Outline of Intellectual Rubbish', Russell has not only pointed out the false beliefs of men, but has also suggested possible remedies to avoid such fallacy.

To settle a matter by personal observation. Russell tells us that although we are prone to irrational views and superstitions, it is not impossible to avoid them by following some simple rules. Firstly we can avoid some foolish views if we have recourse to personal observation. Even a great man like Aristotle made a mistake when he asserted that women had fewer teeth than men. He could have avoided this mistake by simply counting the teeth of his own wife. To think that we know, when in fact we don't know, is a fatal mistake. Hence there is the need of personal observation. Great controversies arise about matters if there is no good evidence either way. In such cases, if an opinion contrary to our own makes us angry, we should be on our guard; we will probably find, on examination, that our belief is going beyond what the evidence warrants.

An awareness of opinion in different social circles. Another way of avoiding certain kind of dogmatism is to become aware of opinions held in different social circles. This can be best done by travelling in different lands to know the opinions of people outside our own social circle. If a person is unable to travel he may freely discuss matters with people, specially those with whom he disagrees, or he may read a newspaper belonging to a party that is not his. If their opinion seems to be perverse and wicked to the person, he should note that both parties may be right,but both cannot be wrong, whereas he may be wrong. Such reflection will surely make him cautious in his opinion thereby making him less dogmatic in his views.

Imaginary dialogue with a person with a different bias. If a person is imaginative, he may have an imaginary argument with a person having a different bias or opinion. This method has one great advantage in that, unlike actual conversation, there is no limitation of time and space. Mahatma Gandhi condemned railways and steamboats and machinery. A man belonging to western countries will hardly find a person supporting the Mahatma's view. So he can enter into an imaginary conversation with the Mahatma to find out if there is any truth in his arguments against use of machinery. This may help a person to realize the possible reasonableness of a hypothetical opponent.

To be cautious of opinions that flatter our self-esteem. Russell points out that a majority of men and women are firmly convinced of the superior excellence of their own sex. If a man says that most poets and men of science are male, a woman retorts so are most criminals. People from a particular country are sure that their own nation is superior to all others. It is false self-esteem which is responsible for these rigid postures. Russell suggests that the only way to deal with such general human conceit is to realize that man is a brief episode in the life of a tiny planet in a little corner of our universe and that in other parts of the vast cosmos there may be beings much more superior to human beings.

To overcome fear. According to Russell, fear is one of the most important sources of error and false beliefs. We find it sometimes operating directly in people inventing rumours of disaster in war-time, or imagining objects of terror, such as ghosts. Sometimes it operates indirectly by creating belief in something comforting, such as heaven for ourselves and hell for our enemies. Fear has various forms—fear of death, fear of the unknown, fear of the herd, and the fear that comes to those who conceal from themselves their more specific terrors. Unless one admits one's own fears and guards oneself against their myth-making power, it is not possible even to hope to think truly and clearly about matters of great importance. Fear can be avoided in two ways. We can persuade ourselves that we are immune from danger, or we can develop sheer courage. The latter is too difficult for people in general. Hence, the first method has always been popular. Primitive magic through the ages has helped mankind through the use of talismans, spells, or incantations to dispel fear. Then came the belief in future and this sought more effective ways of fighting fear. Orthodox Christianity laid down very definite rules for salvation by following which a man was certain to go to heaven. Marcus Aurelius and Spinoza also propounded their doctrines to enable mankind to escape from fear. But some of their doctrines were based upon false belief. They propagated that our true good consists in indifference to our mundane affairs. Whatever may be the case, it must be remembered that almost everybody becomes superstitious under the influence of fear for it robs people of their rationality. Fear makes them cruel. Under the influence of fear sailors threw Jonah overboard; at the time of the Tokyo earthquake the Japanese massacred the Koreans, and the Carthegians threw their children into fire to propitiate Moloch. So Russell is totally justified when he firmly asserts: "To conquer fear is the beginning of wisdom, in the pursuit of truth as in the endeavour after a worthy manner of life."

Q. 13. What, according to Russell, are the main functions of a teacher ? What are the difficulties faced by a teacher in performing his functions and how can they be removed?

Or

"The teacher, like the artist, the philosopher, and the man of letters, can only perform his work adequately if he feels himself to be an individual directed by an inner creative impulse, not dominated and fettered by an outside authority." Discuss

Or

Analyse and comment on the ideas expressed by Russell in his essay 'The Functions of a Teacher.'

Ans. **Teacher's position in the past and in recent times.** The profession of teaching has a great and honourable tradition. In the past a teacher was expected to be a man of exceptional knowledge and there was hardly any control over his thoughts and ideas. The death of Socrates and imprisonment of Plato were exceptions. To fulfil his functions properly a teacher must have a feeling of intellectual independence so that he can instil into his students what he can of knowledge and reasonableness. In ancient days he performed this task, more or less, unhampered. But in the Middle Ages when the Church became all-powerful, there was interference and, as a result, little progress either intellectual or social. With the Renaissance teacher's freedom was restored. But in our more highly organized present-day world a new problem has cropped up. The State has undertaken the task of educating everybody some way or other. As a result the teachers have become civil servants and are obliged to carry out the instructions of the "authority" who have hardly any experience of dealing with children.

State-control very often involves certain dangers which were seen in their full magnitude in Nazi Germany and are still seen to a great extent in Russia. Where such things prevail nobody is allowed to teach unless he subscribes to a dogmatic creed. The result is that in such states young students are bound to become fanatical bigots and dogmatists. And the most deplorable outcome of this sort of education is the decay of cultural internationalism. Hence, those who believe in liberty of thought must be on the alert to protect teachers from such intellectual bondage.

To impart definite uncontroversial information to students. First of all we must have a clear conception of the services which teachers can be expected to perform for the nation or community. To begin with one of the most important functions of a teacher is to impart definite uncontroversial information to the students placed under his charge. It is the basis upon which the other functions are built. It has great value in a technical and complex civilization such as ours, as we require a sufficient number of men possessing technical skill in a modern community. Hence we must have universal compulsory education. But unfortunately governments very often want to instil beliefs on controversial matters in order to produce habits of mind to suit their purpose. Then there is a widespread belief that uniformity of opinion and suppression of liberty make a nation strong and invincible. But Russell points out that insistence upon a narrow-minded doctrinal uniformity has brought about the ruin of many a country. Dogmatists are always a source of great misfortune for our civilization, specially if they are divided into two camps. One may make civilization static and the other may ruin it completely. So it is the duty of a good and honest teacher to provide an effective safeguard against both the rival dogmatic groups. It must be carefully noted that organized party spirit is one of the greatest dangers of our time. This in the form of nationalism leads to war and in other forms leads to civil war. Men in authority would always endeavour to crush those who differ with them. But the teacher should never try to flatter the prejudices of the mob or the officials. A teacher's duty would be to rise above all controversies into a region of dispassionate scientific investigation and then to instil into the young the habit of impartial inquiry. This would help them to judge issues on merit without accepting *ex parte* statements at their face value.

Teachers as the guardians of civilisation by knowing what it means. Russell feels that just to mitigate the heat of current controversies is not the main job of a teacher. They should consider themselves the guardians of civilization. Knowing well what civilization is, they should impart the civilized attitude to their pupils. According to Russell, civilization in its true sense is a matter partly of knowledge, partly of emotion. It is a thing of the mind, not of material adjuncts to the physical side of our living. Russell suggests that as far as knowledge is concerned human beings should be aware of the minuteness of themselves and their immediate environment in relation to the world in time and space. A man should consider his own country to have the catholicity to accept that all have an equal right to live and think and feel in their own way. Then on the side of the emotions, a very similar enlargement from the purely personal is needed. A man should try to appreciate and absorb the thoughts and ideas of great lovers of mankind, the great intellectuals and great artists, the creators of beauty. The civilized man aims at understanding the point of view of others, he should not decry another's views. And this should always be in the mind and heart of teachers—then and only then would they be able to convey it in their teaching to the young hearts in their care.

Russell is, no doubt, just and sincere in his argument that teachers should be the guardians of civilization. But it seems to be rather utopian to expect so much from the teachers of our age. The intellectual and emotional standards of our teachers are far from satisfactory. The teachers themselves are first required to uplift themselves to undertake such noble tasks.

Feeling of warm affection for pupils—to lead to the pursuit of happiness. A worthy teacher must have feelings of warm affection towards the taught and a very sincere desire to impart to them the right type of knowledge without any propagandist attitude. The propagandists never want their pupils to have a clear and impartial view of things or develop the ability to choose freely a purpose which to them appears of value. They are likely to thwart the natural growth of the young souls and thus destroy in them all generous vigour, replacing it by envy, destructiveness, and cruelty. Most cruelty results from thwarting what is good in the early years. Repressive and persecuting passions are really not an inevitable part of human nature, but they are generally the outcome of some kind of unhappiness. So it should be the aim of a good and sympathetic teacher to open vistas before his young pupils showing them the possibility of activities that will be as delightful as they are useful. And these will let loose their kind impulses and prevent the growth of a desire to rob others of the joy and happiness that they have missed. So the teacher should make every endeavour to train children to grow up free from psychological misfortunes.

Hurdles in the way of teachers. Russell expresses his deep concern for the hurdles and difficulties with which the path of right-minded teachers is beset these days. Firstly most of the teachers are overworked and are forced to prepare their wards simply for examination. Thus they get no time and opportunity to give them a liberalising mental training. The overworked and harrassed teachers cannot remain in touch with the recent work in their subjects and so fail to inspire their students with a sense of intellectual delight. Teachers often face another grave difficulty. In some countries some opinions are recognized as correct and others as dangerous. When the teachers' opinions are at variance with the recognized ones they are almost compelled to keep silent about their own idea. As a result the inquiring pupils have to go too often outside the classroom to find out the truth.

Never to conceal the truth. Another must for a conscientious teacher is not to conceal the truth in any way in the course of his teaching. Virtue produced by guarded ignorance is so frail that it fails at the very first touch of reality. The student should be guided to admire and appreciate people who really deserve admiration. But they should never be taught to admire rogues, however powerful they may be, by concealing their misdeeds. Some people are afraid that the knowledge of things as they are will lead to cynicism. But the young should be guided gradually and scientifically. It is morally indefensible to tell lies to the young. Unfortunately in many a country great rogues and scoundrels are transformed into great men by means of false publicity and propaganda by the parties in power.

To produce a spirit of tolerance: Another very important function of a teacher is to produce in his pupils a spirit of tolerance that springs from a desire to understand those who are different from ourselves. This spirit is essential for the survival of democracy. We know that savages and ants put strangers to death. It is quite a natural human impulse to view with horror all manners and customs which are different from ours. This kind of ignorant intolerance is the antithesis of a civilized outlook and spells grave danger for the human race. Unfortunately, almost in every country narrow nationalistic feeling is encouraged at the cost of a broader international outlook. It should be the bounden duty of a teacher to broaden the outlook of young pupils by instilling in them a spirit of tolerance so that they may never become victims of collective hysteria, the most mad and cruel of all human emotions.

Teachers not to blame—Russell's suggestions for improving the teacher's status. In the end Russell opines that teachers can hardly be blamed for anomalies in the realm of education in the modern world. Teachers are not free to teach as they think proper, though they are the persons who know most intimately the needs of the young, So they should be given more freedom to decide what to teach and how to teach it. They should have more independence from the interference of bureaucrats and bigots. The teacher should be treated as a kind of medical man and be given the necessary freedom to cure his patient of childishness. According to Russell, the teacher can be likened to an artist or a philosopher or a man of letters who can rightly perform his work when inspired by an inner creative impulse. He would be baffled if he is dominated and fettered by an outside authority.

Russell as a moralist as well as internationalist. Russell's views and wise suggestions in this essay, 'The Functions of a Teacher', are undoubtedly very instructive and illuminating. Here we find Russell in the role of a great moralist. He has rightly told us that the teachers are the real guardians of human civilization. Unless the teacher is given his proper status and freedom our civilization will be in jeopardy. In this essay we find that the well-being of mankind is his most cherished ideal. That is why he looks upon teachers as the saviours of the human civilization, specially as the turbulence of our times is inimical to the fine flower of culture. According to Russell, "the only way to prevent totalitarianism in our highly organized world is to secure a certain degree of independence for bodies performing useful public work, and among such bodies teachers deserve a foremost place."

Q. 14. Trace, after Russell, the ideas that have helped mankind.

Or

Give a critical analysis of Russell's 'Ideas That Have Helped Mankind".

Or

How does Russell relate his idea of a world government to his discussion of ideas that have helped mankind?

Ans. **Introduction.** Bertrand Russell, an erudite scholar and one of the greatest thinkers of the present age, traces in the essay 'Ideas That Have Helped Mankind' the growth and impact of the most significant ideas that have helped mankind. In this short essay Russell has mentioned most of the important ideas that have come down to us beginning from the pre-historic days. In his introductory remarks he says that man, in certain respects, has become progressively less like animals, particularly in two respects. Firstly, acquired skills, as opposed to congenital, play a continually increasing part in human affairs. Secondly, man's forethought more and more dominates his impulse. But his forethought has not proved to be a source of happiness for Man. However his intelligence has certainly enabled man to get a much greater variety of enjoyments than is open to animals. Russell concludes that whatever may be the case it is man's intellectual and moral qualities that really distinguish him from the brutes. Russell first takes up the helpful ideas developed in pre-historic days and then comes to the ideas that have proved helpful during our historic times. He then divides these ideas into two categories just for expediency: the ideas that contribute to knowledge and technique, and the ideas related to morals and politics.

Ideas that helped before the dawn of history. In the field of knowledge and technique the most important and difficult steps were taken during pre-historic times. And the first and foremost of them was language to help man on the march of civilization. This invention has helped mankind to hand down from generation to generation the inventions and discoveries gradually made. The next great step was the utilization of fire. In the beginning it might have helped primitive man to ward off wild animals and give him some warm comfort. But the long history of cookery also began with its invention. A further great step that has made life pleasanter and secure was the taming of animals, especially the cow and sheep, to domesticate them. An invention of even greater significance was that of agriculture, though it introduced in the beginning some bloodthirsty rites such as human sacrifice. And finally, one of the greatest inventions in prehistoric days was the art of writing. It has helped man to preserve his ideas and achievements for all time. All these great inventions and achievements of pre-historic times have proved to be of the greatest help to mankind for its progress and prosperity during the ages to come.

Amazing achievements during historic times—mathematics and astronomy: Coming to historic times Russell points out that the earliest important steps were taken in mathematics and astronomy. In this respect Babylonia was the pioneering centre in the time of antiquity. Later, in their footsteps followed Greeks, who made the most amazing progress in these fields. But mathematics to them was mostly a gentlemanly pursuit. It was only Archimedes, a great Greek mathematician, who foreshadowed the modern use of mathematics by inventing engines of war to be used against the Romans. Astronomy was also pursued by the Greeks but with no regard for practical utility. It was they who discovered the earth to be round and made a fairly accurate estimate of its size and also found out the ways of calculating the distance of the sun and moon. Aristarchus of Samos, a great astronomer, even evolved the complete Copernican hypothesis. In fact it is to the Greeks that we owe the ways of thinking and investigating that have ever since been found fruitful. The Greeks had even the conception of natural law and had also acquired the habit of expressing natural law in mathematical terms. But unfortunately, after the third century B.C. the Greeks fell back and there was hardly any progress in any field. It was only at the time of Renaissance that the achievements of the Greeks became known and this facilitated the rise of modern science.

Progress in scientific ideas in seventeenth century. Scientists in the seventeenth century made outstanding advances in the study of natural laws; the most prominent among them were Galileo, Descartes, Newton, and Leibniz. Their concepts were the key to many a secret of nature. In fact, modern technique in war and industry, except the atomic bomb, is still wholly based on a type of dynamics that was developed out of the principles of Galileo and Newton. The first of these great principles was the law of inertia established by Galileo. This law unified the principles governing the earth and other celestial bodies. The law states that any body, once in motion, will continue to move as it is moving in the same straight line, and with the same velocity. This great law put an end to all misconceptions regarding the motion of the earth and other heavenly bodies. It dealt a death blow to all ethical or aesthetic bias by laying the foundations of the purely materialistic physics. Every bias of this type had to be discarded by seventeenth century astronomy also. To the Greeks the sun and moon and the planets seemed to be Gods. But Copernicus proved them to be absolutely wrong, by establishing that the earth is not the centre of the universe and that man is not probably the supreme purpose of the Creator.

Challenging ideas from the seventeenth century onwards. Later in the nineteenth century it was geology and Darwin's doctrine of evolution that dealt a mortal blow to the old and orthodox beliefs of common people in general and British men of science in particular. His theory did away with many religious and ethical superstitions regarding the unique position of man in this universe and his everlasting soul. Man's grand conception about his soul was proved to be absolutely useless as far as its role as a discoverable causal law was concerned. For example there are many kinds of experimental methods of determining how men and animals behave under different circumstances. Even the conception of sin has been proved to be quite unscientific. Russell here mentions that by understanding the science of human behaviour our governments are in a position to produce either a population of sane and sensible people or turn mankind into a rabble of mutually ferocious bigots and lunatics.

The second kind of ideas—the importance of moral and political ideas: Now Russell comes to the second kind of idea that has helped or may in time help mankind. By this he means the moral as opposed to the technical ideas. According to Russell, we have made a lot of progress as regards technical and scientific ideas and so have acquired increased command over the forces of nature. But sadly enough we have made very little progress in the sphere of morals. And if our scientific and technical achievements are not properly controlled by our moral and political ideas, they are likely to b[illegible] cause of ruin and destruction to the human race, particularly after t[illegible] ention of atomic and hydrogen bombs. Man is a strange amalgam of angel and devil. On the one hand, he can rise to great spiritual, moral and aesthetic heights, on the other hand, he can also be carried away by the impulses of greed, cruelty and overweening pride. And these evil passions have been the cause of great disasters for mankind. So, without cultivating moral and ethical ideas man will never be able to derive full benefit from our technical ideas or scientific knowledge. In this connection Russell also mentions that our moral ideas often wait upon political developments. Russell then takes up three most important ideas in the second group—Fraternity, Equality and Liberty.

Fraternity or universal brotherhood. The concept of universal brotherhood of man has greatly helped mankind in the moral sphere. This ideal owed its first force to some political development. Alexander, after his conquest of the East, tried to propagate it in his own way. But it was the Stoics of Greece who invented this conception of the brotherhood of man. The Stoics preached that all men are children of Zeus and held that there were no distinctions between the Greeks and the Barbarians. The Buddhists and the Christians also preached the same ideal. Unfortunately, it seems as if these ennobling ideas have had little effect upon mankind, as Buddhism died out in India and the Christians have miserably failed to live up to their great ideals. However, the idea remained alive in every age and for the survival of our civilization man must keep alive this lofty idea of brotherhood of man.

Idea of equality. It may be noted that the watchwords of the French Revolution were Liberty, Equality and Fraternity and they have religious origins. Equality was a characteristic of the Orphic societies in ancient Greece. The Orphics believed in the transmigration of the soul. Hence they believed that a soul which in one life inhabits the body of a slave may, in another, inhabit that of a king. So it would be foolish to discriminate between a slave and a king. Even Plato was influenced by Orphic practices. This point of view passed over from Orphism into Stoicism, and then into Christianity. In the beginning its impact on society was negligible but slowly this lofty idea helped to diminish the inequalities in our social system.

Idea of liberty—liberty of the individual citizen. According to Russell, liberty as an ideal has had a chequered history from the days of ancient Spartans till the days of the Nazis. At different periods, different meanings have been imparted to it. But Russell ascribes only two serious meanings to it. First, it means the freedom of a nation from foreign domination; second it means the freedom of every citizen to pursue his legitimate vocation. But Russell asserts that each of these liberties in a well-ordered world is subject to some limitations.

Russell first takes up the idea of liberty of the individual citizen.

This kind of liberty first entered practical politics in the form of religious toleration. It came to be widely adopted in seventeenth century England after a prolonged and futile war between the Catholics and the Protestants. But the greatest of the theoretical advocates of liberty in that period was John Locke. He endeavoured to reconcile the maximum of individual liberty with the indispensable minimum of government control. Gradually free press, liberty of speech and freedom from arbitrary arrest came to be acknowledged during the nineteenth century, particularly among the western democracies. But Russell is pained to find these noble ideas losing their hold on the minds of men in our present-day world.

The ideas of law and government—Democracy. Russell next talks about two other great ideas in the political sphere—the ideas of law and government. To these ideas mankind owes a lot in the sphere of social organization. Russell defines government as a concentration of the collective forces of a community in a certain organization. This concentration of forces is, on the one hand, able to control individual citizens and, on the other, resist interference from foreign states. Government is more fundamental compared with law as it can exist without law but there cannot be law without government. But unfortunately wherever governments have acquired much power with a view to resisting aggression from outside, they have used it to further their private interests at the expense of the citizens. In the past, autocratic kings misused this political power and, in the present, totalitarian states are doing the same thing. Hence Russell justly points out that democratic form of government is the right device for reconciling government with individual liberty. The most important thing about democracy is that it makes men's tenure in power temporary by making it dependent upon popular approval. Thus it can successfully prevent the blatant abuse of power. Furthermore, democracy ensures freedom of speech, freedom of press and religious freedom and prevents citizens from being punished except by due process of law. It also ensures freedom of economic enterprise.

Idea of international government. Russell has already defined government as a concentration of the collective forces of a community in a certain organization. From this he now comes to the idea of concentration of the collective forces not of one community but more or less of all communities or nations of the world in a particular organization that is a World Government. According to him, an international government is no less important to mankind than a national government, especially after man's great achievements in the realm of science and technology. Modern technique has brought mankind face to face with a new crisis, particularly after the invention of nuclear and other highly destructive weapons of war that are capable of wiping out human civilization in a matter of days. So man is now faced with two alternatives—either to go back to this primitive savage stage or to submit to an international government to ensure steady progress and prosperity in the days to come. Russell concludes by telling us that at present there are only two really independent states in the world, namely, Russia and America, as the recent developments have deprived the smaller states of any real independence. He suggests that all that is needed now to form a world government and save mankind from doom and disaster is the step from two independent states to one. And this should preferably be brought about by mutual agreement.

Conclusion. Russell has lucidly and convincingly discussed about the concepts of liberty, fraternity, equality, law, institution of government and democracy. He has correctly shown how these noble ideas and concepts have helped man in his march towards progress and prosperity. But as regards his favourite idea of an international government it does not seem feasible to us, although we share with him his concern and anxiety over the future of mankind. Firstly there are nearly two hundred sovereign states in the world and they would hardly like to surrender their own entity to an international government dominated by either Russia or America. Russell also did not live to see the rise of China as another great world power. It is also difficult to believe that the two super powers would ever agree to merge with each other to form one super-state by mutual agreement. Besides, Russell apprehended that within a decade or two there might be another world war bringing a catastrophic end to human civilization unless there was a world government to prevent it. But this has not happened so far. In fact the nuclear weapons can be a source of great fear complex and thus serve as a deterrent against war. We may reasonably expect that ultimately collective wisdom will prevail and man will definitely be able to find ways and means to prevent another devastating world war.

Q. 15. "It is now man that is man's worst enemy." In the light of this comment, enumerate the ideas that, according to Russell, have harmed mankind and comment upon them.

Or

Give an account of the ideas which, according to Russell, have harmed mankind.

Ans. **Introduction.** Bertrand Russell, one of the greatest intellectuals and thinkers of our age, has all through his life been a ruthless critic of irrational ideas and the superstitious beliefs of mankind. With his scathing criticism he has exposed the hollowness of such false concepts and ideas and has very correctly and convincingly established how they have harmed mankind from age to age. According to Russell, human misfortunes may be divided into two kinds: first, those inflicted by non-human environment, that is natural calamities and, second, those inflicted by other people. In the first category we may place floods and famines that often cause great harm and hardships for the people. But the misfortunes and hardships inflicted by men on men are far more dangerous and devastating. During the Second World War for six years the so-called advanced nations had been engaged in destroying one another. So Russell is undoubtedly justified when he says that now it is man that is man's worst enemy. And we should realise that the evils that men inflict on one another have their main source in evil passions rather than in ideas and beliefs. Those false and extremely harmful ideas and principles are in most cases cloaks for our evil passions. The burning of heretics in the past was considered righteous but the psychological motivation was that it gave sadistic pleasure to the people. The same sort of thing applies to war—it is a source of great sadistic pleasure to brutal and rigorous people. The same is true regarding the idea of the reformative power of corporal punishment.

Religious and superstitious ideas of the past. Russell draws our attention to irrational religious beliefs and superstitions that have done great disservice to humanity in the past. In ancient days the people believed that human sacrifice would be propitious for the growth of crops. They also considered complete annihilation of conquered races, including their cattle and sheep, to be a religious duty. The Christian saints firmly believed that the pagans and heretics were destined to undergo the most horrible tortures in hell after their death. The gloomy ascetics condemned all sensual pleasures of life. But the ascetic condemnation of sensual pleasures has not promoted kindliness or tolerance or any other virtue. In fact torturing himself a man often begins to feel that it gives him a right to torture others.

Present-day political dogmas. Men may not now believe so strongly in the fiercer forms of the early Christian dogmas, but the world has produced new and dangerous forms of the same psychological pattern. These ideas have now taken a nasty and menacing political bias. Before they succeeded in achieving power, the Nazis lived hard and laborious lives and even after their success their slogan was—'guns rather than butter'. So the Nazis, after depriving themselves of the sensual pleasures of life for long, thought it their right to torture others and this led to the brutal torture of Jews. According to Russell, the same mentality is to be found among earnest communists. They think luxury to be an evil and hard work to be the principal duty. They demand tremendous self-sacrifice from their followers to usher in the regime of peasants and workers. So we find that the Christian dogma that was a combination of asceticism and cruelty has taken new form these days. Such political dogmas have again divided mankind into saints and sinners. For the Nazis Germans were saints and all the Jews were sinners, and the sinners were to be liquidated. So the twin conception of sin and vindictive punishment is the cause of much of the trouble and suffering of mankind.

Sense of self-importance leading to belief in witchcraft. Another very harmful concept is our proneness to imagine our own good and evil fortune to be the outcome of other people's good or malevolent actions. This is due to our sense of self-importance. Hence when some misfortune visits us we are led to think that somebody wishes to do some harm to us out of hatred. It was this state of mind that gave rise to demonology, and the belief in witchcraft and black magic. In the past the belief in witchcraft afforded a most satisfying outlet for our emotion of self-righteous cruelty. With the sanction of the Bible thousands of suspected witches and black magicians were burnt at the stake. Unfortunately these same emotions find an outlet in fear of foreign nations in our present-day world.

Envy and its harmful consequences. Russell asserts that envy or jealousy is one of the greatest sources of some false notions and ideas. Mankind is very much prone to this weakness, so much so that it has caused a complete misconception of economic self-interest, both individual and national. We find that in an office the officials become jealous if a colleague of theirs gets quick promotions even by dint of his hard work. Russell gives us an instructive fable and shows how a baker and a butcher in a town ultimately ruined their own business hoping to become monopolists by ruining the business of other merchants. If we substitute for a town the world, and for individuals, nations, we will have a perfect picture of the economic policy universally pursued in the present day. Every nation has started believing that its economic interest is opposed to that of every other nation. Hence it believes that it must profit only if other nations are forced to be reduced to destitution. This is the psychological root of present-day economic nationalism which may lead to devastating wars bringing about a disastrous end to human civilization.

Passion of pride, cause of many false concepts. Another passion which is responsible for many false concepts and beliefs which are harmful, even politically, is pride. Men are swayed by the pride of nationality, race, class, sex or creed. Every country which is proud of its own nationality looks down upon other nations. Englishmen for a long time considered themselves to be superior to Frenchmen and had the false notion that one Englishman could cope with three Frenchmen. Then comes the pride of race. According to Russell, this is more harmful than national pride. Pride leads the whites to regard themselves as vastly superior to the coloured races. This passion has caused great tension and ill-feeling between the English and the Germans, the Jews and the Christians, the English and the Indians or the Chinese and so on. People do not understand that the belief of each nation in its own superiority and the pride of race have hardly any objective basis.

Next, Russell points out the baseless belief in the superiority of the male sex. Except for his superior muscle, man has no valid grounds to believe in any innate superiority over woman. Even scientists have tried to put forward some fallacious arguments to show that men are more intelligent, more rational, and of the same time less emotional. Unfortunately this tendency at men to dominate over the female sex has had some harmful effects. This male domination made the most intimate of human relations, that of marriage, one of master and slave. Next, Russell talks abou the pride of class, although it is rapidly disappearing these days. In Soviet Russia son of a proletarian has advantages over the son of a bourgeois. In America this pride of class persists although the white people there do not admit it openly. Some sort of snobbery still persists in England, but it is connected with education these days.

Russell then discusses about the pride of creed. This was more evident in the Middle Ages when the Christians and Mohammedans were absolutely pursuaded of each other's wickedness and inferiority. He concludes that all these different kinds of pride make people feel 'grand'. To be happy we require all kinds of encouragement and support to our self-esteem.

Special instruments of the Divine Will. Lastly, Russell speaks about one of the most harmful and dogmatic delusions of men as well as nations. It is that of imagining themselves special instruments of Divine Will. In the hoary past when the Israelites invaded the Promised Land they thought themselves to be carrying out a divine purpose. The Romans believed themselves to be destined by the gods for the conquest of the world. The Muslims believed fanatically that every soldier sacrificing his life in the battlefield for the true faith went straight to paradise. And Oliver Cromwell firmly believed that he was the divinely appointed instrument for suppressing Catholics. In our own day the earnest Marxists think that they are the chosen people to usher in an era of peace and happiness for mankind by establishing the dictatorship of the proletariat. Russell concludes by asserting that dogmatic belief in a divine mission is one of the many forms of certainty that has adversely affected the human race.

Russell's suggestions. As an antidote to all the above false beliefs and harmful ideas Russell has offered us some wise suggestions. He tells us that the most important thing, in public as well as in private life, is tolerance and kindliness without the presumption of a super-human power to forecast the future. Selfishness beyond a point, whether national or individual, is unwise. The defeat and downfall of Germany was due to this very thing. Russell thinks that only an international government can prevent world wars, as human civilization cannot survive more than one more great war. He also believes that democracy is the best possible device for maintaining the rule of law in place of the reign of arbitrary force. Finally he suggests that the present-day world is very much in need of two things. Firstly it needs organization—political organization for doing away with wars, economic organization to help men to work productively, and educational organization to generate some internationalism. Secondly, it greatly needs certain moral qualities to wean away man from his false faith and foolish dogmas and make him a sane, wise, tolerant and generous person. Only then can an era of peace and prosperity be ushered into our troubled and war-torn world.

Conclusion. This is one of the most illuminating and instructive essays from the pen of Bertrand Russell. With his analytical mind, vast knowledge and with his gifts of irony and satire he has exploded all myths and blind and harmful religious beliefs. Arguing sanely and logically he has convincingly told us how our passion of pride—pride of nationality, race, sex, class or creed—gives rise to false beliefs and how these baseless beliefs have caused great hardships and unprecedented trouble and tribulation to mankind. With his great gifts of satire and irony he has exposed and ridiculed those who imagine themselves to be special instruments of Divine Will. It is enough to quote just one sentence to reveal Russell's gift of satire: "It is good to know that God is on our side, but a little confusing when you find the enemy equally convinced of the opposite." Throughout the essay he shows himself to be a strong and stubborn opponent to all sorts of dogmatism. Finally he has given his wise and well thought-out suggestions for discarding all our false and dogmatic ideas—religious, political or economic—and for developing in us the moral qualities necessary to usher in an era of peace, progress and prosperity for the whole of mankind.

Q. 16. What are Russell's impressions of the eminent men he has met?

Or

"The quality of being unforgettable, or personally impres-

sive, has not, in my experience, been greatest in those who have made the greatest mark in history, except in a few cases". Elucidate.

Ans. **Introduction** : Russell came into personal contact with many famous personalities in the course of his life. Most of them, according to what he experienced, did not possess the personality or qualities required to leave an indelible mark on his mind. Queen Victoria he met at the age of two, and he cannot quite remember her impact on him. But he has been told that he showed a respectful attitude toward the Queen even at that tender age. Russell then goes on to sum up his impressions of the poets, philosophers, politicians and others with whom he came into personal contact.

Poets famous and infamous. Russell began to dislike Browning, the famous Victorian poet, even at the age of two. He has been told that at that age he showed his contempt of Browning by asking the poet to stop talking. Later during Browning's last years, Russell met him frequently, but he found nothing unforgettable about the poet. Browning appeared to be a pleasant, kindly man, a smart and domesticated person. But he seemed rather ordinary and did not fit Russell's concept of a poet with divine inspiration. On the other hand, Russell had a scornful hatred for Tennyson, because Tennyson, he felt, 'acted' the poet. Tennyson, during his strolls in the countryside, deliberately ignored the people he met to demonstrate the quality of absent-mindedness usually associated with a poet. This pretension, Russell feels, made Tennyson ridiculous. Russell, however, was much impressed by the German poet Ernest Toller, mainly for his ability to accept suffering impersonally. The other poet he met, Rupert Brooke, was handsome and lively, but he seemed rather insincere and flamboyant to Russell.

Philosophers of eminence and integrity. Among the eminent philosophers, William James seemed the most impressive to Russell. James had no artificiality about him and was not at all conscious of his greatness. He was dignified and was instantly respected by anyone who came across him. Russell remembers some philosophers who, though not very eminent in their field, impressed him through their intellectual honesty. Henry Sidgwick, Russell's teacher at Cambridge, belonged to this group. During his youth, while entering Cambridge, he had to put the obligatory signature to the Thirty-nine Articles of the Church of England, but later, during his days as a teacher, he came to realise that the system favoured the Protestants against the Catholics and hence was biased. He resigned in protest against the system, and his resignation led to a change in the law which ended the old theological restrictions. As a teacher Sidgwick was never dogmatic and was always prepared to take into account the views expressed by his students. This quality, Russell feels, made Sidgwick an impressive teacher.

Men of Science and intellectual honesty. Russell has particular respect for some men of science he has met. They impressed him with their inellect blended with childlike simplicity. These men had ability to disregard personal considerations and possessed an objective outlook. The great scientist, Albert Einstein, a combination of intellect and innocence, was a supreme example of this class of scientists.

Politicians' courage of conviction. Russell gives a somewhat detailed analysis of his impressions of two great political figures—Gladstone and Lenin. Russell has known many Prime Ministers; Gladstone was by far the most impressive. In the sphere of personality only Lenin could come near Gladstone. Gladstone, according to Russell, had a quick and piercing eye that could terrorize any person facing him into humble submission. Russell's grandmother, who was a very formidable woman, was seen to remain speechless with awe in the presence of Gladstone. Once when Gladstone came to their house to spend the week-end, Russell was left after dinner with Gladstone for a *tete-a-tete*. Russell was so awed by the imperious presence of Gladstone, that he could not utter a single word during that brief encounter. Russell has never again experienced that much of fear. Gladstone's political influence had its origin in his sound moral conviction. He believed that all his actions were prompted by noble purposes and he was always guided by conscience. He was also a controversial figure. Half the British nation thought that he was mad or wicked; the rest worshipped him as God.

Lenin, the great Russian leader, despite superficial differences, had many things in common with Gladstone. As regards the differences: Lenin was cruel which Gladstone was not; Lenin ignored tradition, Gladstone did not; Lenin was unscrupulous in politics whereas Gladstone insisted on the observance of certain rules in that sphere. As regards similarities, both believed that they were the human agents of a superhuman power. The actions of both these leaders were prompted by conviction and neither of them would have been prepared to gain personal power through a betrayal of their principles. Both of them, in pursuit of their faith, ventured into realms where they could only make themselves ridiculous.

Of these two great politicians, Gladstone certainly possessed a more imposing personality. To a stranger, Gladstone at first sight would appear to be a remarkable man whereas Lenin, in such a case, would seem a narrow-minded fanatic and a cynic. When Russell met Lenin, he narrated to Russell an incident involving the hanging of some rich peasants. Lenin's jubilant way of narrating it gave the impression that he was a bigot and inhuman. Russell feels that many of the qualities that make a good statesman were missing in Lenin and that he could never have been a success in peaceful times. Lenin succeeded because he could raise the hopes of victory among his defeated and confused countrymen, and could convince them, with calculated logic, that his gospel was the only means by which the world could be saved.

Others : impressive though not eminent. Russell has also been impressed by persons who were not eminent. He has found in many of them, a certain moral quality, a quality of self-forgetfulness, and a desire to pursue the truth. He can remember a rustic gardener, who, though illiterate, was the embodiment of simple goodness. He can never forget a person like E.D. Morel who gave up his job as a shipping clerk at Liverpool to fight against King Leopold's exploitation of the Congo. Morel utlimately succeeded in compelling reforms by rousing public opinion against the exploitation. Such selfless men rarely attain material prosperity, but they are loved and admired by the men who know them.

Q. 17. What is the background of Russell's 'Obituary'? How, according to Russell, would the Press portray him after his death?

Ans. The British Press had always been hostile to Russell for his views against war. When, during his visit to China, Russell fell ill and was in coma, the *Manchester Guardian*, in anticipation of his death, published an obituary for him. Russell wrote an obituary for himself some fifteen years later as a parody of the earlier obituary, and got it published in *The Listener* in 1937. His intention in the imaginary obituary was to show how the English Press had consistently endeavoured to minimise the importance of his contributions and to present him as an eccentric and irrational individual deserving general contempt.

Russell opines that the Press will continue to offer, even after his death, a distorted portrait of the author. The newspapers will, much to his dislike, describe him as a man of aristocratic birth. They will disregard his preference for being one of the masses and will refer to him as the grandson of a Prime Minister, thus depriving him of his individuality. Russell has no regard for public school education, but the Press will mention his lack of it as the reason for his so-called whimsical nature. Of course, the newspapers will have to admit, if only reluctantly, his success as a student, and his important contributions in the field of mathematics, but they will deprive him of some credit by arguing that his mathematical works showed want of insight and spiritual depth. Russell's inclination to adhere to logic will continue to be severely criticised by the Press.

Russell has always been against war. During World War I he pleaded for peace and wanted an early end of the war even if it meant conceding a victory to Germany. The British Press, that has always placed heroic exploits much above the ruinous consequences of wars, took a serious view of Russell's pacifist activities during the war and went on to describe Russell as an anti-national and eccentric individual. The resultant hostility towards him became so intense that he was imprisoned, and dispossessed of his lecturership at Trinity College. Perhaps this attitude of the British Press towards Russell will continue even after his death, writes Russell.

While offering a sketch of Russell's career the newspapers will refer to his brief visit to Russia followed by a longer one to China, where he enjoyed the still existing aroma of the 18th century rationalism. They will minimise the importance of his later works advocating socialism, educational reforms, and a flexible code of morals by pointing out that Russell, by writing them, was simply wasting his energy. They will also warn the readers of the uselessness of the supposedly obsolete rationalism that he wanted to preach through his historical writings.

Russell took no public part in World War II during which period he went to a neutral country. However, in private conversations he used to describe the participants in the war as homicidal maniacs. The Press will refer to his views on war and will remark that such an outlook has fortunately become rare today. It will further point out that Russell was wrong in assuming that those who had died in the war had died in vain.

The newspapers, despite accusing Russell of perversity, will have to admit that he was always governed by certain principles. However, they will try to take away much of credit due to Russell by declaring that those principles were 'curious'. As it is customary to mention in an obituary some virtues of the deceased, that Press will, perhaps reluctantly, point out that in private life he was a jovial conversationalist and a kind-hearted man. It will also inform the readers that Russell had many friends whom he had outlived, that he enjoyed good health till his death, and that he spent the last days of his life in isolation just as Milton did after the Restoration.

The piece is full of the typical satiric wit and humour of which Russell is capable.

V. MISCELLANEOUS

Q. 18. Would it be correct to describe Russell as the voice of eighteenth century enlightenment as well as a Puritan in some respects? Give your opinion.

Ans. Unpopular Essays is imbued by Russell's anti-dogmatism and liberal attitude. His stance is the very symbol of rationality. As a spokesman of Reason, the need to support one's arguments with rational thought and the firm discardance of the illogical, Russell indeed may be called a voice of eighteenth century enlightenment. It may be remembered that the eighteenth century marked a firm shift towards what may be called the 'scientific' age. Russell too is convinced of the efficacy of the scientific way of thinking.

However, having pointed out the closeness of the spirit of eighteenth century enlightenment and Russell's own rational attitude, one must add that Russell's enlightened mind goes far beyond the limits of the eighteenth century rationalists. Russell's rationality has a much broader and liberal base compared to the earlier thinkers. He did not eschew the importance or value of beauty, imagination and the emotions. His anti-dogmatic attitude would not allow him to adopt a rigid stand even in total and self-righteous support of reason alone. He merely demanded a rational approach to life, and consistency of thought. He was far ahead of the eighteenth century thinkers in his just support of the "oppressed" classes against exploitation on an illogical basis. Thus, he speaks up for equality of sexes, races, class and creed. He also went beyond the eighteenth century enlightenment in his advocacy of an 'international government', favouring total peace even at the cost of patriotism. Some of his ideas are thus too modern to be considered as an extension of eighteenth century enlightenment. If reason, good sense and moderation are the eighteenth century virtues which Russell's writings clearly express, he has, at the same time, avoided the facile optimism and excessive reverence for reason that characterised the eighteenth century.

As for the puritan element, one can agree that Russell is a puritan only in so far as the fact that he has a strong moral conviction. He reasons that man's thoughts and actions should have a strong moral base. However, he has none of the puritan's gloomy tendency to suppress life's joy. He certainly prophesies doom for mankind—if it continues in the present manner—but he loves life, beauty and imagination. He has none of the ascetic's disapproval of the sensual pleasures and, indeed, protests against such a suppression of natural instincts.

Russell's enlightenment goes beyond the eighteenth century enlightenment, and if he is staunch supporter of morality, he is also a spokesman for freedom in personal and public life.

Q. 19. "Philosophy........has resulted from the attempt to produce a synthesis of science and religion". Discuss this view of Russell.

Or

How does Russell differentiate between progress and change? Discuss with reference to any of his essays.

Ans. Refer to the discussion of Questions 5 and 6.

Q. 20. "The essence of the Liberal outlook lies not in what opinions are held but in *how* they are held". How far do you agree with what Russell says here?

Ans. Refer to the discussion of Question 5 and the Critical Appreciation of 'Philosophy and Politics'.

Q. 21. Explain what Russell means when he says that teachers are the guardians of civilization.

Ans. Refer to the discussion of Question 13 and the Critical Appreciation of 'The Functions of a Teacher'.

16

Excerpts from 'Unpopular Essays'

From the Preface

Most of the following essays are concerned to combat, in one way or another, the growth of dogmatism, whether of the Right or of the Left, which has hitherto characterised our tragic century.

From 'Philosophy and Politics'

1. The word 'philosophy' is one of which the meaning is by no means fixed. Like the word 'religion', it has one sense when used to describe certain features of historical cultures, and another when used to denote a study or an attitude of mind which is considered desirable in the present day.

2. Philosophy, in this historically usual sense, has resulted from the attempt to produce a synthesis of science and religion, or, perhaps more exactly, to combine a doctrine as to the nature of the universe and man's place in it with a practical ethic inculcating what was considered the best way of life. Philosophy was distingushed from religion by the fact that, nominally at least, it did not appeal to authority or tradition; it was distinguished from science by the fact that an essential part of its purpose was to tell men how to live.

3. The fundamental problem of ethics and politics is that of finding some way of reconciling the needs of social life with the urgency of individual desires.

4. Most philosophy has been a reaction against scepticism; it has arisen in ages when authority no longer sufficed to produce the socially necessary minimum of belief, so that nominally rational arguments had to be invented to secure the same result. This motive has led to a deep insincerity infecting most philosophy, both ancient and modern. There has been fear, often unconscious, that clear thinking would lead to anarchy, and this fear has led philosophers to hide in mists of fallacy and obscurity.

5. Change is one thing, progress is another. 'Change' is scientific, 'progress' is ethical; change is indubitable, where progress is a matter of controversy.

6. The Liberal creed, in practice, is one of live-and-let-live; of toleration and freedom so far as public order permits; of moderation and absence of fanaticism in political programmes. Even democracy, when it becomes fanatical, as it did among Rousseau's disciples in the French Revolution, ceases to be Liberal.

From 'Philosophy for Laymen'

1. It will be found that increase of skill has not, of itself, insured any increase of human happiness or well-being.

2. 'Philosophy' means 'love of wisdom', and philosophy in this sense is what men must acquire if the new powers invented by technicians, and handed over by them to be wielded by ordinary men and women, are not to plunge mankind into an appalling cataclysm.

3. Those who think that science is everything become complacent and cocksure, and decry all interests in problems not having the circumscribed definiteness that is necessary for scientific treatment.... On the other hand, those who pooh-pooh science revert, as a rule, to some ancient and pernicious superstition, and refuse to admit the immense increase of human happiness which scientific technique, if widely used, would make possible. Both these attitudes are to be deplored, and it is philosophy that shows the right attitude by making clear at once the scope and the limitations of scientific knowledge.

4. The demand for certainty is one which is natural to man, but is nevertheless an intellectual vice.

5. What philosophy should dissipate is certainty, whether of knowledge or of ignorance.

6. The pursuit of philosophy is founded on the belief that knowledge is good, even if what is known is painful.

From 'The Future of Mankind'

1. Although the last survivor may proclaim himself universal Emperor, his reign will be brief and his subjects will all be corpses. With his death the uneasy epiosde of life will end, and the peaceful rocks will revolve unchanged until the sun explodes.

2. Assuming a monopoly of armed force established by the victory of one side in a war between the U.S. and the U.S.S.R., what sort of world will result?.. Even if the dominant nation is completely devoid of altruism, its leading inhabitants, at least, will achieve a very high level of material comfort, and will be freed from the tyranny of fear. They are likely, therefore, to become gradually more good-natured and less inclined to persecute.

3.There are, however, important reasons for preferring a victory of

America.. My reason for siding with America is that there is in that country more respect than in Russia for the things that I value in a civilized way of life...freedom of thought, freedom of inquiry, freedom of discussion and humane feeling.

4. An oligarchy which controls all the means of publicity can perpetrate injustices and cruelties which would be scarcely possible if they were widely known. Only democracy and free publicity can prevent the holders of power from establishing a servile state, with luxury for the few and overworked poverty for the many.

5. Liberty must be limited by law, and its most valuable forms can only exist within a framework of law.

From 'Philosophy's Ulterior Motives'

1. The philosopher's temperament is rare, because it has to combine two some what conflicting characteristics: on the one hand, a strong desire to believe some general proposition about the universe or human life; on the other hand, inability to believe contentedly except on what appear to be intellectual grounds.

2. In a man whose reasoning powers are good, fallacious arguments are evidence of bias.

3. Philosophers, for the most part, are constitutionally timid, and dislike the unexpected. Accordingly they invent systems which make the future calculable, at least in its main outlines.

4. Perhaps empirical sobriety is so difficult that men will never preserve it except when they are happy.

5. Philosophy is an intellectual development, and is not compatible with mental maturity. In order that it may flourish, traditional doctrines must still be believed, but not so unquestioningly that arguments in support of them are never sought.

From 'The Superior Virtue of the Oppressed'

1. One of the persistent delusions of mankind is that some sections of the human race are morally better or worse than others. This belief has many different forms, none of which has any rational basis.

2. The idealizing of the victim is useful for a time: if virtue is the greatest of goods, and if subjection makes people virtuous, it is kind to refuse them power, since it would destroy their virtue. But sooner or later the oppressed class will argue that its superior virtue is a reason in favour of its having power, and the oppressors will find their own weapons turned against them. When at last power has been equalized, it becomes apparent to everybody that all the talk about superior virtue was

nonsense, and that it was quite unnecessary as a basis for the claim to equality.

From 'On Being Modern-Minded'

1. The belief that fashion alone should dominate opinion has great advantages. It makes thought unnecessary and puts the highest intelligence within the reach of everyone. It is not difficult to learn the correct use of such words as 'complex,''sadism,' 'Oedipus' 'deviation,' 'left'; and nothing more is needed to make a brilliant writer or talker. Some, at least, of such words represented much thought on the part of their inventors; like paper money they were originally convertible into gold. But they have become for most people inconvertible, and in depreciating have increased nominal wealth in ideas. And so we are enabled to despise the paltry intellectual fortunes of former times.

2. The money rewards and widespread though ephemeral fame which those agencies have made possible places temptations in the way of able men which are difficult to resist, and when all this is open to a men, he finds it difficult to go on doing the work that he himself thinks best and is inclined to subordinate his judgement to the general opinion.

3. Throughout the nineteenth century the True, the Good, and the Beautiful preseved their precarious existence in the minds of earnest atheists. But their very earnestiness was their undoing, since it made it impossible for them to stop at a halfway house. Pragmatists explained that Truth is what it pays to believe. Historians of morals reduced the Good to a matter of tribal custom. Beauty was abolished by the artists in a revolt against the sugary insipidities of a philistine epoch.

4. A certain degree of isolation both in space and time is essential to generate the independence required for the most important work; there must be something which is felt to be of more importance than the admiration of the contemporary crowd. We are suffering not from the decay of theological beliefs but from the loss of solitude.

From 'An Outline of Intellectual Rubbish'

1. The follies of our own times are easier to bear when they are seen against the background of past follies.

2. I find difficulty in the conception of a God who gets pleasure from contemplating such tortures; and if there were a God capable of such wanton cruelty, I should certainly not think Him worthy of worship. But that only proves how sunk I am in moral depravity.

3. Modern morals are a mixture of two elements: on the one hand, rational precepts as to how to live together peaceably in a society, and on the other hand, traditional taboos derived originally from some

ancient superstition, but proximately from sacred books, Christian , Mohammedan, Hindu, or Buddhist. To some extent the two agree.

4. Self- importance, individual or generic, is the source of most of our religious beliefs. Even sin is a conception derived from self-importance.

5. Since evolution became fashionable, the glorification of Man has taken a new form. We are told that evolution has been guided by one great Purpose. At last, in the fulness of time, He produced Man, including such specimens as Nero and Caligula, Hitler and Mussolini, whose transcendent glory justified the long painful process.

6. Every powerful emotion has its own myth-making tendency. When the emotion is peculiar to an individual, he is considered more or less mad if he gives credence to such myths as he has invented. But when an emotion is collective, as in war, there is no one to correct the myths that naturally arise.

7. The discovery that man can be scientifically manipulated, and that governments can turn large masses this way or that as they choose, is one of the causes of our misfortunes.

8. Superstitions are not always dark and cruel; often they add to the gaiety of life. Perhaps the world would lose some of its interest and variety if such beliefs were wholly replaced by cold science. A wise man will enjoy the goods of which there is a plentiful supply, and of intellectual rubbish he will find an abundant diet, in our own age as in every other.

From 'The Functions of a Teacher'

1. Any man who has the genuine impulse of the teacher will be more anxious to survive in his books than in the flesh. A feeling of intellectual independence is essential to the proper fulfilment of the teacher's functions, since it is his business to instil what he can of knowledge and reasonableness into the process of forming public opinion.

2. No man can be a good teacher unless he has feelings of warm affection towards his pupils and a genuine desire to impart to them what he himself believes to be of value.

3. The idea that falsehood is edifying is one of the besetting sins of those who draw up education schemes.

4. The turbulence of our times is inimical to the fine flower of culture. Perhaps we must wait for quieter times before the claims of civilization can again override the claims of party spirit.

From ' Ideas that have Helped Mankind'

1. The curbing of impulses to which we are led by fore-thought averts physical disaster at the cost of worry, and general lack of joy.

2. One of the'grand' conceptions which have proved scientifically useless is the soul. I do not mean that there is positive evidence showing that men have no souls; I only mean that the soul, if it exists, plays no part in any discoverable causal law.

3. Now there remain only two (states) that are wholly capable of independent self-direction; I mean, of course, the United States and the U.S.S.R. All that is necessary to save mankind from disaster is the step from two independent States to one—not by war, which would bring disaster, but by agreement.

From 'Ideas That Have Harmed Mankind'

1. I think that the evils that men inflict on each other, and by reflection upon themselves have their main source in evil passions rather than in ideas or beliefs.

2. I cannot believe, as some psycho-analysts do, that the feeling of sin is innate, though I believe it to be a product of very early infancy. I think that, if this feeling could be eradicated, the amount of cruelty in the world would be very greatly diminished.

3. The world at the present day stands in need of two kinds of things. On the one hand, organization.... On the other hand it needs certain moral qualities.

From 'Eminent Men I Have Known'

1. What I have found most unforgettable is a certain kind of moral quality, a quality of self-forgetfulness, whether in private life, in public affairs, or in pursuit of truth.

17

Symposium of Critics on Russell's 'Unpopular Essays'

1. RUSSELL AS A PHILOSOPHER

Hans Reichenbach: Russell has demonstrated with indomitable courage the strength of his character and the seriouseness of his convictions. An uncompromising man, a fighter for freedom, Russell belongs with the philosophers of action as well as with philosophers of theory. Perhaps the way Russell lives his philosophy is his greatest contribution to our times so deeply torn between thoughts and deeds.

Herbert Read : I do not think that he is a philosopher of any assessable academic status. He has been essentially a teacher; and vitalized thought at innumerable points and has always represented for me and I am sure for many others the embodiment of these Socratic Virtues—self-control, fairness, courage, liberality and truth—which are the characteristics of a mind free from anxiety and fear.

Hans Reichenbach : Russell is one of those rare geniuses who are not satisfied by working in a limited scientific domain, but who delve with the same philosophical earnestness into questions of life and personal action.

Werner Bloch : Russell does not content himslf with presenting the teachings of the philosophers; he joins issue with them as though he were their contemporary; that is to say, not with the superiority of a man taking advantage of the fact that he is living centuries after them, but by putting forward arguments that they should not have overlooked had they been as critical towards themselves as they were anxious to prove that they were right.

II. RUSSELL : A REBEL

Erich Fromm: Bertrand Russell's capacity to disobey is rooted, not in some abstract principle, but in the most real experience there is—in his love of life. This love of life shines through his writings as well as through his person. Bertrand Russell fights against the threatening slaughter not because he is a pacifist, not because some abstract principle is involved—but precisely because he is a man who loves life. For the very same reason he has no use for those voices which love to harp on the evilness of man, in fact thus saying more about themselves and their own gloomy moods than about men. Not that Bertrand Russell is a sentimental romantic. He is a hard-headed, critical, caustic realist, he is aware of the depth of evil and stupidity to be found in the heart of man; but he does not confuse this fact with an alleged innate corruption which serves to rationalise the outlook of those who are too gloomy to believe in man's gift to create a world in which he can feel himself to be at home.

I.F. Stone : Russell has taught us all by word and by example. His first test came in the Boer War, which split the Fabian Society ; the Webbs wavered, even George Bernard Shaw wrote nonsense but Russell opposed the war. When the First World War came, he went to prison as a conscientious objector.

III. RUSSELL'S VALUES

Brian Carr : Russell's objections to dogma can usefully be divided into the intellectual and the moral. The intellectual objection is directed at the insistence that various doubtful propositions are known to be true. The moral objections to dogma are numerous, and one of the most telling which Russell raises is that an insistence on dogmatic claims inhibits social changes which are essential for the happiness of mankind. What this comes to is not so much that present creeds are greatly responsible for the miseries of human existence (though as we shall see.... Russell believes that to be true also). But rather that the opposite attitude of rational scepticism is a condition of the emergence of a happier and more harmonious society; only by the free use of intelligence, unencumbered by any creed, can we discover and initiate the way to individual and social well-being.

Victor Purcell : Russell has examined and criticised accepted values in such a way that our attitude towards politics, morality, marriage, etc. have been insensibly influenced and prepared for change. In an age which is resorting increasingly to mystagoguery, ritualism, and sacredotalism (both religious and lay), he has provided those of us who fined the process abhorrent and intolerable with new philosophic weapons wherewith to fight for our rational survival. He has for long been a beacon of hope in a darkening world.

Max Born : His opposition to the war cost him his academic position, led to imprisonment and forced him to emigrate to U.S.A. He had firmly stood to his convictions and refused to take part in the general outbreak of insanity which swept the world at that time. And ever since he stuck to his principles and acted without fear.

IV. RUSSELL'S IDEAS ON STATE AND POLITICS

Brian Carr : Russell identifies nationalism, a fairly new phenomenon in history dating from the eighteenth century and the French Revolution, as the greatest present threat to civilization. War indeed, and the preparation for it, is one of the primnary functions of the modern state, and patriotic zeal is encouraged in State education to the extent most men are willing to die for their country and believe the myth of its superior excellence over all others. Because nationalism presents this threat, Russell and other pacifists have seen the creation of a single world State as the only solution; pacifism and internationalism have for the most part gone hand in hand: Various forms of World Government have been suggested and some even tried : yet those that have been tried were ineffective in preventing wars. The major feature of Russell's proposal is that World Government be the sole possessor of weapons of mass destruction, with the military capacity to enforce a solution to disputes involving even the largest of the present powers....

Russell argues, correctly, that the State has certain posititve functions, such as the substitution of law for force, the provision of education and general welfare requirements like sanitation, the encouragment of scientific research; but these could be met by a single World State. A second reason could be one of expediency..... Russell believed that a fundamental change of outlook was necessary for the happiness of human race, indeed, for its very existence.

Victor Purcell : It is clear that in Russell's ideal State, with its.... degree, priority, and place, course, proportion, reason, form, office, and custom, in all line of order" is an organism in which the intellectuals and manual workers operate in perfect collaboration [illegible] common end. It has no resemblance to our existing society in which the intelligentsia are ground between the upper and nether millstones of finance and labour. In Russell's state the intelligentsia rule by example, not by military command.

V. RUSSELL AND RELIGION

Brian Carr : Russell's case against religion in general, and Christianity in particular, is many-sided and apparently very strong—it presents the Christian with an unenviable task of defence. One or two lines that might be tried are as follows:

It might be said that, though Russell is right to denounce dogma in general, at least the Christian dogma with their emphasis on love and brotherhood of man have been and continue to be a force for good. But (1) is this so? (Russell has produced a case against it), and (2) whatever good has resulted from these dogmas has to be weighed against the evils attending their enforcement.

Michael Scott : A common failing of preachers is to represent God as like ourselves, only bigger. This is also true of the character and personality of Jesus who often acquires as many of the characteristics of the preacher as the preacher does those of Jesus. If we look at the history of the Christian Church we may be appalled at the discrepancy between the Jesus of the pulpits and platforms and the Jesus of history. It is that discrepancy and the hideous conseqences that resulted from it, not only in the dwarfing of human mind but the dwarfing of the whole scale of human achievements and sense of values, that are difficult to explain. Russell's explanation of this does not seem adequate any more than his explanation of his contemporary world's rejection of many of his ideas and action. The dwarfs around him he is always accustomed to treat as his equals until they do something outrageous and then more than likely it will be his wit rather than his wisdom that is exercised on them.

VI. RUSSELL: A MAN OF REASON AND INTELLECT

Erich Fromm : Bertrand Russell is a man of faith. Not of faith in the theological sense, but of faith in the power of reason, faith in man's capacity to create his own paradise through his own efforts.

Brian Carr : The general intellectual position Russell adopts is one of 'rational scepticism'; the simple and apparently admirable one of not taking something as certain where evidence is insufficient.

I.F. Stone : To browse through Russell's works, reading here and re-reading there, is to see that his life has been one continuous and consistent effort to liberate man by intelligence and by love from his self-destructive illusions and hates.

Michael Scott : To me he appears as a giant among mental and spiritual dwarfs, who are hectically engagd in erecting frankenstein monsters having their own spiritual limitations, powers of perception, scales of value, amd sense of proportion.

VII. LANGUAGE AND STYLE

Hans Reichenbach : These writings show Russell as an accomplished master of language; his pithy and concise style, his dry humour, his simple sentences are as delightful as they are convincing. He is remarkable among philosophers for his literary flair, and one is tempted to compare him with his great compatriot Hume whom he resembles in the style of his writings and in his sober and realistic approach to problems. Indeed, Russell just like Hume has awakened many from their 'dogmatic slumbers'.

Aldous Huxley : No jargon, not a single neologism. Nothing but plain English. There is no hiding behind obscurities, no pretending that the subject is understandable only by specialists and can be talked about only in a private language. Everything is perfectly clear and above board. Bertrand Russell dives deep, but comes up every time as clear as a whistle.

VIII. RUSSELL : THE MAN

Hans Reichenbach : Russell is the descendent of an old aristocratic family whose history can be traced back to the time of Henry VII and which has produced many a famous leader of the Whig Party and many a statesman, such as Russell's grandfather, the Earl of Kingston-Russell. Despite his lineage Russell did not hesitate to break with tradition and, during World War I, to protest vigorously against war itself. He staunchly proclaimed pacifism, was thrown into prision as a conscientious objector, and deprived of his teaching position at Trinity College, Cambridge. Undeterred by such adversity, he published his philosophy in several books such as Principles of Social Reconstruction and Prospects of Industrial Civilization, soon to appear in German translations. His views are close to Brittish Syndicalism. He has also travelled to Russia and China and has described his experiences in several books.

Erich Fromm : Among the few in whom the idea has become manifest in the flesh, and whom the historical situation of mankind has transformed from teachers into prophets, is Bertrand Russell. He happens to be a great thinker but that is not really essential to his being a prophet. He, together with Einstein and Schweitzer, represents the answer of Western humanity to the threat to its existence, because all three of them have spoken up, have warned, and have pointed out the alternatives.

Victor Purcell : Russell has examined and criticized accepted values in such a way that our attitude towards politics, morality, marriage, etc. have been insensibly influenced and prepared for change. In an age which is resorting increasingly to mystagoguery, ritualism, and sacerdotalism (both religious and lay), he has provided those of us who find the process abhorrent and intolerable with new philosophic weapons wherewith to fight for our rational survival. He has for long been a beacon of hope in a darkening world. Because he rejects Christianity, Russell has been accused of turning his back on mystery and the imagination. This is not so. Throughout his writings he has paid the sincerest tribute to creative art and the writings themselves are sprinkled with poetic passages of a high order, but his own function he realizes to be the pursuit of objective truth. As Colin Wilson says, 'Russell prefers the discomforts of scepticism to wild guesses and assertions that seem to be of wishful thinking'. Unfortunately (Wilson adds) most creative artists and thinkers cannot live happily in Lord Russell's state of stoical agnosticism. Russell would deny that his agnosticism is 'stoical' (in fact, he questions the bonafides of the Stoics), and on the contrary believes in the 'pursuit of happiness'. But it is not the case that agnosticism is incompatible with creative art or thought.

Julian Trevelyan : No portrait of Bertie would be complete that did not bring out the impish side of his nature. There has never been any thinker who was at times more disquieting or whose precepts and paradoxes have upset so many apple carts; to have been able to continue in this mischievous vein for sixty years or so is no mean achievement. But underlying this impishness there lies a conviction, one that was so natural to his generation that it was taken for granted by all his Cambridge friends, that man is *au fond* a rational being and will in the long run behave in a rational way.

SELECT BIBLIOGRAPHY

1. A.J. Ayer : *Bertrand Russell*
2. D.F. Pears (Ed.) : *Bertrand Russell*
3. Herbert Gotts Chalk : *Bertrand Russell : A Life*
4. P.E.B. Jourdain : *The Philosophy of Bertrand Russell*
5. P.A. Schlipp (Ed.) : *The Philosophy of Bertrand Russell*
6. R.C. Williams : *Russell Remembered*
7. Alan Wood : *The Passionate Sceptic*
8. A.S. Collins : *English Literature of the 20th Century*
9. C.E.M. Jaod : *Modern Philosophy*
10. R.E. Enger & L. Dennor (Ed.) : *The Basic Writings of Bertrand Russell*
11. Brian Carr : *Bertrand Russell : An Introduction*
12. J. Park : *Bertrand Russell on Education*
13. Albert Schweitzer : *Peace or Atomic War*
14. J.B. Priestley : *Literature and the Western Man*
15. A.R. Vidler (Ed.) : *Objections to Christian Belief*
16. Frederick J. Hoffman : *The Twenties*